STAGECOACH WOMEN

Brave and Daring Women of the Wild West

CHERYL MULLENBACH

TWODOT®

GUILFORD, CONNECTICUT
HELENA, MONTANA

A · TWODOT® · BOOK

An imprint and registered trademark of The Rowman & Littlefield Publishing Group, Inc.
4501 Forbes Blvd., Ste. 200
Lanham, MD 20706
www.rowman.com

Distributed by NATIONAL BOOK NETWORK

British Library Cataloguing in Publication Information available

Library of Congress Cataloging-in-Publication Data
Names: Mullenbach, Cheryl, author.
Title: Stagecoach women : brave and daring women of the Wild West / Cheryl Mullenbach.
Description: Helena, Montana : TwoDot, [2020] | Includes bibliographical references and index. | Summary: "Stagecoach Women offers an expansive overview of stagecoach history in the United States enriched by the personal stories of women who contributed to the evolution and success of a captivating facet of American history. Prepare for a teeth-rattling, romance-shattering journey that jolts away preconceived notions about women and stagecoaches and surprises with its twists and turns"— Provided by publisher.
Identifiers: LCCN 2019039430 (print) | LCCN 2019039431 (ebook) | ISBN 9781493042593 (paperback ; alk. paper) | ISBN 9781493042609 (epub)
Subjects: LCSH: Stagecoach lines—West (U.S.)—History. | Women—West (U.S.)—History. | West (U.S.)—History.
Classification: LCC HE5748.W47 M85 2020 (print) | LCC HE5748.W47 (ebook) | DDC 388.3/228092520978—dc23
LC record available at https://lccn.loc.gov/2019039430
LC ebook record available at https://lccn.loc.gov/2019039431

∞™ The paper used in this publication meets the minimum requirements of American National Standard for Information Sciences—Permanence of Paper for Printed Library Materials, ANSI/NISO Z39.48-1992.

For Richard L. Wohlgamuth

CONTENTS

Introduction

THE OVERTURNED STAGECOACH IS EASY TO OVERLOOK AMID THE IMAGES of blood-thirsty Indians and naked bodies in the 1930s Depression-era mural commissioned by a New Deal arts program that offered jobs to unemployed artists and writers. *Dangers of the Mail* by Frank Mechau Jr. was controversial at the time, and it continued to be in later years as the mural was displayed in public federal buildings. Critics pointed out that the painting reinforced the stereotype of Native Americans as marauding savages who interrupted mail service, and while it's unclear what the artist had in mind with the naked women, plenty of people felt all that nudity was inappropriate in government buildings.

A mural portraying mail delivery during the stagecoach era could have depicted a more authentic reality. Stagecoaches, often driven by women, absolutely played a vital role in the distribution of mail; women of various ethnic backgrounds, including Native American, worked in positions that contributed to the safe delivery of mail, and there were very

Dangers of the Mail
LIBRARY OF CONGRESS, PRINTS & PHOTOGRAPHS DIVISION, PHOTOGRAPH BY CAROL M. HIGH-SMITH [REPRODUCTION NUMBER, E.G., LC-USZ62-123456]

real dangers associated with carrying the US mail—including robberies perpetrated by gun-toting women.

Stagecoaches, otherwise known as shake-guts, were the lifeblood of the nation even before America was an independent country. Horse dealers, harness makers, blacksmiths, wheelwrights, teamsters, maids, and cooks reaped benefits from the stagecoach industry. Newspaper publishers, magazine writers, reporters, book authors, social reformers, public relations promoters, government agencies, and local gossipmongers relied on stagecoaches to help spread their messages. For more than two hundred years everyday citizens, business owners, drummers (salespeople), vacationers, entertainers, prospectors, fun-seekers, and political activists used stagecoaches to travel short distances and cross-country. Women, as well as men, drove stagecoaches, groomed and shod stage horses, hoisted mailbags and boxes of gold bullion, negotiated contracts, bought and managed stage lines, defended (with their six-shooters) their cargo from bandits, and robbed stages. Women also assumed their traditional roles as housekeepers, cooks, and laundresses, and, oh yes, bearers of multiple children.

Stagecoach Women: Brave and Daring Women of the Wild West features the personal stories of the women who contributed to the evolution and success of a captivating nugget of American history. Prepare yourself for a teeth-rattling, romance-shattering journey that jolts away at least some of your preconceived notions about women and stagecoaches and surprises you with its twists and turns.

Chapter 1

The Stagecoach: Job Creator, Money Maker

"A huge uncouth, unmannerly, rough looking being, scarcely human; his visage would frighten a wolf." Stagecoach passenger Anne Newport Royall didn't hold back in her straight-talking description of a worker she encountered at a stage stop in Worcester, Massachusetts, in 1828. She added, "It is surprising that the owners of those lines cannot see their interest to employ none but obliging men to superintend their business, particularly men who are qualified to treat travelers well for their money."

By 1828, when Anne expressed her displeasure with stage travel, including her interaction with a "greasy, black coach, the cushions of which were nails," a "beastly drunk" fellow passenger, and a drunk chambermaid at the tavern, stagecoaching had been operating as a form of public transportation for roughly a hundred years. Despite Anne Royall's unsatisfactory experience, the stagecoach industry as a whole succeeded in many facets of business. Stagecoaching provided jobs, inspired entrepreneurship, facilitated mass movement of people, transmitted news, promoted commerce and tourism, and supported the needs of hopeful but lonely prospectors. It generated widespread economic impact, and it would continue to do so for generations. In time its usefulness was diminished and ultimately eliminated, but for two hundred years stagecoaching was a sustained and profitable contributor to the economy.

It was in the early 1700s that European colonists in North America first began utilizing stagecoaches as a vehicle for hire to carry passengers, mail, newspapers, and small freight. This much-needed endeavor provided a service as well as job opportunities. But the lack of decent roads was a huge barrier.

"There is a large variety in American roads . . . excellent limestone roads which stretch out in three directions from Nashville, Tennessee . . . there is quite another sort of limestone road in Virginia, sloping so as to throw the passengers on one another . . . there are the rich mud roads of Ohio . . . and the admirable road running parallel with Lake Ontario." British tourist and writer Harriet Martineau described her experiences traveling by stage on American roads in 1838. Her encounter with the corduroy roads of America were "happily of rare occurrence" as passengers were tossed about "like pills in a pill box."

New England's earliest roads were mere "trodden paths scarce two feet wide" according to author Alice Morse Earle in her 1900 book *Stage Coach and Tavern Days*. Those corduroy roads were an improvement. Consisting of ten- to twelve-foot-long logs sandwiched as closely together as possible, they offered a mostly dry, but decidedly bumpy, thoroughfare. But Alice had ridden on one, and she agreed with Harriet Martineau, describing her journey as the "most trying ordeal" she'd ever experienced.

It was the talk of the nation when John Loudon McAdam came up with a road surfacing process in the early 1800s that used rock pieces "not to exceed six ounces in weight" and small enough to pass through a "two-inch ring." The world honored McAdam by forever after referring to roads constructed with this ground-breaking technique as macadam roads.

People were inconvenienced all the time by the crummy road situation. In February 1799 Maria Jefferson Eppes, Thomas Jefferson's daughter, had to have been disappointed when she received a letter from her dad saying he wouldn't be able to visit because of the "dreadful" roads. It's not known if she was at all consoled by his assurance that he'd see her in March or April, when he predicted the "roads will then be fine."

A hundred years later, in the late 1800s, shoddy roads continued to be an aggravating feature of day-to-day life in America. Who knows how an impatient Massachusetts teenager reacted when she received the letter from her mother reporting that impassable roads prevented her return home to Cambridge as planned? And if that teen had any thoughts of using a stagecoach to get home, her parents quashed the idea. "Your papa would not trust your life in the stage," her mother wrote. "It is a very unsafe and improper conveyance for young ladies. As soon as your papa can go, you may be sure he will go or send for you." End of discussion.

Disrupted family visits and canceled social outings were one thing, but atrocious roadways also thwarted business and commerce concerns. Shopkeepers and farmers who couldn't get products to and from their markets helped fuel a spurt in the construction of better roads in the 1790s. When pressure on government officials didn't get results, private individuals invested in road improvements.

By the mid-1800s an extensive network of turnpikes had been constructed. Users paid a fee that allowed them to turn a spiked pole stretching across the roadway in order to continue on their journey. Some turnpikes were built by local governments, others by private individuals who invested money in the enterprise and were reimbursed by future toll receipts. Prices varied depending on the number of animals pulling a wagon or stage, the size of the conveyance, and the distance traveled. In the 1790s it cost a four-horse stage eighteen and a half cents to use the Schenectady and Utica Turnpike in New York—a distance of sixty-eight miles. The driver of a one-horse sleigh paid six cents and a horse and rider only five cents. By 1820, with almost forty thousand miles of turnpikes stretching across the country, shrewd investors saw opportunities for making money.

Turnpikes turned out to be a sweet deal for stage owners, who seldom paid the full toll. Many were given as much as 30 percent discounts. In some cases, the toll fees were passed on to the passengers, who ended up paying higher prices for a stage ticket. Some stage owners purchased stock in the turnpike companies and realized financial gain with their investments. At any rate, turnpikes greatly improved stage travel. It meant riders enjoyed mud-free roads, greater speed, shorter distances, and the ability to travel at night.

One of the first public stage services in the colonies was the Boston-Newport line started by Jonathan and Frances Wardell in 1712. Frances had inherited a popular tavern called the Orange Tree Inn in Boston from her father, Francis Cook, in 1701, the same year she married

Benjamin Morse (alternately spelled Morss). When her husband died in 1708, Frances ran the tavern while raising their five-year-old son. After marrying Jonathan Wardell, she continued to run the Orange Tree while her husband managed the stable. Most historians credited Jonathan Wardell with establishing the first public coach in Boston. Starting at the Orange Tree, he drove "once a Fortnight" while the "Ways are passable," charging "Reasonable Rates" for the trip to Newport, Rhode Island.

Numerous stage lines served the colonies throughout the colonial period. What busy, time-conscious New Englander needing to get to New Jersey from Pennsylvania as quickly as possible *wouldn't* purchase a ticket on the stage named the "Flying Machine"? In 1733 some enterprising individual who appreciated the value of market branding offered a service with that name between Philadelphia and Princeton, New Jersey. Of course the Good Intent Stage Company, leaving Philadelphia daily, certainly intended to offer only the best in convenience and comfort. In 1750 there was a service between Philadelphia and New York with a speedy three-day running time, but owners issued the caveat that wind and weather could affect travel time. A Boston–New York line was established in 1772. So stagecoaches were definitely part of colonial life. With the commencement of the American Revolution in 1775 and the capture of Boston, New York, and Philadelphia by the British, stagecoach travel was largely disrupted or completely halted. However, after the ratification of the peace treaty in 1784, stagecoaching gradually picked up again, and by 1789 the golden era of staging had begun in the eastern part of North America.

The heyday of stagecoaching reached its peak in the East and Midwest around 1840 as railroads became more prevalent. However, the stagecoach era was just dawning in the West in the 1850s. As with many commercial endeavors, national events and shifting trends shaped the stagecoach industry's history. While the railroads eliminated many stage lines, the advancement of the iron horse didn't completely wipe out stage services. Stagecoaches continued to transport goods and passengers to train depots from outlying areas. They continued to run in areas not served by a nearby railroad. After all, railroads weren't *everywhere* in America.

As the boundaries of the United States expanded with newly acquired lands, stagecoaches played a pivotal role in moving people and goods. The Louisiana Purchase of 1803 doubled the size of the United States, adding more than eight hundred thousand square miles from the Mississippi River to the Rocky Mountains and from the Gulf of Mexico to the Canadian border. The Gadsden Purchase in 1853 expanded the country by almost thirty thousand square miles, adding territory that became Arizona and New Mexico. The discovery of gold in California in 1849 and in the Black Hills in the 1870s beckoned fortune hunters westward. Prospectors depended on stagecoaches to carry their precious discoveries from mining camps to nearby towns and to bring cherished letters from loved ones to ease their homesickness.

The Civil War gave a temporary boost to stagecoaching as the building of railroads came to a halt. And while the existing railroads transported soldiers and war supplies, all forms of transportation were put to use in this time of need—stagecoaches included. At the close of the war in 1865, the westward movement picked up and resumed in force.

As one historian observed, "stagecoaches sped over the primitive roads of the western prairies, deserts, and mountains." Roads were carved into rugged mountain slopes, and stage stops, called ranches in the West, were situated in strategic locations to serve the needs of western travelers as they had in the East and Midwest. Westward movement helped extend the stagecoach era by about fifty years. That meant the overall economic impact of staging lingered too.

Women and men who made a conscious decision to start up a stage service to meet the needs of a community intended to make money. An offshoot was that others benefitted too—most obviously, people who built these exceptional vehicles. And there were quite a few of them. In 1850 the US Census Bureau identified just over fourteen thousand coach makers; in 1860, over nineteen thousand.

Coach building and related businesses operated throughout the continental United States and even in future states—as at Halley and Hunter coach builders in Honolulu, Hawaii, where the firm offered only the "best materials and workmanship" in 1850. In Louisville, Kentucky, in 1854, carriage dealer I. F. Stone advertised a large selection of coaches made of "superior materials." In 1866 Wilson's Hardware and Harness Establishment in Wilmington, North Carolina, carried "every description of coach builders' hardware," including coach springs and axles. In Houston four coach makers were in business in 1866, and there were eight harness shops. At Donaldsonville, Louisiana, in 1877, coachmaker Joseph Ferrier was ready to "execute at shortest notice all work entrusted to him." And he guaranteed all his work. Worthy Davis's carriage painting shop in Grand Forks, North Dakota, moved into the largest building in town in 1884 because she had so much work. According to the local newspaper, Worthy's decorative paintings on her customers' carriages were of "superior quality" and "first class," and she possessed "rare ability" as a carriage artist. In California in 1886 S. H. Bradley of Marysville boasted the "highest reputation as stage builder of any man on the coast" for his eight-passenger stagecoach specially designed for use in mountains. Anyone who doubted that claim could ask the Small Brothers, who had purchased five new coaches from Bradley and promised to offer their passengers a ride "pleasanter than ever" as a result.

Two eastern cities led the way when it came to coach building. Troy, New York, locals claimed they were responsible for innovative coach-building ideas—seats over the baggage rack and railings around the top of carriages, for example. Stage line owners who had purchased coaches made in Troy used that as an enticement to passengers; owning a coach built in Troy was a badge of honor. At one time there were as many as thirty coach makers operating in the city.

One of those was Eaton, Gilbert and Company. Uri Gilbert and Orsamus Eaton had become partners in 1823, and by 1830 their shop grossed fifty thousand dollars, twice that amount in 1831. Early in 1844 the company had filled an order from Mexico for twelve thousand dollars in stagecoaches and harnesses. Between 1847 and 1853 their coaches were on almost all the mail routes in the country. In 1850 it was estimated that about five thousand were in use in the United States, Canada, Mexico, and South America. Stage companies that purchased coaches from Eaton, Gilbert and Company gave them colorful names—*Beauty*,

Fashion, and *Brilliant*—to reflect the beautiful lines and curves illustrative of the company's graceful carriage bodies.

Troy's impressive accomplishments in stagecoach production justly earned the city accolades and a place in history. About the same time all those coaches started rolling out of Troy, there was a flurry of stagecoaching activity in a town about 150 miles to the north and east. For more than a hundred years the economic picture of Concord, New Hampshire, was colored by a major stagecoach-building establishment located there. Generations of residents were offered job opportunities at the facility that became synonymous with luxury in nineteenth-century travel, and some were women.

On a wintry Saturday morning in January 1899, Maria Foster Putnam submitted an accounting of her hours to the payroll department at the Abbot-Downing Company in Concord. There were certainly more newsworthy events occurring at the time. In Washington, DC, President William McKinley hosted his first reception of the new year at the White House, where the US Marine Band, dressed in their signature vivid red

Maria Putnam
NEW HAMPSHIRE HISTORICAL SOCIETY, GIFT OF MAY NUTTER

uniforms, entertained with a lively performance. Closer to home in Concord, officials was grappling with a resident who was mad as hell and threatening to sue the city for failing to clear his sidewalk of snow after a recent storm. And the police reported a busy night in nearby Portsmouth, where they booked a drunken musician and rescued a fellow who fell overboard at the ferry landing.

But for Maria, payday was likely more significant than any of the events reported in the local newspapers. She may have been eyeing a pair of two-dollar boots from the local department store—much appreciated as she made her way from her house on South Street to the Abbot-Downing facility on frigid New England mornings. Maria's fifteen-dollar paycheck was her reward for eighty-eight hours of work over a two-week period. As a sewer at the coach-making factory, she worked alongside wheelwrights, blacksmiths, painters, and woodworkers to produce some of the finest vehicles in the world. Abbot-Downing had set up shop in 1826 and was considered one of the premier builders of stagecoaches. Stage companies large and small coveted a coach made at the famed facility.

One of Abbot-Downing's most well-known customers was the Wells, Fargo and Company stage line. When the company purchased the renowned Holladay Overland Mail and Express Company from Ben Holladay in 1866, making it the only stage line "of any consequence" between the Missouri River and California, it turned to Abbot-Downing to supply coaches. As the Central Pacific and Union Pacific Railroads raced to complete the First Transcontinental Railroad, Wells, Fargo and Company was there to serve the needs of the Union Pacific. Needing additional stagecoaches to transport people and supplies to the building sites, they once again looked to the legendary Abbot-Downing Company to supply thirty-nine passenger Concord coaches. These charmingly decorated vehicles were delivered to Omaha, Nebraska, on a special train of fifteen flatcars on April 15, 1868. An Abbot-Downing painter had created a different scene on the doors of each coach. The bodies were painted an eye-catching "straw color" and "English vermillion" and were "highly ornamented."

Of course this was long before Maria worked at Abbot-Downing in the late 1800s. But the reputation of the company and the quality of their coaches transcended generations of workers. Maria and her fellow workers in the later decades of the 1800s and early 1900s were upholding traditions that had been established by earlier Abbot-Downing employees.

It was a rich tradition—one that used only the finest materials and meticulous design principals known to professionals at the time. Original owners Lewis Downing and J. Stephens Abbot and their descendants refused to compromise, using the highest quality hand-forged iron as well as ash and white oak lumber seasoned for at least three years. Artists applied layer after layer of paint, varnish, and glazes purchased from the Sherwin-Williams paint company to decorate the coaches with riveting figures and jaw-dropping scenes.

Abbot-Downing offered top-of-the-line Concord coaches for twelve hundred dollars and the less-expensive, far-from-elegant models—the celerity and the mud wagon—each selling for five hundred dollars. Initially the only machines used in the construction of the coaches were horse-powered circular saws and band saws. Skilled craftspersons created precisely measured wheels that ensured perfect balance and could withstand the harshest weather and road conditions. No bolts or screws were used to join the various pieces of a wheel. Rear wheels of the Concord were exactly five feet, one inch high; the front wheels were three feet, ten inches. Precision mattered.

Abbot-Downing coach bodies varied somewhat depending on the model, but basic features were integrated into all their coaches. The driver's seat was positioned to give occupants the best leverage when applying the brakes; an iron rail enclosed the rear and two sides of the top of the coach, providing extra room for packages—and the occasional overflow passenger who relished a rooftop view. The rear platform was encased with waterproof leather and held luggage, mail, packages, and typically not *live* freight. (At least that was the intent when the designers came up with the idea, but there was an unfortunate incident in Kansas of a Poland China boar that had been squeezed into the hind boot of a stagecoach for delivery to its new owner. When a slat on the wood crate carrying the pig broke, the animal made its getaway.)

Most important to the passengers was the coach body and interior. The more luxurious Concord had wood-paneled sides with doors and glass windows. Three leather-cushioned seats accommodated nine passengers. The front and back seats offered cushioned backrests, and the middle bench incorporated a backrest of sorts consisting of a piece of leather suspended from the carriage top and attached on the sides to the doors. The center bench was hinged at each end, allowing movement for passengers to get to their seats or use the doors. The passengers on the center seats had to be prepared to adjust frequently to make those moves possible.

The nine-passenger coach measured a little over four feet in width. Each passenger had about fifteen inches of space to call private. In 1885 the average five-foot-four, twenty-one-year-old male weighed about 125 pounds; a five-foot woman averaged 122 pounds. Not much room to spare, but considering the size of today's humans (195.7 pounds for the average twenty-one-year-old male and 168.5 pounds for the average woman), it afforded enough space to offer a fairly comfortable ride.

A fair amount of fabric was used in the Abbot-Downing coaches, especially in the less-expensive celerity and mud wagon coaches. There were no doors or windows, but the carriage sides did have openings to allow airflow. Canvas curtains were rolled over openings to cut down on dust and cold air. A piece of canvas stretched over a frame served as the ceiling of the coach. Arguably the most important swatch of material was the thick steerhide or oxhide leather thoroughbraces on which the coach bodies were suspended, serving as shock absorbers and making for a more comfortable ride.

All that thick leather and sturdy canvas had to be cut, trimmed, and stitched into specific pieces and shapes. That was what Maria Foster Putnam and coworker Annie Watts spent their days doing between 1884 and 1901. They had the luxury of sewing machines, but it isn't difficult to imagine that their fingers and joints took a beating after years of work. Maria lost her sight in her later years, and one has to wonder if her work had contributed in any way. The Abbot-Downing Company was a source of income for Maria for years, and she has been remembered as a valued employee of one of the most celebrated businesses in stagecoach history.

Job seekers in Concord had a variety of positions to consider at Abbot-Downing. Many required specialized skills—painters, wheelwrights, blacksmiths, and machinists were professionals who produced superb work. Packers and shippers had to be adept at preparing products for shipment cross-country or across the globe, as they did in July 1900 when they sent thirty coaches to Sydney, Australia. The office employed individuals with business aptitudes.

Maud Bradley, Alice Currier, and Alice Sanborn were stenographers at Abbot-Downing in the early 1900s. They took dictation using shorthand, typed letters and forms with a relatively new machine called a typewriter, and transcribed notes from meetings. At the time it was common practice to issue spelling and punctuation tests to individuals applying for stenographer positions. Accuracy was essential at Abbot-Downing, as every coach commissioned by customers carried very specific specifications. Mistakes could cost as little as ruffled feathers or as much as hundreds of dollars. After all, it could have been both embarrassing and costly had one of the women inaccurately transcribed notes from an order, confusing the decorative painting for the grocer's coach with the undertaker's. The painting of the "widow weeping at the tomb of her departed husband" would have been highly inappropriate on the grocer's coach. And the colorful images of ham hocks and pots of beans specified by the grocer would have caused some confusion on the undertaker's coach.

Jonathan and Frances Wardell had no way of knowing what they had started when they initiated their stage service out of their Orange Tree Inn in Boston in the 1700s. Their business was a forerunner in an industry that revolutionized transportation in America with its network of routes snaking across North America. Enterprising men and women with miniscule budgets and nonexistent employees started up services that ran locally; others dreamed of crossing the continent with hundreds of coaches fanning the countryside. Both contributed to the economic health of the nation.

Lines running between major cities, such as the Baltimore–Washington Line and the Boston–New York Line, triggering no ambiguity in the minds of potential customers as to destinations—sped up business and social interactions for thousands of people. While the Good

Intent Stage Company and Shake Gut Line needed little explanation in terms of their names, the June Bug and Defiance Fast Lines begged for clarification. When the promoter of a new line between Philadelphia and Wheeling, West Virginia, announced his intentions, one of his competitors predicted it "would not last until the June bugs come." In 1887 the owners of the Defiance Fast Line defied the opposition by completing their run from Wheeling to Cincinnati, Ohio, "in less time than any other line." Their advertisement said it all: "By opposition the people are well served." Intriguing names aside, these lines offered business and leisure travelers vital services almost universally welcomed by Americans.

And then there were these: Holladay Overland Mail and Express, Butterfield Overland Stage, and Wells, Fargo and Company. Their names weren't as intriguing as some of those smaller regional lines, but they captured the attention of most Americans in the 1800s. And they made a definite splash on the transportation scene, presenting travelers a gateway to a new life in the far borders of the country. As the nation expanded, the need for fast, reliable transportation for people and mail became a rallying cry for entrepreneurs, politicians, and ordinary citizens.

Westerners were disgusted and getting more so by the day in 1850; they wanted faster regular overland mail service between northern California and the East. Newspaper publishers regularly harangued about it, and politicians howled quite a bit about establishing postal routes. For impatient Westerners it was exasperating. Anybody could understand the frustration—it took two months for a letter from Sacramento to arrive in Independence, Missouri! The government's feeble attempts at providing regular, fast mail service were generally mocked by everyone.

In June 1857 Postmaster General Aaron V. Brown established a route between San Antonio, Texas, and San Diego, California. It wasn't located exactly where most Westerners would have preferred; still it was something. At the time, San Diego was considered an out-of-the-way place with only about seven hundred people. And there was something a little different about this new service. The stage line owner chose to use mules rather than horses to pull the stages, and few could resist calling this new service the "Jackass Mail" line. Without a doubt, the animals were to blame for the name, but before long people used it as an opportunity to ridicule the service. People were fond of saying it ran "from no place through nothing to nowhere."

Shortly after the Jackass Mail line began, the postmaster general announced the establishment of another overland mail service that most believed would be better than the jackass service, and it caused a great deal of excitement in California. There would be a mail route traveling cross-country from St. Louis, Missouri, and Memphis, Tennessee (hometown of Postmaster General Brown), through Arkansas, Texas, and New Mexico Territory, into southern California via Los Angeles, Fresno, San Jose, and finally San Francisco. Again, some critics thought it was an unusual route, but proponents said they wanted to avoid the inevitable winter snowstorms promised by a more northern route. The service was required to use horses rather than mules and to carry passengers in addition to mail. The contract was open for bidding.

Meanwhile, John Butterfield had started the Butterfield Overland Mail Company just in time to bid and become the lucky recipient of the six-hundred-thousand-dollar-per-year government contract to provide semiweekly mail across the continent for six years. Butterfield had some financial backing from Wells, Fargo and Company and others, and they called the enterprise the Overland Mail Company, although many continued to call it the Butterfield Line.

Within a year of getting the contract, Butterfield had sunk one million dollars into the venture, purchasing horses and coaches, sinking wells, building way stations, and hiring drivers and station workers. The service was ready to go, and it set out on the 2,757-mile journey on September 16, 1858. When the first stage pulled into San Francisco at 7:30 a.m. on Sunday, October 10, in just under twenty-four days from its start, it was a historic occasion.

However, no one could ignore the fact that there were serious issues confronting sections of the country, and before long those conflicts erupted into what became known as the Civil War. When it became impossible to continue using the southern route to carry the mail, a new route was planned over a central region. Beginning in July 1861, the Overland Mail Company, having been taken over by Wells Fargo in 1860, shared responsibilities of a new service with a line called the Central Overland

California and Pikes Peak Express Company (known as the C.O.C. and P.P. Ex. Co.). The route stretched from the Missouri River to Placerville, California, and ran six days a week, delivering mail in only twenty days. But before long, the C.O.C. and P.P. Ex. Co. line was beginning to face serious financial issues. Then Ben Holladay entered the picture.

Short on education, long on energy, Ben Holladay took advantage of every opportunity he could. Leaving home at the age of sixteen, he earned a living as a store clerk, liquor salesman, and tavern keeper before becoming a supplier of goods to people rushing to the California gold mines and to the Pikes Peak gold rush in Colorado in the 1850s. Using the money he made from these ventures, in 1862 Holladay was in a financial position to buy the struggling C.O.C. and P.P. Ex. Co. The newly named Holladay Overland Mail and Express Company carried passengers and mail. Over the next few years, Holladay expanded and improved his lines, earning him the name "Stagecoach King."

For a time, the Holladay Overland Mail and Express Company, the Pioneer Stage Line, and Wells Fargo's Overland Mail Company joined forces to run the central mail route. But in 1866 Wells Fargo purchased the Pioneer Stage Line and offered to buy out Holladay's Overland Mail and Express Company too. Holladay couldn't refuse the offer: 1.5 million dollars, 300,000 dollars in stock, and market prices for the hay and feed in his horse barns.

Holladay Stage Office
LIBRARY OF CONGRESS PRINTS AND PHOTOGRAPHS DIVISION, WASHINGTON, DC, LC-DIG-STEREO-1S09868

Wells Fargo had been started in 1852 by Henry Wells and William Fargo in San Francisco. Before getting involved heavily in transcontinental transportation in the 1860s, the company provided banking services, including buying gold, and offered express delivery of gold and other valuables. They used steamships, railroads, and stages to get the job done for their customers. Initially they contracted with independent stage owners to fulfill some of their services. But after Wells Fargo bought out Holladay and the Pioneer Stage Line in 1866, the company claimed to have the "largest stagecoach empire in the world."

"Big Horse Market—the Finest of Its Kind in the World"
"The Big Horse Sale—Large Display of Fine Stock and Many Buyers from All Parts of the Country"
"Big Horse Sale! A Car load of Illinois Horses"

All the big stage lines needed thousands of horses to keep their stages running. At Wells Fargo's fifty-three stage stations between Folsom, California, and Salt Lake City, Utah, in 1861, eight horses were kept for each stage running on the line, in addition to animals used for hauling supplies. At this section alone, the company maintained six hundred horses, valued at about 125 dollars apiece—for a total investment in horses of 75,000 dollars. On just one of his several lines in Colorado, owner Bob Spotswood ran five coaches daily; with teams switched out every ten miles, the forty-mile trip required four relays of fresh horses, four to six animals per team. Another line—Gilmer and Salisbury—sent their agents to St. Louis, Missouri, to buy six hundred well-bred horses to jump-start their new stage line between Cheyenne and the Black Hills in 1876. When the Barlow and Sanderson line set up their Canon City to Pueblo stage in Colorado in 1879, the owners brought in two hundred new horses. When John Butterfield invested one million dollars in his overland mail company, he used a chunk of it to purchase two thousand horses. In addition to these big players, the small mom-and-pop stage lines also needed a steady supply of fresh horses to keep their enterprises lumbering over the trails, making horses big business over several decades.

Although a horse sale at a Chicago market was a bit sluggish on Monday, May 25, 1857, it could have been because of low inventory. With only 334 head of horses at seven stables in town, dealers just didn't have sufficient supply to meet demands. Two local trading stables, Robbins and Kelley and Butler and Prescott on State Street, had only forty-five and twenty horses, respectively. Doty's stable had sixty-five head to report, but they had sold thirty that week, averaging 165 dollars per head. Their stock came from great horse-raising states like Ohio, Indiana, and Illinois, with a few from Vermont and New York.

Two years later, in 1859, sales were brisk at a horse auction in Cincinnati, Ohio. Six different stables had sold 383 horses for a grand sum of 43,501 dollars, averaging 115 dollars per animal. Most went to business owners and farmers in Kentucky, Tennessee, and Alabama. Crowds had gotten so problematic at the horse market in St. Joseph, Missouri, in September 1859 that the city council was considering moving the daily sale from its current location. Council members thought that appropriating a couple of town squares near the Missouri Hotel on the corner of Market Square and Edmond Street might alleviate the problem. Proprietor James Conner had recently taken over that hotel, and he promised travelers an experience equal, if not superior, to the first-class hotels in the city. It's unclear how he felt about the odoriferous horse market moving next to his establishment.

In 1875 horse dealers in St. Louis reported that the demand for streetcar and work horses was better in November than it had been earlier in the year, but it was still far from good. No one wanted "common horses and plugs." When sales closed at four o'clock in the afternoon on Saturday, March 14, 1891, at a five-day horse sale in Cambridge City, Indiana, 416 horses had sold for 136,855 dollars. That exceeded sales from the year before, but the average was down from the 1890 sale. Organizers blamed nasty weather for the low attendance.

For decades horses were prized commodities, instrumental to the success of many businesses, including stagecoaching. Buying, selling, breeding, training, and caring for horses provided income for individuals and business enterprises. By 1900 livestock officials estimated that the United States was home to about 21 million horses, Texas having more than any other state with 1.2 million. Illinois and Iowa were close behind, with 1 million each. Pittsburgh, Omaha, St. Louis, and other large cities had vigorous horse markets, but some experts claimed the legendary Union

Stockyards and Transit Company of Chicago, called simply the Chicago Stockyards by most people, was a "mecca" and the "greatest horse market in the world."

When the Chicago Stockyards opened in 1865, horse sales were weak, usually only about thirty horses per week that first year. Most horse dealers worked independently, and the buying and selling in Chicago took place on the city streets—not convenient for either buyers or sellers. In 1886 the leading commission firms organized into a national horse exchange, resulting in "new life" for the industry and leading to the Chicago Stockyards building a horse pavilion. Not surprisingly, in 1905 the number of horses sold had ballooned to more than two thousand per week with a value of more than fourteen thousand dollars. Most of the animals came from western states: Nebraska, Montana, Wyoming, Idaho, even as far west as Washington.

For individuals who liked spending their days roaming the countryside visiting horse ranchers, a job as a horse buyer was a dream. Some buyers were independent agents; others were employed by horse dealers at the stockyards and worked for a salary and percentage of the profits. They traveled regular routes about once a month, starting at the farthest end of their territory by renting a train car that they hoped to fill with horses. After scouting the ranches and small towns at the first stop and making purchases, the buyer sent the car up the road to his next section of ranch country, again purchasing as many horses as possible. A car held about fifteen horses; when it was full, the buyer lined up another car and started the process over again until he had purchased about two hundred horses.

An experienced buyer formed relationships with the local ranchers over time. If he cleared ten dollars on a horse, he was happy; but after paying the freight and feed charges, sometimes it was difficult to accomplish that goal. The ranchers were shrewd businesspeople. They watched the markets carefully and knew that a horse they sold for seventy-five dollars could sell for as much as two hundred dollars at the Chicago Stockyards and other horse sales in big cities. Buyers competed in a tough market, with plenty of competition.

Once the buyer had ten to twenty carloads of horses, he consigned them to a commission merchant at a stockyard. Lucky horses went to the

Chicago Stockyards, where they were treated to spa-like conditions—a sprawling hundred acres with forty-five barns outfitted with seventy-five miles of pipes carrying water to massive drinking troughs. Three hundred stockyard employees tended the horses, keeping them satisfied with quantities of hay and grain, for which the stockyard charged the owner. Some owners complained that the stockyards charged twice as much as suppliers on the open market, but they had no choice—stockyard rules specified that owners could not bring in their own feed.

Horses at the Chicago Stockyards were sold every day in the Dexter Park Amphitheater, a majestic brick and steel domed structure measuring six hundred by two hundred feet, with a two-hundred-thousand-dollar price tag when built. Here again people found a variety of jobs, from grooming to inspecting. Grooms buffed the animals' coats until they shone like satin. But shrewd buyers weren't fooled by a pretty coat and had the opportunity to examine the horses before the auction. They also had twenty-four hours after the sale to allow their veterinarians time to inspect their purchases, returning the animal if defects were found.

Buyers and sellers at the Chicago Stockyards and other large auction houses worked with national horse exchange organizations like the American Horse Association, which had been organized in 1895 to "protect, promote and morally elevate the horse sales industry." This helped establish uniform standards across the industry. Horses were labeled according to four levels of grading: "Sound," meaning the animal was sound in every way; "Serviceably Sound," no lameness or soreness, may have slight blemishes or scars; "Wind and Work," meaning the horse had good wind and would work but was primarily a workhorse; and "Halter," meaning the seller offered no recommendations as to the animal. In other words, the buyer got the horse—warts and all.

The day of the sale brought a gathering of as many as five thousand spectators, including breeders, professional buyers "with the eye of an eagle," the "ever-watchful commission man who is endeavoring to secure the last penny for his country consignor," and "all sorts and conditions of men," all with a common objective: "the acquisition of the ever-potent dollar," as a Chicago newspaper reported. They came from as far away as Germany, Italy, Cuba, and Russia and as close as Illinois, Wisconsin,

Montana, Wyoming, and Idaho. But when the newspaper reporter referred to all sorts and conditions of *men*, that reporter overlooked at least one individual who would have been in the crowd—a "tall and stately blonde" woman who had traveled from her ranch in Idaho to sell her range-bred horses.

The manager of the horse department at the Chicago Stockyards was well aware of one of his most distinguished customers, and it had nothing to do with her appearance and everything to do with her expertise as a professional horse dealer. "I have been engaged in horse dealing for many years and have met with stock dealers from every quarter of the Union," Mr. Hoak said, "but I have never met one to surpass Miss Wilkins in judgement and management of horses. Her skill is truly marvelous."

Kittie Wilkins
MOUNTAIN HOME IDAHO HISTORICAL SOCIETY

Katherine "Kittie" Wilkins, known in many parts of the country as the "lady horse dealer," managed the horse breeding and selling portion of the Wilkins Horse Company in Owyhee County, Idaho. While her brothers and dad raised cattle, Kittie oversaw the horses, which meant she traveled around the country selling her range-bred horses in the 1890s. She sold in large numbers—two thousand, three thousand, and eight thousand once to a Kansas company. Her horses pulled hearses, wagons, coaches, and omnibuses throughout the United States and ended up on battlefields in South Africa and in Cuba.

Kittie told a New York newspaper reporter in 1891 that she started in the horse business at a young age. Her dad had always been engaged in horse dealing, and, she said, "When I was quite a little girl I commenced going around with him when he was selling horses." Kittie went to school for four years in California and studied classical music but ended up back at the Idaho ranch, where she "induced" her dad to let her do the selling. "When I got back to Idaho I was so lonesome I didn't know what to do," she said. "I got over it soon." She became a fierce advocate of range-bred horses. "I hold that in open-air breeding we can obtain just as good results as those who treat their colts like babies," she said. "They are always in the open air and breathe no impurities and take into their system no germs of disease. Not one of them has ever tasted grain or hay until they are rounded up for shipment."

When people expressed surprise at Kittie's role in the horse business, she replied, "Do you know, it never occurred to me before that anybody might think it was an unwomanly business for a woman to be engaged in. But it's my chosen occupation; I enjoy it and am successful in it."

Kate Casey should have known better. At about 2:30 in the afternoon on November 13, 1888, she hired a horse and buggy from L. R. Holloway livery in St. Louis, Missouri. Spending the afternoon and night driving all over town, Kate failed to return the rig to its owner. Instead she abandoned the poor creature on Twenty-first and Morgan Streets, where Police Officer Buckle found the horse and buggy at 8:30 the next morning. Who knows how long the horse had gone without food or water.

When Officer Buckle hauled Kate into the Second District Police Court on charges of cruelty to animals, she was fined twenty-five dollars. Not having the money, Kate ended up in the workhouse.

Considering how important horses were to transportation and commerce in the nineteenth century, it's not surprising that equine experts regularly offered words of advice for the health and well-being of the animals. "Horses know as well as people when they are kindly treated," one horse lover noted. The average person was well aware of treatment that smacked of cruelty: overloading and overdriving (the offense Kate Casey was convicted of), using close-fitting blinds that could irritate eyes, and driving more than two hours on a hot day without a bucket of water.

Even government officials were sensitive to the care and comfort of horses. In Sacramento, California, in 1892 the city council considered the removal of cobble streets because they were known to be "noisy, a dirt gatherer, a sewer filler, and cruel to horses." In Fort Wayne, Indiana, an ordinance that made it unlawful for any person to "inhumanly, unnecessarily or cruelly beat, injure, or otherwise abuse any dumb animal, or overload any team . . ." left no question as to how residents should treat their horses. And in the early 1900s St. Louis animal abusers hoped to avoid the wrath of a woman named Mary Calkins.

At her Golden Chain Home for Animals, Mary and her staff cared for abandoned and abused animals—from cats to a baby elephant. It wasn't uncommon to witness this fashionably dressed woman atop a wagon seat urging a rescued team of horses or mules through the city streets on her way to the police station. The abusers could be certain Mary would press charges, as she did one day in September 1902 when she came upon two drivers drawing blood on their horses as they prodded the animals with the butts of whips.

"If you hit that poor creature again, I'll have you arrested," Mary warned the abusers. Both took off into a nearby stand of timber. "They won't be back," she said. "They thought we'd go away and leave the animals here. Well, we won't. We'll drive them to the police station." A few months later, Emma Bartley, the society's vice president, witnessed two men beating a small horse attached to an ice wagon. "When it fell down, they went to kicking it to make it rise," Emma said. She called police, who

Mary Calkins
ST. LOUIS POST-DISPATCH, SEPTEMBER 28, 1902

arrested the men—who protested the horse had kicked them. The police believed Emma and Helen Sheehan, another witness to the event.

Treatment of stagecoach horses varied among the stage lines. Wells Fargo took pride in their horses, claiming they were always "well-fed, well-cared for, and well-loved." Drivers were required to inspect their teams daily and pamper them with hot sponge baths and blankets in cold weather. They offered classes to teach their workers the best care for horses. Not all stage lines went to those lengths to ensure thoughtful horse care, but every owner knew an injured or sickly horse could mean lost revenue. That's one reason horses were rotated every ten miles on long routes. A skilled stagecoach driver could get his team to do what he wanted merely by changing his tone of voice. A well-tended stage horse could work as long as fifteen years.

April 28, 1908
My dear Mrs. Lydick:
　　I am very much obliged to you for the bridle. I wish I could have seen you in person to thank you. It was most kind of you to send it to me.
　　Sincerely,
　　Theodore Roosevelt

Mary Lydick was thrilled to receive the thank-you note from Theodore Roosevelt. The Nebraska harness maker had spent two years fashioning a fine silk and linen stitched russet leather bridle complete with solid silver bit and buckles for President Roosevelt. She engraved it with his initials: "T. R."

Mary's shop was located in Hartington, Nebraska, where she not only handled the business side of her shop but also took her "place at the bench" alongside the two men who worked for her. She claimed she had never missed a day at work in four years. Edward L. Clark, a customer from Papillion, said, "She can make a complete harness quicker and better than anyone I ever saw. She has made a great many sets of harness for me, and for workmanship they cannot be excelled."

When the US War Department needed harnesses for teams at the western forts in 1906, they turned to Mary for the job. She said she was happy to win the contract and believed that Roosevelt had possibly influenced the decision. Regardless, Mary said, "I thank the War Department for their part of the giving of the contract, and I will do my best to please by doing good work."

At that time the US Census listed about forty thousand men and women as "harness/saddlemakers/repairers" working in factories. Almost seven hundred were women. In New Hampshire alone more than two hundred individuals were considered "wage earners" in the "saddlery and harness" industry; thirteen were women. When stagecoach owners established their businesses, they needed multiple sets of harnesses for their teams, and America's leatherworkers were eager to supply them. When old worn-out harnesses needed repairs, the local harness maker could take care of it. Many harness makers found employment in factories; those with an entrepreneurial bent, like Mary Lydick, set up shop themselves.

At the Nashua Saddler and Hardware Company in New Hampshire, both sexes found "remunerative employment" in the 1890s. Others worked for J. R. Hill and Company in Concord, where, they claimed, "It is an acknowledged fact" that their products were the "best and cheapest harness made in this country." A look at their client list tells it all: Wells Fargo Stage Line, Ringling Brothers Circus, and Buffalo Bill Cody's Wild West Show.

In Troy, New York, Curtis and Rickerson manufactured a wide variety of horse-related products, including double and single harnesses, carriage and sleigh robes, whips, travel bags, and sleigh bells—oh, and roller skates (presumably for humans, not horses). Specializing in unique adaptations intended for decoration, they were the sole agent in the United States for Powell and Smith's patented horse-tail holder. Also in Troy, Covert Manufacturing Company made harness snaps, chain and rope goods, and "horse and mule jewelry"—partly decorative, partly useful.

In 1902, when management at one of the largest harness shops in the country, Chicago's L. Kiper and Sons, refused to consider workers' demands for a 10 percent wage increase, harness maker Maud Dennison joined her fellow workers in a strike. After six weeks, Mr. Kiper relented. Maud's coworkers rewarded her by successfully petitioning the United Brotherhood of Leather Workers and Horse Goods Employees to welcome Maud as the organization's first woman member.

While factories offered jobs for both men and women in the harness making industry, some individuals in the trade chose to work independently as Mary Lydick did. Caroline Overst began working as a harness maker in the 1870s in New York and was still at it in the 1890s, employing two men in her shop. Nancy Curd Barr had learned the harness making trade when her brother left to fight in the Civil War and her dad needed someone to replace his son in the family shop in Newman, Illinois. And Mrs. R. E. Clark of Salem, Oregon, said she learned her craft as a young girl in England. In 1911, as soon as her daughter left for school each morning, Mrs. Clark donned a regulation harness maker's apron and headed to work at J. W. Johns's shop. "I make every part of the harness and do all kinds of harness repairing," she said. "I can assure you there is at least one woman in the world who knows more than to put a collar upside down on a horse or put the crupper over his head."

It's not surprising that there was also a great need for blacksmiths and wheelwrights during the stagecoach era. The 1850 census listed more than thirty thousand wheelwrights; the 1900 census showed more than two hundred thousand blacksmiths, including almost two hundred women in the trade.

The big stage lines such as Wells Fargo operated company shops employing people in those trades. And main streets in most small towns and big cities sported signs for blacksmith and wheelwright businesses. Those local business owners supported the day-to-day needs of smaller stage lines. Every stagecoach was filled with iron parts that sooner or later required maintenance at the blacksmith shop, and each coach had four wheels constructed of wood and iron—materials that took a beating on the rugged terrain everywhere in the country. Some of those wheelwrights and blacksmiths were women.

The daughter of a non–English speaking immigrant wheelwright captured the attention of the *New York Times* in 1895. Both she and her dad remain nameless, but her story was newsworthy at the time. "You see my father has never learned to speak English, so I had to learn the different parts of the wagons and tell him what the English words are," this mystery woman told the reporter. The family's wheelwright and wagon shop employed several men, whom the daughter supervised. She knew the business from the ground up. "I've known all about the work since I was a little girl," she said. Because she knew the skills a successful wheelwright needed to have, she had high expectations of the workers she hired. "He ought to make a pair of wheels in two days and a half, and if he takes four days for it, I know he is slow and that much time is lost," she said.

Anna Albrecht was another New Yorker who made a living as a wheelwright, while at the same time raising three kids. She and her husband owned the shop, where the kids played and helped out after school. Maybe not the safest environment for kids, but they seemed undisturbed "by the clang of steel on steel or the whirl of sparks" as their mom was busy swinging heavy hammers and "fashioning iron and steel at white heat."

"I have found time to bear my husband three fine, healthy children, brought up at the forge, you might say," Anna said. "When we are not busy in the shop and I am not busy at home, I go out and canvass for trade for my husband." The Albrecht's hard work paid off—they owned their shop and a house free and clear.

Throughout the country during the stagecoach days, female blacksmiths also plied their trade. Wells, Fargo and Company was headquartered in San Francisco and employed company blacksmiths; it's not clear if they hired women as smithies. But for those stage lines in San Francisco that patronized the local blacksmiths, Annie Bole was available. She was only fifteen years old in 1888 when she brushed her hair back from her face, rolled up her sleeves, and donned a leather apron every morning. Plunging a mound of iron into the fire, Annie hammered away at the red-hot mass, creasing it into the shape of a horseshoe as the sparks flew around her. "I've seen dozens that tried it, but none of 'em had the natural talent for making horseshoes that the young lady's got," the shop owner said about Annie.

At Santa Rosa, California, Serina Ann Faber toiled from morning to night amid the sparks and smoke and "din of ringing anvil." She was considered an expert at using a sledgehammer as she practiced her skills on coaches and wagons and wheels. "Yes, I know it is somewhat of a novelty for a woman to work in a blacksmith shop as I do, but I like it just the same," she said as she wielded the hammer on the anvil.

Celia Holbrook was only seventeen years old when her dad died; her mom had died eight years before, leaving her to raise her four younger siblings in Sherborn, Massachusetts, in 1903. Luckily, her dad had a blacksmith shop where he employed several assistants; Celia took over the business. With a large family to support, she was happy to win a contract with the post office to carry mail from the railroad station to the post office, four miles round-trip each day.

By 1905 stagecoaching had faded from the transportation landscape in many places; however, there still were plenty of stagecoaches in operation in Arizona. In fact, the government was looking for stage drivers to bid for mail contracts in a number of locations. There were at least five routes available running out of Prescott. They paid quite well—ranging from 144 dollars to more than a thousand. Routes varied in length and frequency. The one from Prescott to Juniper, which ran three times a week, paid $1,035.55. A couple of stage lines provided passenger and freight service in Prescott too. Hocker and Baker stage company made daily trips between Prescott and Walker. And Jas. M. Sloan's stage left from Shumate's store in Prescott every day at two o'clock for a trip to Walker. The fare was one dollar.

Fortunately for these stage owners, there was a top-notch blacksmith in town. Mollie Thompson White pumped bellows, ran a drill press, and swung a sledge at an anvil to weld and reshape iron in her blacksmith shop in Prescott. She was adept at all sorts of things. "I can handle horses all right, though they do get a little fractious at times," Mollie said. "And I do all the buggy painting that comes to the shop." On Sunday, Mollie and her husband headed for the nearby hill country to do a little small game hunting; Mr. White admitted that Mollie was a much better shot than he.

Mining operations during the last half of the 1800s and into the 1900s, especially in Arizona and other places in the West, needed those who could transport both people and supplies, so it was only natural that individuals who had rigs and a team would see an opportunity to make money. Stagecoach lines transported miners and small cargo items, but bigger and sturdier wagons were required for some of the heavy equipment and ores brought out of the mines.

Arizona Mary standing next to her team
USC DIGITAL LIBRARY. CALIFORNIA HISTORICAL SOCIETY COLLECTION

A woman known as "Arizona Mary," whose real name has been lost to history, worked up to fifteen hours per day guiding her wagon and sixteen-ox team through the mountain mining camps of Arizona in the late 1800s, carrying supplies to the camps and returning with the ores the miners had pried from the earth. While little is known about this hard-working woman, enough has remained of her story to raise her to the level of legend. She was described as a slender figure, with a "firm mouth" and a "resolute way" and dressed in a simple frock with a deep-brimmed bonnet atop her head and a large white kerchief about her neck. As owner of the outfit, Mary was responsible for maintenance of the wagon and oxen as well as coordinating her work. It was said she had trouble with neither. Nor was she stymied by the occasional road agent who was attracted to her valuable cargo. She handled them calmly and bravely with the aid of her trusty gun. By 1900, when newspapers carried a feature article about Mary, she had been at her trade for several years and had no intention of stopping. According to reports, her business was valued at "five figures."

About the same time that Arizona Mary was reported to be pulling in comfortable amounts of money with her freighting business, Mrs. John Ferris (sometimes spelled Farris, and whose first name is a mystery) was making a comfortable living with her freight business, first in Colorado and later in Wyoming. She was a common sight in the late 1800s, driving her team through the streets of Telluride, Colorado, hauling timber to the mines. By 1900, with twenty years of driving under her belt, she and her six-horse team were pulling a freight wagon between Battle Lake, Wyoming, and the railroad stations. She was known to camp out in the wilds when her trips required overnight runs, and her work could be dangerous. In 1903 she was hauling a load of lumber from a sawmill when the top layer began to slip down. Mrs. Ferris tried to stop the fall but got caught under the lumber, dislocating her knee. The injury required a short break from her strenuous work, but before long she was back at it—loading and unloading heavy cargoes as she had for years.

Fate smiled on Arabelle Sewell one day in 1884 when a "swashbuckling" cowboy named Dave Mackey rode into John Marts's stage way station in Odee, Kansas, where she worked as a cook and food server. Belle had been taken in by the Marts following a harrowing trip across the prairie with her parents. The Sewells were traveling to New Mexico when outlaws stole the horses pulling their covered wagons. They relied on their milk cows to lead the wagons to safety, but Belle had walked much of the trip on bare feet. It's unclear what happened to her parents, but she was taken in by the Marts as a foster child. She was working at the way station when Dave struck up a romance, and Belle ended up marrying him. It turned out well for her: a paying job when she needed one and a good mate for life.

Way station. Tavern. Ranche. Over the two-hundred-year history of stage travel, stage stops went by a variety of names, but they generally served as a place for drivers to switch horses or for passengers to eat a meal, spend a night, or delight in the private luxury of an actual outhouse after enduring the behind-a-tumbleweed facilities of the stage trail. Proprietors made money, and their businesses offered job opportunities for cooks, servers, and maids. While the promise of romantic encounters like Dave and Belle Mackey's couldn't be expected at every stage stop, there were certainly paying jobs to be had.

Kitty (sometimes spelled Kittie) Gibson spent a lifetime living and working at a stage stop. Her birth name was Catherine Burns, and she was believed to be a granddaughter of an enslaved woman. Her dad was part French, part Native American. One version of her story has her being adopted as a young child by a woman named Elizabeth Gibson, who moved from Ohio to Indiana with Kitty. Elizabeth's brother, David, operated a tavern along the Calumet River in northern Indiana, and Kitty worked there from about the age of twelve. The Gibson tavern was a stop for travelers heading to Chicago from the East. Before the Michigan Central Railroad tracks were laid all the way into Chicago, a stagecoach picked up passengers near the Gibson tavern and took them into the city. It was a popular way station for travelers to refresh with food and sleep. People noticed "the little black-eyed Indian woman," who impressed them with her "cheerfulness and quiet demeanor." When the Gibsons died, Kitty inherited two and a half acres of land and a house, where she lived until 1914, when she died at the age of eighty-nine. She had begun to sell off her land in parcels to support herself in her old age. The way station where the little girl had worked serving travelers became her home and a source of income for the rest of her life.

As the pervasiveness of the stagecoach in American society increased over the years, the average woman and man looking for ways to make a living found many opportunities associated with stagecoaching. The stagecoach industry reached into many facets of American life, in large cities as well as small towns and rural areas. The economic impact was significant for some, less for others—direct for some, indirect for others. The owners of stagecoach constructing enterprises realized considerable economic benefit over decades, while a blacksmith operating near a stage stop welcomed any work that came his or her way as a result of steady stage traffic. While these individuals experienced economic gain related to staging, they and others offered valuable goods and services to the stagecoach industry, helping to sustain it for years.

It's a brain-tickling exercise to imagine the economic impact of the stagecoach over time. But the human stories of the day-to-day lives of ordinary and extraordinary people whose livelihoods depended on and contributed to stagecoaches help us understand how impactful these vehicles were to the economy and growth of the country.

CHAPTER 2

Stagecoach as Purveyor of Information

KING GEORGE III COULDN'T HAVE BEEN HAPPY WHEN HE RECEIVED THE report from his postal inspector in the American colonies in 1773. Hugh Finlay had spent ten months traveling throughout his territory, which stretched from Quebec, Canada, to St. Augustine, Florida, to get a feel for the post office situation, and what he learned probably reinforced the belief that the colonists were an unruly bunch of rebels. It seemed more than a few stage drivers were enabling colonists to skirt the postal service when it came to paying for letter delivery. Rather than enrich His Majesty's coffers, many colonists relied on local stagecoach drivers to devise ways to bypass government rules. Stage passengers were often in on the deception as well—agreeing to carry a letter in a coat pocket or satchel, claiming it was a personal letter of recommendation if asked by prying inspectors. And while letter carrying by private entities was opposed by the post office, packages were not a problem. It wasn't unheard of for an inspector to find a letter attached to a box wedged into a stage's baggage boot. Upon further investigation, the package itself might contain nothing more than a bundle of paper or straw. Yes, with the help of cunning stage drivers, colonists went to great lengths to avoid paying the greedy Crown to carry a letter to a friend or relative.

In Salem, Massachusetts, everyone knew about the stage driver who was happy to deliver as many letters as he could easily accommodate, causing very few letter writers or business correspondents to use the post office. Without a doubt, his activities were putting a dent in post office revenues in Salem. When Inspector Finlay asked the postal clerk why the driver was allowed to continue his illegal practice, the clerk explained that there wasn't a jury around that would convict the fellow. Not only that, he claimed, the informer "wou'd get tar'd and feather'd."

The Crown's postal authorities may have thought they solved the exasperating stage driver dilemma in one location when they offered a job to an exceptionally successful stage driver/clandestine private letter carrier. Although it meant an annual investment of ten pounds Sterling for his salary, the post office not only eliminated an irksome competitor but also reaped the benefit of the established customer base he brought along.

But the Crown's post office officials were waging a losing battle. Stage drivers weren't the only violators of the postal guidelines that discouraged private mail carriage. Because butchers traveled frequently to buy and sell livestock, they also carried a letter or two now and again, charging far less than the post office. Likely the most audacious abusers of the system were the postriders themselves, employees of the post office hired to carry correspondence by horseback. Many were open to accepting a letter from a writer along the route, happy to carry it for less than their employer charged!

Inspector Finlay explained all this rebellious behavior on the part of the American colonists as their attempt to "hinder all acts of Parliament from taking effect in America," adding: "They are, they say, to be governed by laws of their own framing and no other."

If the king's inspector was correct, one would think the illicit acts against the post office would cease after the hard-fought Revolution. But they didn't. That rebellious spirit so manifest in the years when Great Britain ruled the colonies persisted in the early days of the new republic. Those stage drivers who had operated covert letter-carrying services simply resumed those activities under the new United States of America. It may have had nothing to do with defying the government and everything to do with making money.

The new American government had passed an ordinance in 1782 outlawing the delivery of mail by private individuals. If postal officials weren't already aware of stage drivers and others bypassing the post office to deliver mail, stage proprietor Nathaniel Twining spilled the beans when, in the course of memorializing a friend to Congress in April 1785, he mentioned that the deceased had a lucrative arrangement with merchants who paid a subscription to this private citizen to "convey all Packages and Letters." At the same time, Twining proposed to right the wrong committed by the fellow who was no longer able to defend himself. He offered to continue the unlawful service through a *lawful* contract under the auspices of the US Post Office. Twining's business proposition sparked a debate that lasted for months.

Postmaster General Ebenezer Hazard wasn't convinced that using stagecoaches for mail delivery was a wise business decision. He believed they were slower and would be more costly than the postriders already in service. And he was aware that stages usually catered to their passengers, who expected to stop occasionally and didn't typically appreciate night travel, whereas he wanted the mails to go through as quickly as possible. However, after a bit of wrangling among politicians, Hazard relented; contracts to deliver US mail were awarded to stagecoach proprietors, including Twining and some associates. But Hazard was never happy with the situation, and by 1788 he was again using postriders.

Hazard might have continued defiantly rejecting the use of stagecoach companies as mail carriers had it not been for the intervention of a fellow named George Washington, who was about to become the first president of the United States after ratification of a new constitution in 1789. Hazard's decision to revert to postriders coincided with the period in which states were voting to ratify the new US Constitution, and news regarding the results was spreading far too slowly for many citizens and politicians. Some blamed it on Hazard and the slow-moving postriders. One of those dissatisfied citizens was George Washington, who was home at Mount Vernon waiting to hear results. When he blamed the "new arrangement in the post-office"—that is, "the contract for transporting the mail on horseback, instead of having it carried in the stages"—for being "unfavorable to the circulation of intelligence," Hazard must have known that he would be out of a job under the new president's administration. And he was.

In 1790 the new postmaster general, Samuel Osgood, sent a letter to Secretary of the Treasury Alexander Hamilton in which he gave his assessment of "evils" that plagued his department and that he had inherited from his predecessor. "Stage drivers and private post riders may have been the carriers of many letters which ought to have gone in the mail" was number five on his list of six problems he identified as causing concern. "The injury the general revenue has sustained in this way is greater than I had expected," Osgood warned. And he admitted that "perhaps no complete remedy can be devised for this evil."

Osgood explained that stage proprietors were at a disadvantage, as their initial investments in horses, coaches, and drivers were considerable—as much as twenty thousand dollars, according to one of the contractors. Every one-hundred- or two-hundred-mile mail route cost the stage owner several thousand dollars. With no guarantee of winning a mail contract over multiple years, the investment was risky, causing owners to charge high rates for their mail service. Osgood claimed that his hands were tied because he was required to offer the mail contracts to the lowest bidders, who often were "poor people" who didn't have the means to fulfill the service "as it ought to be."

At the time, the postal service had about twenty mail-carrying contracts in place. Over the next hundred years the number ballooned, offering many Americans—both rich and not-so-rich—opportunities to be part of a vast communication network that helped knit the country together by delivering the US mail. Many of those enterprising individuals were women.

"That's the craziest thing I ever saw. There could not be any fact like this. It starts out being a slander against the pioneer women, as I view it. Obviously, from this picture they were riding along naked and the Indians scalped them for indecency. The presumption might be the Indians were so shocked by this party of nude ladies with some gentlemen riding across the desert in a large bus that they scalped them," John Collier, commissioner of Indian affairs, said.

He wasn't the only person surprised by the painting hanging near the office of the postmaster general in Washington, DC, in 1937. The mural, titled *Dangers of the Mail*, had been painted by Colorado artist Frank Mechau as part of a New Deal art program that provided jobs to unemployed artisans. The mural was controversial at the time—mostly for its nudity—and has been since because of its stereotypical portrayal of Native Americans as violent savages. And many questioned the idea of women riding in a stagecoach without clothes in a blizzard. In reality, mail carriers faced many dangers, mostly from the weather and treacherous roadways or white bandits who pillaged the mail for valuables. Women *were* part of the story, but more likely as carriers of the US mail. Polly Martin was one of those fearless individuals.

"I have carried a great deal of express matter—some pretty heavy packages. Once I carried a corpse. The box was pretty long, and projected over the rear of the wagon some distance. It was a kind of a dark, stormy night. When we got to the graveyard, we drove through it over to the back side, and unloaded the box," Polly told a *Boston Globe* reporter in 1884.

Polly had been delivering mail in Attleboro, Massachusetts, since 1860. In addition to US mail, she delivered telegrams, express packages, and passengers. "Well, I had some adventures, that's a fact," Polly told the reporter.

There was that Thanksgiving night when the Methodist minister asked for a ride to the parsonage after a delightful evening with parishioners. It was a night as "dark as a pocket," Polly recalled, when she overtook a gang of five or six men by the roadside. As one of the fellows jumped into the road and tried to grab the reins, Polly used her whip, fashioned from branches of an apple tree braided together. As the outlaw attempted to enter the coach, Polly "pounded him in the face" with a stick "until the blood ran down" his face. The horse kept going, and Polly kept pounding that face. Finally the intruder's foot caught in the wagon wheel and he fell to the ground, the wheel crunching over his foot. "He had tackled the wrong customer that time," Polly said.

Polly admitted that she had carried a revolver for a time but had never used it. She preferred to intimidate with her voice and fists. When a customer questioned her practice of tossing his bag filled with gold onto the floor under her feet, she soothed his nerves by remarking, "I should like to see anyone try to get it away from me. He would have a good job."

Polly said she seldom had problems with the passengers she squeezed in around the mailbags. She almost always had five or six humans in her cargo. "Some have been so drunk that they had to lie down on their backs in the bottom of the wagon," she said. Folks liked to tell a story about an impatient young fellow Polly picked up who started to harangue the horse for not going as fast as the man wanted. "Look here, young man, you just stop swearing or get out," she reportedly told the passenger. As the story went, the next time this fellow rode with Polly, he swore at the horse in French, and was thus immune from Polly's reprimand.

The US Post Office contract paid Polly 134 dollars per year for her Attleboro route. For sixteen years she braved all kinds of weather to ensure that her customers received their mail. "It seems like a long time to look back on, and I wouldn't want to go through it again," she said as she reminisced to the *Globe* reporter.

Seventeen-year-old Florence S. Markham had a government contract to deliver mail between Stockbridge and Interlaken, Massachusetts, beginning in 1889. She was the sole support of her parents, but her 108-dollar-per-year mail contract wasn't enough to cover all their expenses. She looked to other sources to supplement that income. "It's the little incidentals, the carting of goods and passengers between the villages, that has made the job pay," Florence said. But toting the freight, express packages, and passengers' baggage was heavy work. On top of that, Florence cared for the horses that pulled her coach, feeding and harnessing them, in addition to maintaining the stable yard.

Making the six-mile trip twice a day could be grueling in the New England springs, when she often drove through driving thunderstorms, but the winters were brutal. Often the roads were impassable for the horses; when the drifts were too high, Florence swung the mailbags over her shoulder and made her way through the snow by foot to meet the mail trains.

By 1913 Florence had never taken a day off work and had never missed a train, so Postmaster Steve Burghardt must have been shocked when she requested a vacation day in June to marry Archibald Boyd. Newspapers reported that after her four-year, three-hundred-dollar-per-year mail contract was publicized, she had received a hundred marriage proposals from across the country. But Archibald and Florence were old friends, and her attractive postal salary probably had nothing to do with their decision to marry.

When Florence decided to retire in 1917, she told people she had enjoyed a pleasant career as a mail carrier. "I don't mind admitting that I am forty-five years old. I have found the life has had some advantages. It keeps one in perfect physical health," she said. "I suppose I have ridden close to 80,000 miles between these villages in the last twenty-eight years," she added. Newspapers reported that she had won the admiration of people in her community of Stockbridge for her success in doing "a man's work"—not surprising, as it was well known that Florence was a suffragist. Florence looked forward to taking time to grow flowers and "do a few things I have been planning to do for ten years or more," she said.

Stories abound about another female mail carrier who reached legendary status. As is often the case when it comes to legends, fact and fiction blur. Mary Fields, a woman with a reputation "along the lines of the rough and tough Calamity Jane," captured the attention of residents

Mary Fields
URSULINE ARCHIVES, GREAT FALLS, MONTANA

in and around Cascade, Montana, in the late 1800s and early 1900s. The portrayal of Mary as a cigar-smoking, gun-toting, coarse-talking, freight-hauling mail carrier survived into the twenty-first century.

Much was made about Mary's physique: a heavy-set frame stretched over six feet of height. A photo of Mary cradling a rifle in her arms reinforced the stories that she relied heavily on her guns as protection from dangerous situations and to settle disputes involving humans and animals. There was the account of the night Mary used her rifle and six-gun to fend off a pack of hungry wolves when her freight wagon overturned on a desolate roadway. The time Mary and a coworker engaged in a duel to decide who would perform chores was reportedly what led to her dismissal from that job.

As tantalizing as the stories about Mary were, there was no need to embellish stories about her life. The gritty reality of her existence was sufficiently intriguing to make her memorable. Mary Fields, who became known as "Stagecoach Mary," was born into slavery somewhere in the southern United States in the early 1830s. At some point she became a free woman and, after the Civil War, made her way to Toledo, Ohio, where she worked at a convent as a groundskeeper. She had a close friendship with one of the nuns, Sister Amadeus, and when the nun was sent to Cascade, Montana Territory, to run a mission in 1884, Mary followed.

Absent the benefit of Mary's own voice through journals, letters, or oral records, historians have relied on the writings of others to paint a portrait of Mary's life in Montana. A priest wrote about her in his diary in 1887, describing Mary's reaction to a skunk invading the mission chicken yard, killing sixty-two little chicks under Mary's care. "Mary was horrified but did not retreat but at once took a hoe and made fight on the skunk and killed the beast." When the priest asked Mary how she avoided being sprayed by the skunk, she replied that she had approached the creature "from the front, not the rear." One of the nuns at the mission wrote Mary's biography entry for the Cascade County, Montana, history book. Another photo of Mary holding a rifle appears in the book, and the nun wrote that Mary worked at the mission for about ten years before "her terrible temper, rough ways and the many complaints to the Bishop by those who were unlucky enough to arouse her wrath" led to her dismissal.

The same nun indicated that Mary moved into the tiny town of Cascade, where she eventually secured a job delivering freight and mail from 1895 to 1903 between town and the mission from which she had been fired. One of the residents of Cascade recalled Mary hauling supplies and food from town to the mission. He said she "often spent the prairie nights fighting her way through storms and braving great dangers."

Reports of Mary's freight and mail carrying years, when she was in her sixties, resemble the experiences of other women with similar jobs in other places. Obsession with getting the mail through no matter the weather. Braving blizzards, floods, and wild creatures including wolves. Shouldering mailbags when her horse team couldn't get through the snowdrifts. Never missing a day of work. Tending the horses that pulled the coaches. Sitting high atop the stagecoach seat, Mary skillfully "managed the two teams of horses." And according to the *Great Falls Tribune*, Mary's horse-handling skills were phenomenal. Apparently, she could use her six-shooter or whip with equal dexterity when removing a fly from her lead horse's ear. Not only could she remove the pest, friends said, she "could break the fly's hind leg with her whip lash and shoot its eye out with a revolver."

After Mary retired in 1903, the local newspaper occasionally ran articles about her. They described a woman who wore a man's coat and hat—but drew the line at trousers—and who enjoyed drinking buttermilk and tending her flower garden overflowing with pansies. The paper described her as a rabid baseball fan who declared that an umpire who made a decision against the home team deserved "the gallows," or at least a "licking." When she died in December 1914, the *Tribune* claimed her funeral was one of the largest ever held in Cascade.

There are so many unanswered questions about this woman who became a legend. Did she hold any precious memories of a loving family? Was Sister Amadeus a true friend, or was the relationship a servant-mistress situation? Did Mary have any other friends? Was she a dog lover, as one might surmise from the widely distributed photo of Mary with a cute black-and-white pooch perched at her feet?

Brushing aside the romanticized particles of Mary's experiences leaves future generations with a narrative of a woman who started life under the most horrific disadvantages imaginable and worked tirelessly under rugged conditions her entire life. A writer in *Negro Digest* magazine wrote in 1950 that Mary was "in the best sense, a pioneer woman. She was rough and she was tough."

The 92,500 people living in Wyoming in 1900 didn't think they were unreasonable in expecting regular mail service delivered on time. The Casper post office reported as much as seven hundred pounds of mail arriving every Monday, yet people living in outlying regions complained that they hadn't seen a newspaper in a week, and someone had spotted undelivered bags of mail stacked up at the Lost Cabin post office. The mail contract between Casper and Winthrop called for runs three times a week and paid the carrier $632.04 per year. When the Casper to Berthaton route was running, the carrier earned almost fifteen hundred dollars per year. When the government opened up bids for the Casper to Lander route three years before, there had been plenty of competition. Bids ranged from fifty-four hundred to seventy-three hundred dollars per year. So everybody knew the government was throwing good money at mail contracts in Wyoming.

Some people blamed out-of-state mail contractors for the unsatisfactory service. Eastern tenderfoots submitted ridiculously low bids to fulfill mail routes in Wyoming, not knowing the rugged conditions they would face in the western territories. After winning the contract and arriving in the state, the greenhorns were in for a rude awakening. Ravines and gullies, mountains, and wide-open stretches of sparsely populated areas greeted the newcomers.

When the government opened bids in Wyoming in 1901, it placed some very specific restrictions on the process. The bidder was required to live on or contiguous to the route and to personally supervise the performance of carriers. This was intended to eliminate "syndicate bidders" and encourage locals to submit bids. Wyoming residents had more faith in their local mail carriers, and William and Agnes Clark were perfect examples of responsible locals.

The Clarks' Concord coach, the Golden Chariot, carrying passengers and mail, was a "Winner" if residents were to believe the ads running in the *Natrona County Tribune* in 1897. Over the years the Clarks fulfilled all aspects of the stage business—owners, drivers, horse suppliers and breakers, and stage stop operators.

Agnes handled the reins over "a four-span of wild-eyed broncs" day and night over the Casper to Lander or Thermopolis line three times a week. After a time, mail arrived daily on the train into Casper, and Agnes increased her runs to accommodate. "We carried mail, express, . . . passengers ranged all the way from drummers, Indians and herders, to governors, ex-governors, and state and federal executives of various sorts," she recalled years later. "There were few bridges in those days, and the hills and gulches of Natrona and Fremont County made the trip a hazardous one." Agnes often drove the stage overnight, and when she returned to the ranch, she tended to household chores and raising her thirteen children.

As their business expanded, the Clarks invested in two big coaches at nearly four hundred dollars apiece and had about three hundred horses

Goose Egg Ranch, 1949
GOOSE EGG RANCH, THOMAS G. CARRIGEN PHOTOGRAPH COLLECTION P86-19/2546, WYOMING STATE ARCHIVES

on their ranch to keep the big stagecoaches and several hacks moving over the countryside. In 1901 they decided that the higher cost of horse feed necessitated higher passenger fares for the stages. The ten-cents-per-mile rate increased to eleven cents per mile to accommodate an annual increase in feed costs of about two thousand dollars.

The Clarks lived at different locations over the years: at Goose Egg Ranch, where they raised cattle and lived in a big stone house that operated as a stage ranch at times; at a ranch at Hobart; and at a homestead near the Powder River. They held mail contracts for eight years, at times driving themselves and at other times hiring drivers to transport passengers and the mail. The 140-mile Casper to Thermopolis run took thirty-six hours and left Casper at 9:00 p.m., traveling fourteen miles to the first relay station, where horses were switched out and the mailbags dropped. It was a five-minute stop in the middle of the night, and the stage sped on to the next stop—the Clark ranch at about 2:30 a.m. When Agnes was not driving the route, she and her daughters provided breakfast for the stage driver and passengers. After a short break, everyone climbed back into the stage to continue the long journey through Hell's Half Acres—an area rich in deep ruts and high peaks that was "truly half an acre of hell"—to the Wolton Hotel, operated by Thomas and Henryetta Hood, for a short transfer of mail and express packages, and then on to the Round Hill station, where passengers could grab a delightful meal prepared by Luella Demorest while husband George tended the horses. Here the route split off into two directions—to Lander or Thermopolis. The Thermopolis route took passengers over the "burning sand of the desert" and some of the roughest roads of the entire trip to Lost Cabin, an old abandoned gold mine. The stage then headed for a mountain peak up ahead, but not before descending a steep hill that tested the skill of any driver, and that passengers swore they would never attempt again, choosing to walk down next time. Next stop was a ranch where M. L. Bishop tended stock for William Clark and where horses were switched. Passing through a ranch operated by Minnie Rider and her mother, the stage proceeded to De Ranch to drop mail and then continued up the mountain until finally reaching the peak, only to gingerly make its way down after a short rest for the horses. On the way down, the stage stopped at a ranch operated by Joseph and Ellie Burgess, who welcomed passengers with an excellent meal provided by Ellie—some said as good as a meal served at the Palmer House in Chicago. After another night's drive "over hills, through canyons, around crooks and curves," the stage reached Thermopolis, where the "completely tired out and exhausted" passengers searched for a bed. The entire trip required at least twenty men and women and 125 horses, all overseen by William and Agnes Clark, who kept the US mail moving no matter the weather.

William and Agnes were celebrating Christmas Day 1901 in Cheyenne when they were served with papers notifying them of a lawsuit brought against them by Harry Weller, a traveling salesman from Omaha, Nebraska. He was asking for 23,345 dollars to cover expenses for a broken collarbone and "injuries too numerous to mention" that he had received some years before when he fell from one of the Clarks' "soft-cushioned, air-springed coaches" on a trip to Wolton. Weller claimed the stage had flipped over, and as he managed to crawl out from under the overturned coach, he realized the seriousness of his injuries. William Clark had a slightly different version of events, ready to testify that his passenger had been "heavily burdened with John Barleycorn," having consumed about two quarts of whiskey during a two-mile stretch. Weller claimed to have witnesses who would swear he'd had nothing to drink. The parties settled before the case ever went to court. The Clarks paid Weller 250 dollars for damages.

———

"Neither snow nor rain nor heat nor gloom of night stays these couriers from the swift completion of their appointed rounds." The unofficial motto of the US Postal Service was taken seriously by the women and men who fulfilled mail contracts across the country. From Connecticut to Colorado and New Mexico to Oregon, hardy women earned admirable reputations as dedicated purveyors of the nation's correspondence, urging plodding horses through spring's muddy mountain roads and shoveling their way through winter's blinding snowstorms. At times fighting off would-be robbers and threats from wild animals, they were a resilient mixture of pluck and fortitude.

"Yes, I meet some pretty tough-looking customers sometimes, but they never touch me. If they did they would find out how serious a thing it is to interfere with the US Mails," Charlotte Waldo said about her rugged Connecticut mail route in 1894.

In New Mexico, Harriet Anderson proudly claimed, "I'd as soon think of starting out without my mailbags as without my revolver."

"Afraid? Why, no! Whatever should I be afraid of?" Rose Sturgeon said of her thirty-five-mile mail run between Denio and Andrew, Oregon, in 1898.

"I took up this work because it promised a good living, that's all," May Robertson matter-of-factly explained her rationale for taking on a daily mail run between Meeker and Buford, Colorado, in 1912.

— ◆ —

Some called Charlotte Waldo's thirty-six-mile round-trip Ashford to Bolton Hills run the worst mail route in Connecticut in 1894. Each morning except Sunday, this woman of medium height with a build that suggested "great strength and endurance" donned her huge black eye goggles, secured a well-worn sailor hat adorned with a white ribbon and huge bow atop her shortly shorn hair, and slid her feet into a generously sized pair of men's shoes. Ready for her twelve-hour journey over some of the rockiest trails of Connecticut, she affixed to her visage a "resolute, determined look."

At 6:00 a.m. Charlotte set out from the Ashford post office on her rendezvous with the mail customers and postmasters along her route. There was not a hint of underhanded practices by this veteran mail carrier; as customers intercepted her along the route with letters, Charlotte settled them snuggly in her pockets, dutifully bringing them out at the next post office for the postmaster to cancel and place in the mail pouch with the other canceled letters. At some locations she veered off to the side of the road, grabbing strings hanging out of a small box set on a post. One swift tug of the strings landed the large waterproof mailbag safely in her wagon. At other stops along the route, residents with just a letter or two for mailing placed them in a long narrow box fastened to the end of a post. A heavy stone held the letters in place, and a white rag attached to the box alerted Charlotte. Up and down steep hills of an old turnpike road, Charlotte delivered and collected hundreds of pieces of mail each week, arriving in Bolton Hills about 9:00 a.m., just in time to meet the mail train for Hartford.

After the mail was loaded onto the train, Charlotte had a short respite of sorts—taking her horses to a nearby barn for a quick curry and rub-down. Both Charlotte and her horses enjoyed a hasty meal brought from home. By noon Charlotte started on the return trip. For her efforts she was paid 150 dollars a year.

Hundreds of miles from Charlotte Waldo's Connecticut mail route, another woman—a "wild western type," according to the *Buffalo (NY) Courier*, a twenty-five-year-old with a pretty face and rosy complexion—carried mail westward from Magdalena, New Mexico, to several small settlements in the San Augustin plains. Harriet Anderson held the reins over her trusty team, Don and Donna, as they carried the US mail through the hundred-mile journey over a harsh, unforgiving wilderness in 1895. Harriet's dad had won the contract to carry mail, but when he was sidelined with health issues, Harriet slapped a pistol belt stuffed with a six-chambered revolver around the waist of her blue serge dress topped off with a stylish Eton jacket and tackled the job. Locals said she could draw her revolver as quickly as any professional, and she proved it by unloading all six bullets into a playing card posted at thirty paces.

"I've never had occasion to use it in earnest, but I always feel safer to have it with me," she said. "I've got to protect the property that is in my charge, and I'd do it with my last breath and my last cartridge."

She was more likely to use her weapon on a wild coyote than a human being in the lonely region of the New Mexico plains during her twice-weekly trek. And there was the time she shot a bear alongside the road as he pawed his way up a tree trunk. "I halted my team and banged away. But he scrambled off into the brush so quickly that I didn't have a chance to shoot again," Harriet said. "Poor fellow, I was sorry afterward that I shot, because it's likely that I lamed him."

Harriet admitted that she also followed some advice from her mother as she made her way on her mail run. "My mother always makes me carry, very secretly, though, a little flask of brandy, because she says it might be the saving of my life some time."

"Modest as her flower name, yet brave and self-reliant" is how the *San Francisco Chronicle* described barely twenty-year-old Rose Sturgeon, mail coach driver in Denio, Oregon, in 1898. Thinking she would teach school as a way to supplement her family's income, Rose changed her mind when her dad's friend suggested she may like to become a mail carrier. "I considered it a joke at first, but afterward I got to thinking about it and I concluded I'd rather do that than teach school. I've always been used to horses and to driving, and I'm not timid about being alone, and so I asked by father's friend to get a job for me."

Her route ran through a ranching and mining area, but the ranches and mines were few and far apart; it could be a lonely drive for the young woman when she didn't have stage passengers. "Most of the time I go alone. I am fond of horses and my team is company for me. I don't think I'd ever feel lonely as long as I could see all outdoors and the sky up above," Rose explained.

Unlike Harriet Anderson, who followed the advice of her mother, Rose chose to ignore Mrs. Sturgeon's motherly concerns when it came to guns on her daily trips to Andrews—a thirty-mile drive. "I don't carry a revolver or anything of the sort. I did at first because my mother wanted me to. But the thing was always in the way. There wasn't any place to put it, and I didn't want to buckle it around me because it looked so—so sort of mannish, you know—and it would slide out of the seat, and so after a few times I quit carrying it," she said.

Bad weather didn't bother this plucky Oregon girl. On snowy, windy days she wrapped up in warm clothes and a fur hat, driving as fast as her horses would go. "It's pretty good fun to come rattling along through the rain or snow as fast as your horses can travel," Rose said. "It makes you feel alive clear through."

She never seemed to regret her decision to drive the mail stage rather than spend her days in the schoolhouse. "It wasn't any hotter on the road between Denio than it was anywhere else and not nearly as uncomfortable as it would have been inside a schoolhouse," she said.

"I think I've got a pretty nice job. I like it better than anything else I could possibly do, and I mean to hold on to it just as long as Uncle Sam will let me," Rose said.

——

Newspaper readers across the country in 1912 might have wondered if the tiny community of Meeker, Colorado, was a hotbed of women's rights based on news stories emanating from the tiny town of eight hundred. There was that provocative divorce suit brought by a woman who claimed her husband had failed to provide her financial needs and had assaulted her with a "deadly weapon" when she asked for a small amount of money. Cross-examination brought out information that may have swayed the jury. Apparently the woman had asked her husband for one hundred dollars for a political contribution; when he refused, she proceeded to "pound it out" of him. He, in turn, struck her with a feather duster. The jury denied the woman the divorce. But the details of the case were only part of what made the news noteworthy. What was even more remarkable was that the judge, both attorneys, the clerk of court, and all members of the jury were women.

Other headlines from across the country at the time also suggested that Meeker was more than a little liberal minded in terms of women's roles:

"First Girl Stage Driver," in a New York newspaper
"Girl Drives the Meeker Stage," from the Ogden (UT) Standard
"Girl Runs Coach Line," a San Antonio, Texas, newspaper

Twenty-one-year-old May Robertson had signed a one-year contract to deliver mail between Meeker and Buford, a thirty-mile daily run over dangerous, lonely mountain roads. According to the *Ogden Standard*, May held the ribbons over "four bronchos [*sic*] of unwarranted dispositions" in addition to handling baggage and seating of passengers. Ranchers along her route depended on her for their transportation needs as well.

47

When May's dad and local businessman A. G. Robertson purchased his stage line to deliver passengers and mail, he fully intended on hiring a man to drive the coach. But May insisted she wanted the job, and he relented. One of her justifications for getting the job was that she understood horses better than anyone. She illustrated her competence one day when her driving skills saved a group of passengers from serious injury. Jolting along a rough mountain road pulling a coach-load of eastern tourists, May's team was terrorized by a passing automobile. As the horses veered to the precipitous edge of the winding road, May wound the reins around her wrists and braced her feet against the dashboard, struggling to subdue the frightened animals. Just as the stage approached a sharp turn in the roadway, May righted the nervous team, avoiding what could have been a very serious accident. It was stories like this that compelled travelers to declare there was "no better driver in the West."

"I always liked horses, and they have always seemed to like me," May said. "I never have any trouble, even with the wildest animals."

May admitted that she was simply looking for a way to make a living when she persuaded her dad to let her drive his stage route, but she understood that holding the ribbons over a four-horse team wasn't right for everyone. "I don't know as I would advise stage driving for every girl," she said, "but I imagine that there are lots harder and less remunerative employments."

"There is scarcely a poor owner of a miserable log hut who lives on the border of the stage road, but has a newspaper left at his door . . . ," an Englishman observed about his American friends and their relationship with newspapers in 1814. And that afforded even the common man and woman an opportunity to acquire "a general acquaintance with the world." Enabled by the stagecoach industry, that relationship only flourished and expanded over the years. A prominent communication tool for decades, newspapers, distributed by stage proprietors and drivers, helped educate and inform—as well as attempt to persuade and dissuade—readers about events close to home and around the world. And as that English traveler noted, it was a common sight to witness "boys and girls running out of the farm-houses at the sound of the post-horn, to catch the numerous newspapers," undoubtedly ensuring future generations of readers.

Before 1792 Americans living in remote areas acquired their beloved newspapers at the hands of private riders or stagecoach owners, who accommodated the printers by transporting bundles of papers in saddle-bags or stage pouches, sometimes at no cost. But with passage of the Post Office Act of 1792, newspapers were also distributed by postal contractors at a cost of one cent for up to one hundred miles. Newspaper publishers now had choices in terms of how they could get their papers out to subscribers. But the new law created a strain on postal resources, partly because local postmasters were awarded 50 percent of the postage on newspapers as part of their salaries, so the US Post Office encouraged the continued private transportation of papers.

There were disadvantages for subscribers who received their papers from the private carriers. In their efforts to get the paper out as quickly as possible, printers often sent insufficiently dried papers out to customers, resulting in smudged print. Additionally, wet papers were heavy papers, and stage drivers might choose to leave a weighty bundle at the drop-off site rather than weigh down their coach on a muddy or snowy roadway. In contrast, the US Post Office refused to accept newspapers that were not thoroughly dried. Also, many private carrier stage drivers stored the newspapers on the exterior floorboard under their feet, meaning they were subject to weather and muddy boots, whereas the US Post Office strongly recommended that newspapers be carried inside the coach.

It was common to drop newspapers off at locations, such as stage taverns, where paid subscribers would pick up their papers as soon as possible to prevent nonsubscribers from walking off with a copy before subscribers arrived. In 1825 the *North-Carolina Star* in Raleigh called out those thieves who resorted to the "shameful practice," claiming the robbers not only stole personal property but also deprived subscribers of the news the paper contained—an even more vile offense. In contrast, US Post Office carriers delivered papers in sealed bags hoping to discourage such treachery, and fined any unauthorized individuals who opened the bags.

Another problem associated with private newspaper carriers had to do with politics. Some private carriers distributed only papers that espoused a particular political viewpoint, refusing to hand out papers with opposing views—even when they had the papers on the stage. Sometimes the publishers asked the drivers to partake in the scheme; other times, the drivers themselves had strong political convictions. The US Post Office frowned on this and required contractors to deliver different political newspapers with "strict impartiality," although at the time it was questionable that a government agency had the right to regulate private newspaper carriers.

Throughout the eighteenth and nineteenth centuries, the stagecoach and newspaper industries were inextricably linked, enjoying a symbiotic relationship that stimulated reward for both. Notices about the startup of new stage lines, sales of stage taverns, stagecoach schedules—stagecoach-related business owners utilized local newspapers to inform citizens of important announcements. City governments publicized ordinances related to staging operations.

"Henry Stousser respectfully informs the public, and his old friends and customers, that his stage between Baltimore and Annapolis will run three times in a week and will perform the passage by a change of horses, with the greatest speed that possibly can be." Henry's notice appeared in the *Maryland Gazette* in September 1790.

Joseph Robinson announced his business was for sale in November 1815 in the *Carlisle (PA) Weekly Herald*: "Clark's Ferry Tavern and Farm to let. Wishing to relinquish my present line of business. Consists of everything necessary for tavern-keeping. The tavern is unquestionably the best stand, and has the best custom of any from Philadelphia to Pittsburgh. The Juniata mail stages stop two nights every week."

Stagecoach owners in Sacramento, California, had no excuse for not knowing they were required to license their coaches in 1852; the *Sacramento Daily Union* ran city ordinance pronouncements front and center on page one in July 1852: "The owner or owners of every stage coach or other vehicle carrying passengers to or from the city shall pay fifty dollars per quarter, and shall have printed on each vehicle so licensed in some conspicuous place, the number of the same as registered by the license officer."

The *Austin (TX) American-Statesman* ran the schedule for the Blanco Stage Line in January 1890: "Austin and Blanco Stage Line leaves Austin daily except Sunday at six a.m. For passenger rates and express matters apply to D. C. Dunn."

A Colorado woman made use of both stagecoaches and newspapers in her quest to educate citizens about causes dear to her heart, at the same time sustaining a livelihood for herself. Caroline Nichols Churchill embodied the essence of an astute newspaper entrepreneur and passionate women's rights activist in the late 1800s and early 1900s. Stagecoaches and newspapers were vital communication tools she employed to facilitate the success of her endeavors.

"You leave that door instantly or you will have a ball put into your carcass, if not more than one," Caroline Churchill advised the two men who appeared at the door of her room at a stage stop in Georgetown, Colorado, at two in the morning in 1879. "You have our room," they claimed. That was not the response Caroline wanted, so she fired three balls into the door and never saw the men again. The next night men in the adjoining room were up most of the night carousing and smoking cigars, the smoke so bad as to "smother a woodchuck." Because she firmly believed that it was never her duty "to keep a man's secrets for him," she published the experiences in her newspaper. A few weeks later she ran into the owner of the business, who informed Caroline that as a result of the bad publicity her newspaper article elicited, he had been forced to close his establishment.

Born in 1833 in Canada, Caroline began teaching at the age of fourteen and married in the early 1850s because "people did not know what else to do with girls." In the relationship for several unhappy years, she never remarried after her husband's death. She lived for a time in Minnesota, where she taught and operated a millinery and dressmaking business. Her only daughter was raised by a sister, giving Caroline "an opportunity" to pursue her future endeavors. In 1870 she moved to California and for the first time devoted her energies to traveling and writing about her experiences, mingling detailed depictions of natural beauty and human interactions with her observations as a feminist.

In her book *Little Sheaves: Gathered While Gleaning After Reapers*, she offered readers glimpses of "brilliant-hued wild flowers" and "yawning precipices" as she rode a six-horse stage between San Jose and Santa Cruz piloted by a veteran driver who stopped at appealing spots along the way—all for the price of one dollar. The accommodating fellow, who, to Caroline's delight, prohibited smoking both in and outside the coach, stopped at a stream to allow passengers to fish for trout and at a farm where two brothers raised grapes, pears, and peaches and proudly led the travelers over their grounds covered in shade trees, shrubbery, and vine-covered arbors. When the stage reached Santa Cruz, Caroline wrote glowingly of the town of three thousand inhabitants and its fine beach and commodious hotels.

At the same time, Caroline refused to suppress her views about society, calling out the Santa Cruz newspaper editors as "belligerent" men who resorted to "fists instead of pen and ink to settle their difficulties." She continued to ask questions that were certain to earn her a reputation as a radical feminist: "Why is it that a man may be one of the lowest dregs of a foreign nation—may drink, smoke, chew, swear, gamble and whip his wife, and even be guilty of the hitherto crime of having a black skin—and still be any man's equal at the ballot-box?" She seldom missed an opportunity to express her opinions, often about men she considered unworthy of any form of praise: "This individual, like most men, supposed that things seen by women were as good as not seen at all" and "It is surprising how men neglect to guard the morals of each other, while the meanest loafer among them is always more or less concerned about the morals of the gentler sex."

Caroline continued in much the same vein in *Over the Purple Hills*, providing vivid tales of travel and proselytizing on her perspectives of a male-dominated world. Once she related a near mishap on a steep mountain trail where the stagecoach team nearly upended the coach when frightened by a sound in a nearby brush "so compact that I could not have walked a rod if a grizzly bear had been in prospect." While it seemed obvious to the passengers that peril did indeed appear imminent even though the male driver assured them that there was no danger, she remarked, "I belong to a class of women who have not unlimited confidence in the assertions of man at any time."

While her disdain for men remained a central theme in her writings, she frequently displayed her compassion for animals. On a trip through Yosemite Valley, the stage driver promised Caroline the choice spot on the seat next to him; she enthusiastically complied, despite a near confrontation with a male passenger who coveted the seat. The outside perch gave Caroline a prime position to observe routine stage travel practices, including the switching of horses at stops every ten miles. At one stop she watched as a fresh little horse was brought from the livery and stable boys proceeded to settle the harness over the animal in preparation for the next section of the trip. Caroline commented on its "baby or colty" appearance as it took its place next to the larger horses. The driver admitted the little fellow had "outworked three common teams already," and he hoped to get another summer's labor out of the pony. Caroline wrote, "I just wish it were possible for me to purchase the creature and place it in some horse heaven, abounding in clear streams and alfalfa grass, where it should do no more staging."

It was also on this trip that Caroline later recalled she had met some brave frontiersmen who had caused her to momentarily "regret that I am not a marrying subject." She further explained, "Believing as I do in the Darwinian theory, and knowing as I do that I have not thrown off the biting hen stage of evolution, I will accept no offer of marriage until hen pecking becomes more popular."

Following a two-year tour throughout Missouri, Kansas, and Texas to promote her books, Caroline stopped in Denver for what she thought would be a temporary visit; however, she fell in love with the place and decided to stay. Long having a dream to publish a newspaper, in 1879 Caroline started the *Colorado Antelope*. If anyone was curious about the intent of the publication, that curiosity was quickly sated by a casual perusal of the masthead: The *Colorado Antelope*: "A paper devoted to the interests of humanity, woman's political equality and individuality."

Early on, Caroline set the tone for the newspaper's content with the splash of that masthead, as well as a paragraph titled "Advantages Which the Antelope Has Over Other Papers" in a January 1880 issue. "Its editor is the oldest and handsomest in the United States. It has the only lady editor who wears a seven by nine boot and dares tell her own age. It has the only lady editor who dares so far defy underlying principles of political subjection as to write and publish a joke perpetrated upon herself." And if that didn't entice readers, she added, "it is the wittiest, spiciest, most radical little sheet published in the United States." In 1882 Caroline changed the name of her paper to the *Queen Bee*, but the message did not change. She spent the next eighteen years writing, publishing, and promoting her work.

She traveled extensively throughout the western United States seeking out subjects and causes for scrutiny in the next edition of her paper and revealing what she saw as social injustices in American life—always promoting or selling subscriptions and advertisements along the way. (A Deadwood newspaper criticized her for devoting only a few inches of print to actual news, while "roasting" a resident for not subscribing to her paper.) She visited jails, penitentiaries, hospitals, and county homes, observing to her readers that in most institutions men were in positions of authority. She suggested that women should have a paid lobby in Washington every session of Congress to "look to the interests of their own sex." And she wrote, "We are living out the adage all have heard reiterated so many times, that two heads are better than one if one is a woman's."

Writing in her autobiography, *Active Footsteps*, Caroline modestly concluded that she was "Not really great in anything but perseverance, firmness and self-respect," but that she had always longed for a "more ideal civilization." At the age of seventy-six, she believed she had given the "best years" of her life "towards this attainment."

———

"I guess some woman must a done him 'long back and he feels sort o' spiteful against 'em all." That was the rationale for Ol' Jake's distaste for women passengers on his twenty-mile Lake City to Wagon Wheel Gap, Colorado, stage run in 1880. The driver was a known "woman hater," and when Carrie Adell Strahorn requested a seat up top with the driver, the ticket agent warned her about the surly fellow. Pulled by six "full of ginger" horses, the stage tottered over the mountain roads as Carrie clung to the seat straps "with a tenacity of a life and death effort." She reported that

Charles M. and Nancy C. Russell, Philip R. Goodwin, Carrie Adell
Strahorn (standing on right), and woman, 1910

Jake "drove like fury," venturing "within a hair's breadth of going off the bridges" and would "turn out to the very edge of a precipice" on a whim. As Ol' Jake urged his team around a tight curve and down a steep mountain grade at full speed, the six male passengers bounced around inside the coach, emitting curses that could be heard on the top seat. Barely avoiding a tip over as the coach veered around a turn, the driver admitted to Carrie that they could easily have hit a rock and become "food for the bears." "I knew he was trying to make me scream with fright, which I as stubbornly refused to do," Carrie recalled.

When Jake realized there was no scaring this woman, he remarked, "Well, I guess you've been on a stage before, for you don't seem to scare very easy."

Carrie, who had traveled thousands of miles by stage, replied she had been on a stage once before but did not have a grizzly bear for a driver, so this trip was a new experience for her. Later, Ol' Jake was overheard telling some of his fellow drivers about the time he tried to scare a woman (Carrie) on the Lake City run, but "a lot of our drivers'll scare a damned sight quicker than she would," and she "didn't yell a once."

When Carrie married Robert "Pard" Strahorn in 1877, he had just been hired by the Union Pacific Railroad to set up an advertising and public relations department to explore and publicize the West through his writings and guidebooks. He had insisted that his employer allow his new bride to accompany him on his travels by stage across Utah, Colorado, Wyoming, Idaho, New Mexico, Montana, Washington, and Oregon, as well as Alaska, Hawaii, and British Columbia. By the time Carrie demanded that the word "obey" be left out of the marriage vows, Pard already was aware that he was marrying a remarkable woman. Over the next forty-plus years, the couple traveled the West and wrote about their experiences, partly in hopes of encouraging easterners to settle in the great frontier. Newspapers, including the *Chicago Tribune* and the *Omaha Republican*, carried their columns. "The real home for many years was in the saddle or stage-coach," Carrie wrote in her two-volume memoir, *Fifteen Thousand Miles by Stage*, in 1911.

In the 1870s, when the Strahorns began their journey, stage stops were often crude and uninviting. Freight boxes or kegs served as seats, blankets were scarce commodities shared by several travelers, dirt floors became slick with mud from leaky roofs. Canvas sheets hung from the ceiling offered the only privacy and scant relief from snorers or fussy babies. Carrie became adept at identifying wide variations of snores: One sounded like the "escape valve of a steam engine" and another the "squawk of the guinea hen."

The proprietor of a stage stop in the Rockies offered shelter from cold winter nights and charged a dollar for his hospitality, but the place suffered from a severe shortage of blankets. When a guest drifted off into a deep sleep, his precious blanket would be surreptitiously eased off his sleeping form and given to a new arrival. When people complained, the proprietor replied that he had never promised a blanket with his beds. At a stop called Root Hog, so called because it was so filthy no other name would suffice— "dirt roof, dirt floor, and dirt everywhere else, and filthy dirt at that"—the travelers chose to eat food they had brought in hampers rather than a meal from the proprietor, whose face was covered with a frowzy beard, his hair "matted around his head and neck until he looked more like some untamed animal than a man." The next stop was somewhat cleaner, although all nine stage passengers slept in one room with narrow strips of white muslin hung around the beds for privacy, the mattresses and pillows stuffed with wild hay.

At Mrs. Corbet's stop in Montana, stage passengers were greeted by the owner brandishing a pistol as she encouraged them to enjoy a meal at her table for the price of a dollar per person. If they chose to eat their own packed lunches, she refused to let them into her establishment for water, telling them to use the nearby river, located down a steep embankment. And just because a stage traveler was lucky enough to find a stop offering private bedrooms with doors, there was no guarantee there were locks. At one stop, the owner, Mrs. Burns, after partaking of a cup (or two?) of toddy was known to enter guests' rooms unannounced. At other stops, guests knew to wedge pieces of furniture under the doorknobs to discourage uninvited guests during the night.

Fly-speckled dinnerware made more unappetizing by greasy handprints greeted stage travelers at a stop in Montana. In Idaho the Strahorns were tempted by the simmering scents of ham at a stage stop at the end of a day in which an axle broke on the stage and the stage horses were nearly drowned in mud. As hungry as the travelers were, everyone at the table was surprised when the Strahorns politely passed on a platter of ham slices as it was handed to them. But Pard and Carrie had witnessed the cook drop a slab of meat on the dirty floor before slapping it onto the platter. On a trip to Boise City after a night without supper, the Strahorns were eager for their breakfast. Their hostess carried into the dining room a loaf of bread dough she had pulled from under the covers of her bed. "I always put the bread in my bed when I get up in the morning," she explained, "because it is so nice and warm that it makes it rise quicker."

Snakes, mice, and rats were frequent companions at stage stops. On a trip to the Sawtooth Mountains in Montana, Carrie recalled a night at a deserted cabin where the travelers took refuge from a storm. As soon as the candles were extinguished, "hordes of rats and mice . . . scampered in the rafters" and across the beds, jumping "into our faces." At another stop, a mother traveling with her baby checked on the child who was on the floor, seemingly very content. She was horrified to find a rattlesnake coiled around the baby's body. The snake reacted when the baby squeezed, and within a few hours the child was dead.

All those miles of stagecoach travel provided Carrie reams of adventurous tales and daring escapades only dreamed of by most Americans in the 1800s. In 1880 Carrie boarded an eleven-passenger stagecoach in Georgetown, Colorado, for a seventy-mile trip to Middle Park; the coach was overcrowded with five children and seven adults. As the coach ascended the steep mountain pass that looked from below like a "mere scratch on the rocks," three of the kids got sick to their stomachs. About fourteen miles into the journey, a stop was made at a stage post office to let the kids stretch their legs; the driver got down to adjust some mail packages in the boot. The rest of the passengers stayed in the coach as the driver draped the reins loosely over the brake handle. As soon as the six-horse team realized they were unfettered, they made a dash for freedom. With the frantic passengers fearing for their lives, the stage bounced and rattled over a mile of corduroy road with jagged logs protruding on each side of the trail. Finally, one of the passengers managed to climb out to the driver's seat and grab the reins, working with all his might to control the runaways. A young boy who had been sitting on the outside driver's seat was thrown off the coach, falling between the wheels as the horses raced over the road. With the horses finally tamed, the passenger/driver turned back to the post office, where he encountered the driver running to catch the runaway coach. The boy was badly injured and remained at the stage stop while the rest of the passengers continued to the Middle Park Hotel, where they "washed away" their memories of the unpleasant ride in the hot spring baths of Hot Sulphur Springs.

Later that year, Carrie and Pard departed for a sixty-five-mile trip to Gunnison City on a stage crammed with eleven inside passengers and six on the roof. Carrie wasn't reassured when she learned the passenger directly overhead was a 250-pound man. Once again, motion sickness affected two of the inside passengers, who spent the entire day with their heads hanging out the windows "to dispose of the last week's ration." When one of the wheels struck a boulder and nearly caused an upset, two of the passengers up top landed in the canyon below the trail. Both climbed back to the stage, and before long bottles of brandy began to appear from above as the pair attempted to find relief for their painful bruises. Not long after that incident, the stage began to pitch toward the drop-off and was saved by one of the outside passengers, who grabbed a tree limb to right the coach. As darkness loomed, the driver asked the passengers to follow his orders without exception as they approached some especially dangerous spots in the road. Carrie was sitting alongside the driver and recalled coming close to being "hurled top down into the Gunnison River" at one point. It was after dark when the driver shouted for the passengers to lean to the north, but their luck had run out. Carrie was pulled from the brush to avoid being dragged by the horses, which were trying to right themselves from the overturned coach. Fortunately, no one was seriously injured, but another female passenger blamed Carrie for falling on her and causing great distress. Carrie hoped the woman would bite her tongue as the stage was restored to its position and they continued on their way. However, according to Carrie, the woman's tongue "wagged on worse than before."

As the Strahorns traveled the West over the years, they visited Omaha, Helena, Butte, Yuma, Leadville, Tucson, Seattle, and Spokane in addition to other emerging frontier towns. At each stop Carrie recorded her thoughts, offering a picture sometimes tinged with negativity, at other times with glowing optimism. She lamented leaving Los Angeles "for the cheerless wastes of Arizona" and referred to Yuma as the "worst looking, most squalid town one could imagine." Seattle was a "veritable mudhole with its cowpath streets" and Spokane "one of the most picturesque" spots in America. Helena, Montana, said Carrie, was a place where "No one could feel like a stranger." And Leadville, Colorado, was the "magic word that drew thousands of people into the vortex of dissipation, vice, and plunder." There was the terror-filled night in Blackfoot, Idaho, when the Strahorns were greeted by shots and howls from visiting cowboys, who rode their horses through saloons and stores, shooting at random and leaving a "cyclonic wreckage" in their path. (One of the town's merchants, who had experienced previous visits from the cowhands, had constructed a building with a wide entrance and exit at opposite ends of the establishment so that rowdy cowboys could ride straight through without turning their bucking broncos in the middle of his merchandise.) Carrie was well aware of Cheyenne's reputation and recalled a joke popular among old-timers about two freighters meeting on a nearby trail when one noticed the other carrying a load of twenty barrels of whiskey and one sack of flour. "What in hell are you going to do with so much flour?" the crusty old driver asked his fellow freighter. Santa Fe caused Carrie to begrudge the time she had to take to eat and sleep, as there were so many delightful sights to explore. And in Carrie's opinion, Taos was "the most picturesque inland town in the Southwest." Everywhere she went Carrie succumbed to the natural beauty of the western lands—"maddening salt plains," and mountains that "kiss the sky," as well as countless "marvelous bits of scenery hidden in the remote nooks of uninhabited places in our loved country."

Carrie was told more than once that she was treading into territory where women had no business traveling, but it never stopped her. When the Strahorns made their first expedition into Yellowstone in October 1880, the park superintendent refused to allow Carrie to follow Pard on one leg of the trip as heavy snow fell. Refusing to miss out on any part of Yellowstone, after her husband and the superintendent set out, she followed some distance behind on her horse. By the time she caught up with them, they were already on their return trip; Pard turned around, and together the couple explored "up and down o'er hills and vales," witnessing the "awful grandeur" of the park.

Together Carrie and Pard, through his guidebooks and her newspaper columns in the *Omaha Republican*, helped lovers of adventure who were "carried on wings of avarice, romance, adventure, and discovery and even fairy tales" to consider a move from their comfortable lives in the East to the uncertainty of the wild West. With great pleasure, the couple watched as people responded, "to the magic work of the pen."

Carrie explained her part in this grand adventure: "The joys of motherhood have often been envied as fond parents watched the budding and maturing intellects of their children . . . but it is no small compensation to help make towns and cities spring from earth in answer to the demands of an army conquering a wilderness as it follows the trail of the pioneer."

On days the stage came to town, residents lost at least an hour of work—for the time spent ogling and then for the time devoted to talking about the event after the stage left town. The stage brought much-appreciated bundles of newspapers and mail, but those sources carried news that might be a week or more old. Even more anticipated was the "unpublished news" shared by the driver and passengers—more up-to-date, and possibly juicier, gossip. And if townsfolk missed the stage, the stage stop proprietor was a lucrative source of information gleaned from the stage occupants. There were always the local curiosity seekers who loitered on the sidewalks or in the hotel lobbies to pick up news, so within a few minutes of the arrival of the stage, there was an "eager buzz of gossip drifting away to the homes and byway," as one writer put it. For more than two hundred years, the stagecoach was a vital vehicle for communicating news, ideas, and, yes, gossip. From colonial days until well into the twentieth century, men and women shared the responsibilities of transmitting precious cargoes of human interaction. By way of conveyances with four wheels led by a team of horses, male and female couriers faithfully held the ribbons through snow and rain and gloom of night.

CHAPTER 3

Travel by Stage:
Teeth-Rattling, Bone-Jarring

It's not difficult to imagine the sheer terror experienced by the passengers on a late-night stagecoach in January 1822 as the coach careened through the dark countryside near Havre de Grace, Maryland. The drowsy passengers awoke to the sudden realization that they were in a driverless coach, horses racing full tilt over the rugged terrain. A frantic discussion ensued among the rattled riders: Jump from the lurching coach, or ride it out until the horses stopped on their own? At that point, no one questioned what had happened to the driver and his armed guard. Stopping the stage was their only concern. One fearless passenger offered to attempt the risky climb to the driver's seat and regain control of the runaway team. Miraculously, the courageous individual managed to secure the reins and wrestle the agitated team to a halt, just as a galloping horse carrying the missing stage driver overtook the coach. The guard was nowhere in sight, but his blunderbuss remained safely wedged on the driver's seat despite the perilous ride. It turned out that the driver and guard had stopped at a tavern for "the purpose of refreshing themselves" and failed to notice the stage disappearing into the night with its cargo of sleeping passengers. When they realized the coach was nowhere to be seen, the driver set out to find the missing coach; the guard decided to stay at the tavern.

Stagecoach accidents were not uncommon, and as with the unfortunate Havre de Grace incident, they were frequently caused by drunk or reckless drivers. Stage racing was another recurrent problem over the decades of stage travel and a contributor to serious accidents. Sometimes the offenders were simply foolhardy drivers who delighted in showing off for their passengers. And while it's true that many were merely thrill seekers, others were employees of stage lines that were in keen competition for limited routes. Although stage proprietors bragged about hiring only the safest and most experienced drivers, they also wanted to outshine any competitors in the area. One way to do so was to deliver the fastest service. Drivers shared that goal, and often raced to reach their destinations before the rival lines. Often it was the passengers who paid the price with injuries or even death.

William Lattin, a stage passenger from Washington, New York, chose to stay on a coach driven by a man who took pleasure in a rousing race with fellow drivers. He'd already upset his stage full of passengers one night in November 1818, causing all but William to disembark before reaching their final stop. Enjoying the thrill of a good race, William stuck with the driver. When they entered into a "spirited contest" with a wagoner as they neared Troy, New York, the two men were thrown from the driver's seat. The driver survived, but William's body was found sprawled in the roadway about eleven o'clock that night.

Nineteenth-century newspapers spared no ink when reporting on stage accidents caused by racing drivers, and editors called for action to rein in the abuses. J. P. Garcia was driving with his wife and child down Broadway in New York City one morning in March 1833 when two racing stage drivers plowed into his carriage, shattering the vehicle, injuring the horse, and greatly endangering the Garcia family. "It is high time some energetic measures were taken to put a stop to the daily and hourly races of which Broadway is the scene," the *Evening Post* declared.

The *Selma (AL) Daily Reporter* warned stage passengers to avoid a coach driven by a "full blood Irish scamp" named John Dillon, who drove for the Mail and Telegraph Stage Line in 1838. It was reported that "with a crack of the whip and a wild whoop," he had tried to pass a coach from the People's Line, causing its horses to take fright and run at full speed for about three hundred yards before coming to a "tremendous crash." Passengers on the People's Line swore that Dillon had acted intentionally. Everyone knew the two stage lines were fierce competitors, and the paper called for the Mail and Telegraph line to fire Dillon and adopt a rule that mirrored the People's Line position on racing: Stage racing was "absolutely prohibited," and "every driver must be discharged immediately that may attempt to run his horses." The paper scolded the drivers for putting passengers at risk for the sake of making good time and coming in three-quarters of a minute before their competition.

Even the most conscientious stage drivers couldn't avoid some of the pitfalls that resulted in accidents. Abysmal roads and foul weather, as well as unexpected tree stumps, swollen creek beds, rickety bridges, and snowslides, all took a toll; low-hanging tree limbs knocked topside riders from their perches. Water created its own unique challenges for stage riders. Before bridges became common, stages forded streams—a dangerous undertaking that could result in death for horses and passengers. Even where bridges had been constructed, the engineering techniques of those early builders left much to be desired: Throw a few sturdy logs across a creek and hope for the best. But there was always the chance a horse would wedge a hoof between the logs, causing a catastrophe. Or if someone had gone to the trouble of nailing a few planks together to form a bridge, they weren't regularly maintained. Nails fell out; planks floated away. Ferries were an option in some locations, but they were time-consuming and could be costly.

Mother Nature could be blamed for many stage catastrophes, despite the actions of skilled drivers. As stage horses attempted to dodge debris in a swollen arroyo in Tucson, Arizona, in spring 1877, the driver fell from his seat; he landed under a wheel, which passed over his arm, fracturing the bone near the elbow. The runaway team raced over the desert road and likely would have met with disaster if not for a courageous freighter driving a loaded wagon pulled by a team of hefty oxen who happened to come along. The quick-thinking fellow positioned his intimidating rig in the path of the runaway coach, causing the frantic team to come to an abrupt but jarring halt. A new driver was brought to take the place of the injured man, and the stage was soon on its way. And on a snowy night in 1886, a stage with nine passengers leaving Leadville for Aspen, Colorado, was caught in a snowslide fifteen miles east of Aspen. The stage lunged over a two-hundred-foot precipice. When a rescue party found the passengers, four were unhurt; the other five were expected to die from their injuries.

Winter weather in cold climates and mountainous areas could impede stage and rail travel for months. Trains simply stopped, whereas determined stage line owners turned to stage sleds to carry resilient passengers. "The United States cannot stop in their westward march on account of snow storms," the *Leavenworth (KS) Times* reported in March 1869. Intended as a harsh criticism of rail travel that had come to a halt as a result of heavy snows, the newspaper continued in the same vein: "The people wanted a highway of commerce, travel and mail transportation that can be used three hundred and sixty-five days in the year. But they have not got it." However, snow sleighs were getting through on the thirty- to fifty-foot snow base in Dakota, Utah, Nevada, and California—an "almost continuous wilderness" region the paper predicted "never will be settled."

Brave passengers sprang to action when disaster seemed imminent. Sarah Eagan was traveling with her four-year-old granddaughter between Butte and Anaconda in Montana in 1883 when their stage overturned. Sarah broke her arm and suffered bruises about her head and face. Her granddaughter was spared serious injury when a fellow passenger, Henry Joost, seized the little girl and jumped from the coach, risking his own life to spare the girl. In 1907 a fearless passenger on a stage running between Byersville and Pepperwood, California, probably saved lives when he took control of a perilous situation. When the driver became too drunk to drive, a sober but cowardly substitute had stepped in. After rounding a sharp corner too fast, he panicked, dropped the reins, and jumped—leaving the stage and its passengers to fend for themselves. A passenger who was sharing the driver's seat grabbed the reins and turned the skittish horses into a bank as the coach capsized. One passenger fell between a jumble of rocks, which broke his ribs but prevented the stage from crushing him. Another rider had a severe scalp wound, and his wife suffered a cut above her eye and a broken right elbow. Elsie Carr from Oakland suffered a back injury, and Dr. Russ Bullock from San Francisco had a four-inch laceration on his head.

Travelers were well aware of the dangers they might encounter when they purchased a ticket for a local trip or an overland journey, both "teeth-rattling" experiences, but they were willing to take the risk. Over the years fares fluctuated, impacted by demand, seasons, competition, and the going rate for good stage horses, oats, corn, and hay. Fare for the 115-mile run between Iowa City and Des Moines, Iowa, was ten dollars in 1857; the Wells Fargo overland stage charged three hundred dollars for a ticket between Omaha, Nebraska, and Sacramento, California, in 1867. At that rate, Rebecca Yokum's family had a sizable investment in their move west in 1860, even considering reduced fares for children. Fifteen-year-old Rebecca set out on a Butterfield Overland stage from Spring-field, Missouri, with her mother and three brothers, planning to join her dad, who had gone ahead to Santa Clara, California, the year before. The kids ranged in age from three to seventeen years of age. The cross-country trip offered its share of challenges, according to Rebecca's recollections: a lost lunch basket, expensive meals of moldy bread, overcrowded coaches, a dunking in a river, and baggage left behind to lighten the load. By the time the family arrived at their destination, Rebecca's mother had held the three-year-old on her lap for twenty-one days, no one had bathed or changed clothes, and a sound sleep was only a faint memory.

Any number of issues could disrupt plans when travelers were rely-ing on stagecoaches for transportation in the 1800s. Kate McCormick and Maria Higgins purchased tickets in June 1873 for a 380-mile trip from Corinne, Utah Territory, to Deer Lodge, Montana Territory. The Gilmer and Salisbury line was well known in the region. Their rates were reasonable and their drivers reliable. They carried the US mail, so almost nothing stopped them from their route, and they utilized sleds in winter months to ensure delivery of mail and passengers. Kate and Maria paid about fifty dollars apiece for their tickets and were aware they could each bring a bag weighing up to twenty-five pounds at no cost and would be charged $1.50 for each additional pound. However, a dangerous malady was sweeping across the region that could jeopardize their travel plans.

The winter of 1873 had been an especially tough one for stage lines—deep snows with drifts up to thirty feet, blinding snowstorms, slow going that caused missed connections. Corinne had endured a forty-hour snowstorm at the end of January. By June, when Kate and Maria were making their travel plans, snow wasn't much of an issue; however, another serious barrier to travel threatened stage lines throughout the first half of 1873. An epizootic epidemic was swiftly spreading throughout the West, causing interruption of business and the closing of horse-related establishments, including livery stables and stage routes.

In January the Helena newspaper warned citizens that they should be prepared for temporary shutdown of stage services, as there were reports of an imminent arrival of the dangerous disease. Already in outlying areas, stage lines were scaling back services because of sickly teams, and livery owners reported that nearly all their horses were disabled. In February, Gilmer and Salisbury personnel said it was their intent to "use every exertion to deliver the mail regularly"—if they could find healthy stock to pull their stages. All along the lines, signs of the dreaded, highly contagious disease were evident. Some lines were reducing services, and drivers were advised to avoid overheating their horses to prevent fatalities. A traveler who had made the Corinne to Deer Lodge run reported that he had witnessed "a solid sick" among horses on the line below the Snake River.

Maybe it was just a public relations stunt, but in March O. J. Salisbury, general superintendent of Gilmer and Salisbury, had taken a trip along their line and reported back that "the great horse scourge was rapidly decreasing," meaning the company would begin regular mail service again. That pronouncement may have been a bit premature, maybe wishful thinking on the part of the stage operators. Later in the month the *Helena Weekly Herald* seemed to disavow Salisbury's claim, reporting that the disease "without doubt" had made an appearance at the Pacific Stables in town, where the entire stock showed signs of the disease, including heavy coughing among the animals.

Horse experts offered a variety of cures for the epizootic scourge, including feeding the animals raw potatoes with a few oats sprinkled over the top as garnish. Billy Child, the Gilmer and Salisbury agent in Helena, had consulted with a horse doctor who recommended keeping stables well ventilated and flushing horses' nostrils with a strong concoction of vinegar and salt every two days. He also suggested a recipe of alcohol, melted hog lard, turpentine, and iodine, to be smeared on the animal's chest every twelve hours.

By the end of May, all signs seemed to indicate the threat was over for horses in the area. The newspaper reported that the disease had run its course. Only a few weeks before, hardly a horse had been seen on the city streets, but things seemed to be back to normal. Gilmer and Salisbury had announced its summer schedule. Kate McCormick and Maria Higgins probably saw this as a sign that it was safe to purchase their tickets on the Gilmer and Salisbury line and that there would be no interruptions in their travel.

Early in the stagecoach era, people joked that the cost of a ticket was "ten cents a mile and a fence rail" because passengers were encouraged to bring a fence post to pry the coach free should it become stuck in a muddy quagmire. It was common for drivers to ask passengers to get out and walk to lighten the load, sometimes for miles; baggage was often tossed out too. On a nasty, rainy night in 1857, a driver on the Newton to Montezuma, Iowa, stage asked passengers to alight and hold lanterns as beacons to help guide the stage through a muddy slough. Most riders accommodated by walking stretches of the forty-mile trip; the exceptions were "a red head and the fur hat man"—two dandies who had paid to ride and weren't about to walk. When their destination was reached, the driver went directly to the tavern and swore he would not go a mile farther.

In the West in the 1860s, drivers who carried volumes of public documents sent from Washington, DC, to outlying areas of the country devised creative solutions to combat mud and slush, including building what they jokingly referred to as "bridges built of pub. docs." When they found themselves hopelessly stalled in a sea of mud, they pulled out the sacks marked "Pub. Docs.," opened the bags, and distributed the "massive books from the Government printing office" in the mud. Building "a solid foundation with them," they were able to get enough traction to move the stage forward.

Seating arrangements on a stage followed an unwritten protocol. Everyone was expected to stay in his or her original seat unless one was vacated. Those who had traveled the longest had preference. Middle seats were more easily accessed and promised less lurching. Rear seats offered a back rest, and riders who coveted front seats knew they were less likely to suffer from tumbling baggage in case of an accident. Kids could be a problem for some travelers. As one cranky rider noted, "Two children, however small, always occupy more space than one grown person." Furthermore, "though they are charged at half price there are no such things as half children."

The process for reserving a seat on a stage varied from place to place too. If a line had a company office in a town, passengers went there to purchase a ticket in advance. The agent kept track of everything in a book, where riders registered their names when they paid their fares. Typically, passengers were allowed baggage weighing up to twenty-five pounds but

Feeding teams on Placerville stage route, 1866
LIBRARY OF CONGRESS PRINTS AND PHOTOGRAPHS DIVISION, WASHINGTON, DC, LAWRENCE & HOUSEWORTH COLLECTION, LC-USZ62-20153

were charged for any amount above that; one company set the rate at two cents for each thirty miles. On the day of the trip, passengers came to the office to board the stage, or they may have arranged a pickup location along the route. Some drivers picked up random passengers who flagged them down along the route.

One of the aspects of staging that some found appealing and others viewed with distaste had to do with the "democratic" nature of stage travel. As one writer stated in 1825, stagecoaches were "made for no particular class in society, but for the young and the old, the rich and the poor, the great and small, male and female, of all ranks and conditions." That presented a problem for some. British traveler Sir Henry Huntley complained about the "absence of classes," and the "dirty citizens" he was forced to share coach space with on his journey between Sacramento and Placerville, California, in the mid-1800s. Frank Marryat, another Brit, offered his opinions about a fellow passenger "who traveled under the protection of an ill-looking dog," a "quarrelsome and bumptious" rider armed with a revolver, and a couple of traveling miners who "squirted their juice at passing objects on the road with astonishing accuracy."

An unnamed woman in Brooklyn, New York, may have disputed the democratic nature of stage travel based on her experiences one day in 1853. She beckoned to a driver of a coach running between Brooklyn and Greenpoint; when he stopped she entered the coach, joining two other passengers. At some point in the journey, the driver became aware that the woman was "colored." Ordering her out of the stage, he pulled the woman from her seat, causing her to fall in the street. His actions resulted in an indictment and conviction for assault and battery, which carried a five-dollar fine.

Despite passengers' dissatisfaction with stage travel, the experience had its positive aspects. Firsthand accounts in diaries describe beautiful scenery and closeness with nature and opportunities to see new places from different vantage points, especially when riding at the height of the driver's seat: "the Great Salt Lake, a shining mirror, spotted with purple mountains of islands, framed in pale, violet peaks draped with gauzy clouds of purest white," and carpets of wild roses, orange and pearly white lilies, as well as red and white petunias. Immigrant Mary E. Cook wrote in her diary on her way to Montana Territory in 1868 about "truly grand" scenery: a river "bordered with a profuse growth of cottonwood, pine, choke cherry and hemlock," scenery that surpassed anything she had ever seen.

For some the social interactions among passengers from different parts of the country or other parts of the world were priceless, causing one writer to claim, "America went to school in the stage." After all, stage passengers could interact with fellow travelers who were politicians, army chaplains, attorneys, travel writers, immigrants seeking new homes, and land speculators. Topics of discussion took the form of religious doctrine, politics, and geography. Passengers who filled the coach with endless questions were viewed as either curious, inquisitive, or prying—depending on one's perspective. Such close quarters over extended periods made it nearly impossible to avoid at least some interaction with fellow riders.

Early twentieth-century author Alice Morse Earle wrote that stage-coach travel offered riders a "closeness of association" which made for a sense of companionship and intimacy that only "fellow-sufferers who had risen several mornings in succession with you, at daybreak, and ridden all night, cheek by jowl" could appreciate. Earle wasn't the only writer to suggest the possibility of romance blossoming on a stage ride. As she put it, "Many pleasant intimacies and acquaintances were begun on the stage-coach; flirtations, even courtships, were carried on."

In 1849 a writer for the *Knickerbocker*, a literary magazine published in the early 1800s in New York City, profiled a romantic reunion of lovers on a stagecoach ride in a story titled "The First Kiss." It may have been a work of fiction, but it struck the hearts of those who wanted to believe in possibilities.

In the story, a young man named Walter Marshall couldn't help but notice a female traveling companion—a "perfect vision of loveliness"—on a journey by stagecoach in Connecticut in the early 1800s. The two flirted unabashedly during the entire trip, and when they found themselves alone in the coach, Walter planted a kiss upon the young lady's "warm rosy lips." He was unaware that the woman was Mary Fuller, an acquaintance he hadn't seen since she was a child and he a young teenager. After the two shared "at least a hundred" kisses, the stage stopped at the Fuller house, where Walter was stunned to realize his fellow traveler was the Mary Fuller of his youth. Three months later the two were married, but not before the bride admonished her groom, "Walter, dear, it's understood in the vow, 'No more kissing strange girls in a stage-coach!'"

A stage leaving Dodge City, Kansas, one winter day in 1879 carried only two passengers, a Texas cattle rancher named John F. Tuttle and a woman whose name has been lost to time but who was described as "attractive." The fateful encounter led to love, but with an unexpected ending. John was on his way home to Springer Ranch, where he and his partner, Frank Chapman, operated a stage stop in addition to their livestock operation. As the stage made its way toward Springer Ranch, a blinding snowstorm moved in, making travel impossible. As nightfall blanketed the prairie, the two passengers and the driver huddled together inside the coach, trying to keep warm as the storm raged around them. By morning the snow had stopped and the stage was able to continue toward Springer Ranch, but the shared experience had caused John and the attractive woman to become romantically inclined toward each other. He convinced her to become a housekeeper at the ranch and stage station. Unfortunately for John, his newfound housekeeper fell in love with his partner, Frank. The two men quarreled, and John bought out Frank, thinking that would leave an opening for him to rekindle his relationship with the woman. But the woman had completely lost interest in John and fallen madly in love with John's ranch foreman, Tom Raines. When Tom threatened to kill John, the rancher decided he'd had enough and sold the ranch. Although love had blossomed for a short time during that frigid interlude in the Dodge City stage, the two were never able to reignite the sparks that flared that stormy night.

Unlike Walter Marshall and Mary Fuller, and John Tuttle and his lost love, a long stagecoach ride shared by a man and woman in 1893 held no hope for romance, but it did lead to a very personal conversation about love gone wrong. As author Alice Morse Earle imparted, long monotonous stage rides could kindle intimate conversations between passengers—especially when one was an inquisitive writer and the other a wronged spouse. J. L. Harbour, a writer for *Frank Leslie's Weekly*, probably couldn't help himself when he shared a ten-hour journey through the

Rocky Mountains with Elizy Bradley on a wintry day in 1893. He started asking questions and learned his companion had tales to tell of her thirty years as a western pioneer with her husband, Bill. "Well, if me an' Bill Bradley ain't had experiences I dunno who has," Elizy began. There was the long wagon ride from Iowa during which she gave birth to her first baby and nearly drowned at least three times as they forded streams. "You couldn't have had many worse experiences since," J. L. prodded. So Elizy let him have it: snowed in for six months at a mining camp where an avalanche cut off one end of the cabin while the pair slept; living on nothing but cornbread for weeks at a time while dreaming of fresh rhubarb from back home in Iowa; keeping nine boarders in an eighteen-square-foot, one-room cabin for an entire winter (and doing all their washing and mending and caring for them when they were sick); running a laundry, post office, bakery, newspaper office, dressmaking shop, and toll gate; and teaching school. And because it was a ten-hour stage ride, Elizy had time to mention the "five months an' three weeks" when the Bradleys "never saw a livin' soul but our two selves." Not long after, Elizy gave birth to their second baby. "I've kep' up my end of the row in all our little experiences, an' Bill Bradley knows it too," Elizy informed J. L. To which the writer replied, "Why, of course, he must know and appreciate it too, Mrs. Bradley." "You think so, eh? You know where I've been now?" she asked. "I been down to Denver fightin' a divorce-suit Bill Bradley begun agin me on the ground o' incompatibility o' temper growin' out o' the fact that he sold a mine a year ago for $300,000, an' Elizy Ann Bradley ain't adapted to him now." But, Elizy confided in J. L., she believed the real reason her husband suddenly felt the two "ain't suited to each other" was that all their experiences "ain't made no beauty nor no fine lady" out of her.

——◆——

Anne Royall, once described as a "shrill-tongued" journalist who "dared think her own thoughts and proclaim them from the house tops," spent much of the early nineteenth century traveling throughout the United States by stage, writing about her observations and publishing books about her experiences. One of her favorite targets was stage stops. In Hagerstown, Maryland, she stayed at what she called "the worst public house" in the area; it's where she was forced to deal with a drunk chambermaid and her "ignorant, proud, squat, scornful and sluttish" mistress, as well as a "ruffian barkeeper." And in Schenectady, New York, she had just gotten settled into her bed in a room at a stage stop when a "great rough fellow" opened the door and stalked in, "followed by his doxy rough as himself." As the passionate pair made their way to another bed in the chamber, Anne sat up in her bed and ordered them out. The would-be lovers left, but not before issuing a complaint to the barkeeper, who had come to see what the commotion was about and demanded to know why Anne refused to let the pair share her room. To make matters worse, the next morning Anne had a run-in with the innkeeper, who had accidentally put her luggage on another stage to Albany, not her next stop. He invited her to spend another night or two at his inn while waiting for the return of her bags—all a devious scam to get a few more dollars from her, according to Anne.

A writer opined in 1886 that the nation's old stage taverns were "influential centers for political thought and discussion" where many brilliant ideas were fostered over the years. Another declared the taverns were "one of the most important institutions" in the life of the nation. While the brilliant ideas part may have been debatable, there undeniably were an abundance of taverns in the East during the heyday of stage travel. On a sixty-three-mile stretch between Philadelphia and Lancaster, Pennsylvania, there were sixty-two. There were four hundred taverns on a 270-mile run between Baltimore, Maryland, and Wheeling, Virginia (now West Virginia), and on a five-mile stretch of road near Little Falls, New York, twelve of the thirteen buildings were taverns.

Stage stations, way stations, stage stops, taverns, ranches, road ranches, stage stands—the structures located at regular intervals along the stage lines were known by a variety of names, but they had a common purpose: providing a change of horses for a stagecoach driver. At the least, they also offered passengers an opportunity to take a short break from their travels. Some provided meals and/or a bed for a few hours' sleep. They likely included a barn or livery stable and at least a one-room building for passengers. Alcohol was often available. These stations were constructed of any number of materials—brick, limestone, wood, sod, log, or adobe.

Some were quite grand looking; others were squalid. They were located in towns and cities or out in the middle of nowhere. The colorful names conferred on these establishments were intriguing: In the East there were the Bag 'o Nails, Goat in Boots, Load of Mischief, Goddess of Liberty Tavern; in the West were Frog Tanks, French Woman's Ranch, Burnt Ranche, Raw Hide Buttes, Buzzard's Roost, and Dirty Woman's Ranch.

Postlethwaite's Tavern in Lexington, Kentucky, a rambling log structure, was furnished with cherry and walnut furniture built by local craftspeople. The Cosmopolitan Hotel in Tombstone, Arizona, offered stage travelers twenty-five neatly furnished rooms; a parlor piano was available for use by guests at the Scott House in Deer Lodge, Montana; the Pumas House in Quincy, California, carried the choicest liquors and cigars in its bar, and its stable offered the best accommodations for horses. Whiskey, peach brandy, wine, beer, and gin were popular drinks for stage travelers in the Kentucky Bluegrass region, but passengers opposed to strong spirits could patronize the LaFayette Temperance Hotel, an establishment based on "temperance principles." Those establishments were all in populated areas.

Although the Latham Station near Greeley, Colorado, was located in a desolate area, it was famous for miles around. Not only were the meals superb under the direction of cook Lizzie Trout, a nearby rancher sold supplies, including liquor, to locals as well as stage passengers and drivers. He famously promised that although he might run short on the "luxuries of life," he would always have the "necessaries" (beer, wine, and whiskey) in stock. The Mulberry Ranch near Dodge City, Kansas, was one of the cruder road ranches—a two-room hut with dirt floors. Four stakes driven into the floor with a board across passed for a bar; the shelf behind the bar held a few bottles of whiskey. Walls were covered with newspapers to cut down on cold winds whistling through the gaps in the wallboards. In 1857 renowned author Hinton R. Helper described a California hostelry built of "unhewn sampling, covered with canvas and floored with dirt." The interior consisted of one room crammed with tables and benches for dining and sleeping berths stacked directly above one another, each supplied with a two-foot-wide straw mattress, uncased pillow, and a blanket. Just because a stage stop offered luxuries such as sheets and feather-filled mattresses didn't ensure freshly washed sheets. It was a common practice for maids to sprinkle used sheets with water while smoothing them with a warm flat iron—ready for the next guest.

Meals at stage stops were a constant source of discussion among travelers. A certain overland stage route through the Great Plains frequently stopped at a place offering meals for weary, hungry travelers. The cook was known for her delectable biscuits. If anyone had paid attention, they might have found it peculiar that the driver, who had driven this route many times, always refused a meal at this stop—"a weak stomach," he claimed. By the next stop he appeared to have recovered and ate heartily. It might not have bothered some people, but the driver couldn't forget the time he had witnessed the cook rubbing her hands over the cats and dogs that hung out around the station and then, without washing her hands, thrusting them into the gooey biscuit batter, kneading with all her might.

tough beefsteak, boiled potatoes, stewed beans, a nasty compound of fried apples, and a jug of molasses
dried fruit pies with paste board crusts
half-cooked beans, heavy bread, stale butter

There were plenty of complaints about stage stop meals, but there were just as many compliments. In Nebraska and Kansas fried bacon, ham, elk, and buffalo steaks were served along with that highly prized delicacy: boiled buffalo tongue. Eggs, chicken, wild turkey, fresh vegetables, and creamy butter were offered as regular fare at some rural stops. At the Half-way House in Montana, passengers said that Meta Miller's table "groans with an abundance of good grub." In 1886 in Wilburn House in Kansas, Sallie Hutchison was well known for her first-class accommodations as well as her delicious meals. And Mrs. Mose Hayes's fruit pies couldn't be beat at Springer Ranch in Texas.

Passengers riding the stage from Cheyenne, Wyoming Territory, to Custer City, Dakota Territory, in 1876 could expect a variety of culinary experiences. Fagan's Ranche offered meals at fifty cents per person, and fresh fruits and vegetables were part of the fare. Chugwater Ranche promised a "well-stocked bar" and "good meals;" however, the coffee was less than perfect, according to some reports. At Kelly's Ranche stages stopped for meals prepared by Mrs. Kelly, a Native American woman who had married Hiram B. and cooked at the stage stop, where her meals were described by one passenger as "quite good enough for hungry people." At Fort Laramie the Markles operated the Rustic Hotel, where both humans and horses could partake of a decent meal, one dollar for humans. Corn for the teams ran $2.25 per bushel, with hay $3.50 per hundred pounds.

At the Hat Creek Ranche, passengers sat on old boxes for chairs around a couple of unplaned pine boards and were charged seventy-five cents for a meal that consisted of a tiny portion of fried dried meat, a few cold biscuits, "some very stale bread of a light chocolate color, a little syrup, and a dark concoction called coffee." A specialty at Hat Creek was their dried field corn cooked for about five minutes without salt, butter, or milk and served with a potato dish that required hours to prepare. The cook started with potatoes that had been exposed to a slight frost. Making sure they were entirely covered with water, she put them on to boil slowly until they were half done. The pot was removed from the stove and set aside, with the potatoes soaking in the water for four to six hours. Next she threw out the water and pared the potatoes as quickly as possible into one-quarter-inch slices. Placing them in a dry skillet (no butter or grease), she heated the potatoes until they were "slightly warm on one side." They then were placed on a cold plate with a little salt and served. If there were leftovers, the cook found the dish an "excellent substitute" for hog swill— quite popular with the pigs who needed fattening up.

In 1878 a young couple traveling to their new home in Deadwood, Dakota Territory, stopped at Chugwater, Kelly's, and Hat Creek Ranches and took advantage of the hospitality offered at all the other stops along the way. They relied on another form of nourishment to make the meals at the deficient stops more palatable.

"I am quite convinced that wine and other liquors are really necessary to use while crossing the Plains, as one cannot drink water and the thirst becomes intolerable. Nor do I blame anyone for wanting the beer." Anna Gerard offered these nuggets of wisdom shortly after enduring a rugged stagecoach ride from Cheyenne to Deadwood in late summer 1878.

Throughout the four-day trek she fought waves of sickness, grasping for any antidote to relieve her discomfort. Sometimes wine, beer, or brandy with lemon provided relief.

As the stage moved over plains and rocky bluffs, the coach's constant rocking and jolting only intensified Anna's wooziness. Riding up top with the driver seemed to help her condition. "I didn't care whether I died or lived. I was so miserable," she lamented. "We were jolted up and down till I really thought there would be nothing left of us but the pieces." Most stage stations offered beer or wine, and the Gerards usually purchased some to add to the supply they had brought and that fellow passengers shared. Between bouts of nausea, Anna managed to appreciate the scenery and the entire experience shared with her husband, Joseph. And he did all he could to ease her misery, including surprising her with a bouquet of wildflowers he'd gathered in a lush meadow.

At Chugwater Ranche she found a quiet corner to comb her hair and wash her face—grateful for the clean towel provided by the owner. At Fort Laramie every place was closed, preventing the purchase of badly needed brandy. Raw Hide Ranche provided a hearty breakfast of biscuits and boiled eggs in addition to a take-out package of beer and cake for sustenance until the next stop, and at Hat Creek they purchased drinking water for twenty-five cents. The owners of Land's End station welcomed the travelers, despite having themselves arrived only a few days before from Pennsylvania. The woman produced a commendable meal for twenty from her damp, dirt-floor cabin lined with shelves and a block of wood for a table. She had been battling muddy floors after recent rains that had flooded the structure, and the gunnysacks she used as makeshift carpeting didn't solve the problem.

Travel was delayed when a swollen stream prevented fording for a couple of days. Wrapped in blankets to ward off the chill of the summer night, Anna found it impossible to sleep—there wasn't room to stretch out in the coach crammed with other passengers. Another delay occurred when the stage became mired in a slough of mud, forcing the passengers to remove all contents of the stage as they struggled to pry the horses and coach out of the slick mess. It took a full hour of strenuous effort, plus another break for a rest after the feat was accomplished.

According to her diary, Anna was more amused than frightened when armed guards joined the stage at one point on the trip. Maybe her flippant attitude came from having seen "a belt with fire weapons" strapped around the waist of most every man she met on the trail. Had she known that an attempted robbery had occurred only days before on the very route they were traversing, she may not have been so dismissive of the guards.

A stage with four passengers aboard had been traveling several miles from Deadwood when a gang of masked bandits popped up from behind a clump of brush and started to fire at Captain Eugene Smith, the guard traveling with the coach and riding a few yards ahead—fortunately with a revolver in his left hand and a rifle in his right. One of the passengers on the stage described how the "brave man sitting coolly in his shirt sleeves, with a handkerchief around his neck" sat upon his horse "answering lead with lead" as he single-handedly returned fire at the outlaws concealed behind the brush along a creek bed. The witness described bullets whistling over his head as he sat upon the driver's seat of the stage. Even after Captain Smith's horse was mortally wounded, the brave guard calmly issued one last shot in the direction of the desperadoes and then "turned coolly around and walked to the coach, mounted the box and ordered the driver to drive on.

"I never saw such cool, desperate courage exhibited before in all my life," the witness said about Captain Smith's actions that day. But it was a close call, and the proprietor of the Gerards' coach wanted to be prepared for the next time—thus the addition of the four guards Anna wrote about in her diary.

Later, Anna was more curious than alarmed when they met an "iron clad" stage making its way from Deadwood loaded with a valuable cargo of gold and silver from the mines. Joseph talked the mine manager who rode with the treasure into a tour of the specially designed vehicle meant to prevent or at least discourage would-be robbers.

The unusual coach toured by the Gerards was the first of two commissioned by the Cheyenne and Black Hills Stage Company. It had been put into use just three months before. (The second would hit the trails in September 1878.) Luke Voorhees, superintendent of the stage company, contracted with the Master Safe and Lock Company of Cincinnati to construct the sixteen-by-thirty-inch safes with three-inch-thick walls. They were fitted with Yale combination locks expected to thwart even the most determined bandits. Voorhees asked the A. D. Butler stagecoach manufacturers to build two coaches with steel-lined interior walls and portholes from which guards "armed with weapons of all kinds" could fire at marauding road agents. Guards or messengers of the special coaches were handpicked "brave, fearless men" who had reputations as crack shots. Two of them—Daniel Boone May (better known as Boone May) and Scott "Quick Shot" Davis—bore "honorable scars as evidence of their pluck."

It was the simple pleasures that gladdened Anna's heart during the arduous journey to her new home that summer of 1878: a bouquet of wildflowers from her husband, a clean towel to dry her face, a couple of hairpins from another female passenger when she lost her precious few. Still, when the Gerards reached Deadwood, Anna had formed an unmistakable opinion about future travel. "When we go back, we are going in a wagon and camp along the road, but I won't go in a stage," she announced.

A decade later, a woman traveling overland by train and stagecoach probably could relate to Anna's sentiments. Unlike Anna, Mattie's adventure ended with a return to her former life; however, both women endured both the pleasures and the distresses of stagecoach travel.

Passengers on Thomas McEwen's stage line out of Baker City, Oregon, in 1889 endured a jolting ride over narrow, chuckhole-filled roads during the twenty-eight-mile trek to McEwen Station. Driver Rusty Red was skilled at guiding his team over the treacherous trail, pulling to the side when he met freighters with their cumbersome loads. But long before the two vehicles met, passengers were serenaded by the faint echo of tinkling bells reverberating over the mountain passes—a courteous alert of the approaching wagon pulled by a team of horses with bells attached to their harnesses. Midwest couple William and Martha (Mattie) Piper withstood the trip in the summer of 1889 on their way to a new life in Oregon.

When the stage finally reached McEwen Station, the Pipers were relieved to see a small settlement consisting of a hotel, blacksmith shop, dance hall, icehouse, and a corral filled with surplus stage horses. Initially the station had been intended as only a stop on the way to their home-stead—twenty acres of timber with no buildings—but when fire destroyed most of the timber on the Pipers' land, they abandoned their plans for homesteading. Thomas McEwen offered the Pipers a room in the hotel and jobs. William went to work shoeing horses and driving stage. Mattie

Street scene in Deadwood, 1876
COURTESY DEADWOOD HISTORY, INC., ADAMS MUSEUM COLLECTION, DEADWOOD, SOUTH DAKOTA

worked in the hotel serving food prepared by Little Red—no relation to stage driver Rusty Red (they both happened to have red hair)—in the hotel's dining hall. McEwen raised cattle and hogs, so delicious pork and hearty steaks were frequent menu items. Fresh milk also rounded out most meals.

The Pipers' journey to Oregon had been a trying one for sure. They had started out from Downs, Illinois, in 1886, when Mattie was a teenage bride. Their intent was to travel by rail and stage to Oregon, but a pickpocket in Kansas City stole most of their savings, leaving them with only fifteen dollars. Hearing of jobs in nearby Lawrence, Kansas, the young couple made their way there and worked for two years, William in farm fields and Mattie as a housemaid. When they finally had saved enough money (train tickets were seventy-four dollars for two) to renew their journey west, they left at ten in the morning on July 1, 1889. Their cross-country trip exposed the couple to vistas neither had seen before. Vast plains of prairie grasses, bleached animal bones strewn along the tracks, cowboys herding cattle, acres of wheat, oil wells, Indian reservations, mountains, high trestle bridges—all filled the Midwest couple with wonder.

In the end the Pipers' Oregon experience was short-lived. There were highlights such as hikes into the mountains, a tour of a working gold mine, a Christmas dance, and a New Year's Eve party that lasted into New Year's Day with dancing to a violin and banjo band and culminating with an eggnog breakfast. But with socializing consisting of visits from an old mountain man whose garlic-and-whiskey-laced breath could scare off wolves, rescuing Rusty Red from near death during a snowstorm, and becoming stuck in snow on her way to the clothesline, not to mention once-a-month mail delivery and chilling screams from nearby mountain lions, Mattie decided the life of a western pioneer wasn't for her. It didn't help when William found himself looking into the wrong end of a Remington pistol wielded by a masked bandit in October 1889. After rifling through the mailbags and taking all the valuables, along with about seventeen hundred dollars in cash and gold dust, the robber threw the empty mailbags into the coach and ordered William to leave and "not look back." By May, Mattie was on a train back to Lawrence; William joined her six months later.

Newspaper and magazine publishers during the height of the stagecoach era found that their readers were captivated by stage travel; this led to traveling writers and reporters conducting on-the-spot interviews of fellow passengers, who then became the subjects of entertaining articles. Stagecoaches were used to move across the country as well as for short day trips between local communities, so there was never a shortage of material for writers. A sampling of passengers on any given day or night provided a snapshot of a variety of individuals who used stagecoaches for myriad endeavors; for example, to attend social events, perform civic duties, and conduct professional business. In pre–Civil War days, wealthy southerners hired stagecoaches to transport belles and beaux to lavish resorts called "the Springs" in Kentucky. Graham Springs, Crab Orchard Springs, and Blue Licks Springs were favorites. The waters were valued for their medicinal purposes as well as for social events, including fishing and dancing parties. They became gathering places for the elite, with hotels to accommodate five hundred guests in stylish dining rooms and spacious ballrooms.

In the West, where socializing could be a challenge due to the distance between ranches and towns, stage stops became community centers. Young women, hungry for any opportunity for social interaction, thought nothing of purchasing tickets on the closest stage to ride as many as fifty miles to attend a dance at a stage station. They might take the return stage later in the evening or stay overnight with friends, catching the next day's stage home. Travelers passing through were often surprised to find such large gatherings in seemingly isolated regions, but locals didn't let a simple thing like distance stop them from having fun. In addition to facilitating much-appreciated social affairs, stagecoaches were instrumental in helping voters exercise their civic duties. Political activist Abigail Scott Duniway relied on stagecoaches to help her spread her passion for women's suffrage.

"Free Speech, Free Press, Free People"—the motto for Abigail's weekly human rights newspaper, the *New Northwest*, was prominently displayed on the front page of the Portland, Oregon, publication from

1871 to 1887. The suffragist and advocate for social justice was a regular passenger on stagecoaches as she traveled to spread her messages and gather news. Riders on The Dalles to Canyon City stage shortly before election day in October 1880 might have gotten an earful from Abigail, who was embarking on a journey throughout eastern Oregon and Washington. She certainly expressed opinions and perceptions with her readers, describing the scenery—"the great white peaks of the Cascade Range keeping eternal guard over the seemingly illimitable vista"—and referring to herself as "a native-born victim of 'taxation without representation.'" Her narrative as the stage went "careening, bumping, and crashing" over the "labyrinthine maze of serpentine curves" and hills covered with a "shaggy coat of bunch-grass, like the uncombed wool on the back of a Cotswold buck," was peppered with commentary about individuals she met at each stage station. Effusive with compliments for John and Eliza Shearar (alternately spelled Sherar), who operated a toll bridge and "cosy and pleasant" overnight accommodations, Abigail couldn't refrain from asking, "Can anybody tell us why Mrs. Shearar, who is as heavy a tax-payer as her husband, should not vote as well as he?"

Election Day found Abigail at Bake Oven stage station, run by Thomas and Ellen Burgess, where she delivered a talk about women's suffrage to a crowd of teamsters. And she observed the voting process as male voters—"gentlemanly judges who presided over the destiny of the voters"—cast their votes and women, who were "determined to vote for the next President," watched. The next stop on the stage line was Antelope Station, where Nathan and Sarah Wallace operated a post office. When the stage arrived, Abigail noted that passengers were greeted by a shivering Sarah, who had left her bed to distribute mail while "her protector and head," otherwise known as her husband, "snoozed cozily beneath the blankets." Abigail couldn't resist opining that Nathan undoubtedly got the postmaster salary; she sarcastically speculated that he probably "'thinks too much of women' to permit them to vote." Surprisingly, Abigail expressed no opinions about William and Bercia Saltzman, the operators of the next station at Burnt Ranche, other than that they provided a well-kept establishment with a cheerful fire and hearty breakfast. After

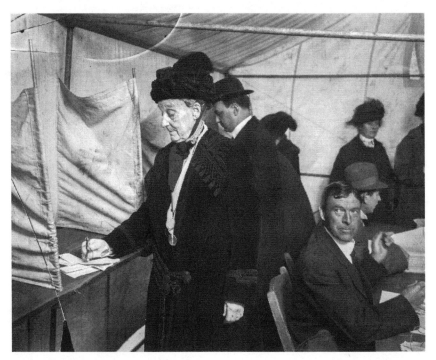

Abigail Scott Duniway voting in 1912
OREGON HISTORICAL SOCIETY, ABELL AND SON, CATALOG NUMBER ORHI 4601A

a few hours' sleep, she was refreshed and eager to climb into the stage for the next segment of the journey.

Abigail's efforts to expand voting rights to Oregon women did not result in victory until 1912, when the state's voters approved women's suffrage by 52 percent.

Women in Wyoming had been voting since 1869. A transplanted New Yorker living in Wyoming in 1881 wrote about the unusual situation she witnessed in the western United States, where women were well informed about political issues and weren't afraid of voting in opposition to their husbands' views. She had actually seen men stay home to watch the kids and tend to house chores so their wives could go to the polls. The writer observed "colored servant girls" sharing stages with white voters on their way to vote, although she believed they voted in line with their mistresses.

Stagecoaches played a vital role there too. When Frank Hamilton ran for justice of the peace in the late 1800s, his supporters borrowed a stage from the Chugwater station, about fifty miles north of Cheyenne, to transport voters to the nearest polling location, about a mile from the station. With only two harness-broke horses and two wild broncos available to pull the stage, everyone knew it would be a reckless trip as the tame animals tried to offset the rowdy ones. But "twelve or fifteen men" who worked at the ranch along with "three ladies and the colored servant girl" climbed into the coach for the ride. When they arrived at the poll, wagons were rolling in carrying voters from miles away. At the end of the day, men and women gathered at the Chugwater station for a supper and dance in honor of Frank.

Election days in Cheyenne found women spearheading drives to get voters to the polls by knocking on doors and sending coaches and wagons into outlying rural areas. Newspapers reported that women could be found at the polling places throughout election day, sometimes "electioneering" for votes. Winning candidates credited women with delivering the votes, and stagecoaches could literally be credited with delivering the voters.

Businesspeople used stagecoaches to conduct their day-to-day enterprises, relying on coaches to supplement rail service or reach otherwise inaccessible potential consumers, thereby expanding their customer base. Photographers in the 1870s set up shop on Main Street and waited for customers to come to them for family portraits; others took their business on the road. Elizabeth Kirby Withington established her Excelsior Ambrotype Gallery in Ione City, California, to meet the needs of locals, but she also traveled by stagecoach into outlying regions and into the nearby mountains to practice her art. Her distinct creative spirit was revealed not only in her beautiful photographs but also in her ingenuity in getting her cumbersome equipment to remote locations.

Elizabeth had moved to California in 1851 to join her husband, who had gone a couple years before during the early days of the gold rush. Within a few years of her arrival, Elizabeth was looking for a way to bring more income into the family; photography became her passion. In her quest to learn all she could about photography, she traveled to

Mrs. E. W. Withington,

STEREO ARTIST,

IONE CITY,

Amador County, - - - *Cal.*

Photo by Elizabeth Withington
PETER PALMQUIST COLLECTION OF WOMEN IN PHOTOGRAPHY. YALE COLLECTION OF WESTERN
AMERICANA, BEINECKE RARE BOOK AND MANUSCRIPT LIBRARY

New York in 1856 and brought her newfound knowledge back home to California.

Ione City was a booming little community, a stop for both stagecoaches and railroads, but Elizabeth looked beyond the boundaries of the little town and recognized the beauty of the natural landscapes and the quaintness of surrounding mines and homesteads. To get to these sites rich with photographic potential, she used the only resource that could transport her over the rugged terrain: stagecoaches.

But carrying her bulky photographic equipment as well as dangerous liquids to remote areas required more than a little grit and a great deal of resourcefulness. She designed and constructed unique containers to safely transport the delicate tools of her craft. Varnish, ammonia, nitric acid, alcohol, and lamp oil were meticulously wrapped in strong cloth sacks with a carpet bottom—all "snug and secure." Cotton batting helped absorb the jolts ("and some awful ones they get," Elizabeth admitted) caused by notoriously bone-jarring stagecoach trips. "But I never have had a bottle broken when traveling," she added. And what photographic endeavor could occur without a large tub to process plates? Elizabeth designed a special crate to hold her "Newell bath-tub," making it possible to operate without a traditional darkroom. She improvised with black calico dresses and a traveling shawl when in need of something to block the sun.

"Last but not least in usefulness is a strong black-linen cane-handled parasol," Elizabeth explained. "It is at hand if a view must be taken when the sun is too far in front, to shade the lenses with, or to break the wind from the camera."

Elizabeth's innovative photography techniques and her unusual eye for beauty began to gain recognition outside Ione City. Two national publications recognized her work. *Photographic Times* magazine ran a short article about her in August 1874, and *Philadelphia Photographer*, a journal published by an officer of the National Photographic Association of the United States, ran her article in 1876 detailing her techniques. Unfortunately, Elizabeth lived only another year; fortunately, many of her photographs have survived.

Meals fit for hogs and humans, unwashed sheets, staggering drunk drivers, amorous intruders in bed chambers, quagmires of syrupy mud, deadly snowslides, petulant passengers, cranky kids—the negatives were endless. But breathtaking scenery, access to otherwise inaccessible locations and social gatherings, intermingling with erudite individuals from all parts of the globe, and the prospect of finding love were also part of the teeth-rattling, bone-jarring adventure of stagecoach travel in America.

CHAPTER 4

Salty, Resourceful, Big-Hearted Bosses

"Fire, Pye, fire!" Elizabeth Pye urged her husband, John, as he froze with fright at the sight of a robber in the couple's bedroom. "I cannot, I cannot hold the gun," John Pye cried. It was 1805 and the scene played out in the Pyes' stage tavern near Albany, New York. In the end, Elizabeth Pye pulled the trigger on the gun that fired a bullet into the body of the would-be robber. The citizens of Albany overall agreed that Elizabeth "deserved a better and braver husband." However, they felt justice prevailed when Elizabeth outlived her husband by many years and married her barkeeper, a fellow forty years her junior. And while people couldn't say with certainty that Elizabeth's new husband had a courageous spirit, they said he was a "very fine" young man.

In a time when stage travel dominated, opportunities for individuals with an ounce of entrepreneurial spirit abounded. With endless miles of country to traverse and hungry, tired travelers looking for a good meal and a few hours in a comfortable bed, gutsy risk-takers went into business for themselves. Owning stages and stage stations presented unique challenges that were best met by a proprietor who possessed a great deal of pluck and more than a little grit. Elizabeth Pye proved she had what it took, and over the next hundred years, countless women and men bought, sold, managed, and operated stage enterprises. Typically, the names of the men were widely publicized at the time and have survived the years; women proprietors, however, were usually identified by their husband's name: "Mrs. John Pye" or "John Pye's wife." And where women were not allowed to own property, just the husband's name appeared on legal documents. Only through a fair amount of effort can the women's names be unearthed. These inequities in the historical record can't disguise the fact that women were not only vital to the operations but also frequently the impetus, and that they contributed significantly to the entrepreneurial aspects of the era.

Operating stage businesses could be a demanding life. Stagecoach owners dealt with upkeep of the coaches, hiring reliable drivers, and tending horses. It required an investment of time and money to purchase equipment and real estate. And there were nagging issues such as laws that held stage owners liable for passengers who traveled on the Sabbath and court decisions that held owners responsible for lost packages and injured passengers. Stage station owners dealt with a plethora of issues, including grumpy passengers demanding meals at all hours of the day and night, and highwaymen, like the bold intruder who entered Elizabeth Pye's bedroom. The legal roadblocks could be especially exasperating.

The Connecticut legislature grappled with the issue of people traveling by stage on the Sabbath in 1817. It had become a troubling dilemma for stage owners, who were in violation of state law when they transported passengers on their mail stages on Sunday. Passengers who originated in states without the Sabbath travel ban were forced to depart the stage when it crossed into Connecticut, causing them to incur additional costs for rooms and meals as they waited for Monday to arrive. Critics pointed out that the ban perpetrated even more serious breaches of law—profane cursing and swearing—as passengers were forced from the stagecoaches upon their arrival in Connecticut. Some suggested retaining the law but placing the penalty on the travelers themselves rather than the stage owners.

Early in the stagecoach era, courts had issued directives regarding the liability of stage proprietors in terms of bodily injuries to passengers as well as damage to packages. In 1821 a Virginia court decided that stage proprietors were liable for all packages entrusted to their care, despite notices issued by stage companies that all baggage was accepted at the passenger's risk. An 1839 case, *McKinney v. Neil*, was a landmark decision that held stage owners responsible for providing reliable coaches, harnesses, horses, and drivers. Subsequent decisions largely placed the burden of proof on stage owners to prove their innocence. Accident victims merely had to prove they were a passenger who had paid a fare and been injured by the upset stage. Rashes of lawsuits brought against stage owners prompted one loyal driver in 1866 to joke that should his coach upset in the future, he would examine each passenger, leaving the dead ones alone and finishing off the injured because "corpses never sue for damages, but maimed people do."

Despite the challenges associated with owning stagecoaches and stage stops, fearless entrepreneurs of both genders recognized the potential rewards offered by providing a service needed across the country, especially as people moved ever westward. The demand for stagecoach transportation and stage stops every ten miles along a route sparked the entrepreneurial spirit in countless men and women. Jane Melvin was one of those individuals, and she was barely past childhood when she made her foray into a stagecoaching enterprise.

Twelve Mile House
HISTORY COLORADO CENTER

Smoky Hill Road was a busy pioneer stage and wagon route stretching from the Missouri River to Denver in 1868 when sixteen-year-old Jane Higgins married John Melvin, who had taken up a 320-acre homestead to raise cattle and horses. The couple immediately added ten rooms to their three-room log house, which they called the Twelve Mile House, so they could take advantage of the brisk traffic passing their door on Smoky Hill Road. A stage stopped at least once a day, dropping mail and delivering passengers, some of whom purchased meals and a room for the night. The addition included a large kitchen with two cookstoves kept in constant use by Jane; a ballroom furnished with rugs, drapes, and furniture; and a barroom used for the usual purposes as well as a post office so that John could perform his duties as barkeep and postmaster at the same time. In addition to looking after the needs of stage passengers, Jane provided housekeeping duties for as many as ten hired hands who boarded at the station located just twelve miles southeast of Denver. They helped with milking the couple's seventeen cows and other chores some of the time, but also spent hours in the barroom smoking and imbibing, according to Jane's recollections.

"Although still a child of seventeen, I was cooking for large numbers, caring for my infant son, doing all the washing, baking, cleaning, sewing and mending," Jane said in a 1935 interview.

It wasn't an entirely dreary existence for the Melvins. John, an avid horse racer, built a track on the property where guests enjoyed thrilling entertainment as cowboys showed off their racing and roping skills. People came from the city to dance and picnic under the Melvins' shade trees. And there were the dances in the ballroom where guests dined and danced for five dollars apiece. Those dances meant additional work for Jane, who spent days roasting hams, pork, and beef in preparation for the arrival of guests. The menu included homemade bread, fresh-churned butter, oyster stew, coffee, and of course liquor. Jane's pies and cakes were a hit; she prided herself in baking at least thirty-six large cakes of several varieties for the dance parties. Always the thrifty businesswoman, she sold any leftovers for a dollar apiece. The dances famously lasted into the night and, more times than not, into the second day. One might think that by the day of the event, Jane would be ready for a rest; however, she was very young and wasn't about to miss an opportunity for fun. "In spite of my heavy work I never missed a dance from dusk until dawn," she remembered.

During the time a railroad was being built near the Twelve Mile House, Jane was exceptionally busy, rising at three o'clock in the morning and finally falling into bed at eleven o'clock at night. With the help of one hired woman, she served meals to eighty very hungry men each day. However, the coming of the railroad was a mixed bag for the Melvins. It meant additional income while the construction of the rails progressed but also meant the end of the brisk stage business once the railroad was completed. The ever-resourceful Melvins used their large dwelling to house their four children and turned their full attention to stock raising.

———

Advertisements in Dakota Territory newspapers made sure readers were aware of the Bull Dog Ranch, located about seventeen miles from Deadwood in 1879. J. J. (John) Erb's name was prominently displayed as proprietor; and the bar amenities—imported liquors and cigars—couldn't be missed. The ad assured travelers that there was "No Better Supplied Table in the Black Hills." Before long the line became more than a mere slogan—people actually were impressed with the Bull Dog's outstanding meals and its "champion cuisine director," who turned out to be Mrs. Erb. Even the name of the place was the brainchild of the female half of the business; it was said that Sarah kept a couple of bulldogs in full sight to scare off potential intruders who might consider stealing her chickens. It may not be a stretch to claim that the entire reputation of the Bull Dog was largely due to Sarah Erb's business acumen. And while her name never appeared in the newspaper advertisements, it did begin to show up in print quite frequently. In time, her expertise in the culinary arts was overshadowed by her notoriety as a gunslinger and rabble-rouser. In the case of Sarah Erb Hammond, her entrepreneurial spirit took some peculiar twists and turns!

The Erbs' establishment was a popular stopping off place for travelers heading to the Black Hills, including bandits, who seemed to know the place was a likely source of valuable loot. Robbers visited the Bull Dog more than once. About 10:00 p.m. on a May night in 1879, three masked men approached the Bull Dog ranch house, where John and Sarah were settling in for the night. Initially the couple wasn't alarmed when they heard movement out in the horse corral—late-night paying guests were common. But when three masked men entered the house demanding any and all valuables, the proprietors—encouraged by two pistols aimed in their direction—handed over fifty dollars in cash and jewelry valued at about three hundred dollars. As the bandits perused the premises one last time before fleeing into the night, one noticed John's gold watch and chain dangling from his pocket. Explaining that it was a family heirloom and a distinctive piece of jewelry that would likely be difficult for the bandits to sell without being noticed, John hoped to dissuade them from taking the watch. It worked, and the watch remained in John's possession. As an additional deference to fairmindedness, the robbers promised John that if the other jewelry proved to be a problem, they would leave it in a place where he could retrieve the stolen goods.

Sarah's behavior during the entire episode was remarkable; she remained cool and calm throughout the ordeal. When the bandits noticed a banjo hanging on the wall and asked who played, Sarah pulled the instrument down and began to serenade the group. She later admitted she was attempting to detain the culprits, hoping they would inadvertently reveal clues to their identities. But in the end, they made off into the dark night. John headed out the next day to follow their trail but failed to find the robbers.

Despite the Erbs' successful business partnership, by summer their marriage had begun to crumble, and their ugly situation played out in the local newspapers. There was the unfortunate incident in Deadwood, where Sarah had gone to seek a legal separation. When John followed her into a pawnshop as she disposed of some of the couple's possessions, Sarah pulled out her revolver and aimed it squarely at her husband's face. According to the *Black Hills Daily Times*, John "cut out like a quarter horse."

Fueled by their mutual rage, the couple set out on their missions for revenge. John swiftly sold the Bull Dog Ranch; its contents, including farm implements and the stock, went to a neighbor at nearby Ten

Mile Ranch. When Sarah found out, she went on the "warpath," according to the *Black Hills Daily Times*. Heading out to Bull Dog Ranch, she convinced the new owner to disclose where the stock had gone. At first the fellow claimed ignorance, but his memory was jogged when Sarah embedded a bullet in his little finger. He recalled that her estranged husband had taken the herd to Ten Mile Ranch. Off she went, and on the way she encountered Officer Paul Rewman, a local constable whom she mistook as one of John's pals. Details of the interaction were a little murky, but the newspaper reported that Sarah held up the lawman and then proceeded to Ten Mile Ranch, where she once again used her pistol to inspire the proprietor to round up her stock so she could take the animals into Deadwood. When she got to Deadwood, Sarah was arrested for allegedly stealing the gun she had been using to terrorize her victims. The newspaper reported that she was disarmed of any weapons before entering the packed courtroom at her arraignment, but that didn't mollify the citizens of Deadwood—every time she made abrupt gestures with her hands, the spectators headed for the door.

Sarah was released on a five-hundred-dollar bond but failed to show up for her court date. She did make a court appearance later, when she and John divided up their property. Only a few days later, Sarah was again in trouble with the law; she was accused of trying to murder a fellow named John Duckworth, but the charges were eventually dismissed.

By July 1880 Sarah appeared to have moved on from her old life with John Erb and owned a ranch about five miles from Fort Meade. Maybe she recognized the value of market branding, as she once again named her property Bull Dog Ranch and adorned it with a hand-painted sign of a bulldog. The *Black Hills Daily Times* reported that it was "one of the best kept ranches in the territory." In August a newspaper notice indicated that she had remarried—this time to one of her ranch hands, George Hammond, who was at least a decade younger than she. By September she was in the news again—again on the wrong side of the law as a result of bigamy charges brought by John. By some accounts John claimed he believed the couple was simply separated rather than divorced. One newspaper claimed the divorce settlement had specified that Sarah could not remarry during John's lifetime. Sarah either thought she was legally divorced or didn't care. When local lawman Gale Hill went out to Bull Dog Ranch to confront Sarah, she chased him off with her six-shooter. She ultimately was acquitted of the bigamy charges. Over the next several years, Sarah lived a checkered existence plagued by legal run-ins, including problems with creditors, accusations of appropriating goods belonging to the US government, and assault and battery charges. Sarah's name was absent from newspapers after 1882, and it's unknown whether she ever again used her business skills to serve the traveling public.

When a young girl named Olivia Antonini left her home in Italy and traveled to San Francisco, California, with her family in the late 1850s, no one could have guessed that her name would one day be linked to one of the most elusive stagecoach robbers of the Old West. But the deliberate, day-to-day business acumen coupled with a generous spirit she embodied as an adult deserved just as much acclaim.

The Antonini family settled in northern California, where Olivia's dad worked as a miner. In her late teens she married Gerolamo (James) Rolleri, whose family had also emigrated from Italy. Together the couple built a family and a reputation as honest, hardworking business owners. The couple raised cattle on their ranch, operated a ferry that transported stages over the nearby river, and ran a general

Olivia Rolleri
CALAVERAS COUNTY HISTORICAL SOCIETY

store catering to the needs of locals as well as drummers (salespeople) and miners. They also raised eleven kids. In 1883 Olivia's little inn was a popular stopping place for stages, including those running between Tuttletown and Copperopolis. Her fabulous Italian cooking was famous for miles around.

At the same time the Rolleris were making their mark on this part of California, an intriguing stage robber was the subject of intense fascination throughout the West. The bandit known as Black Bart had made a living robbing Wells Fargo's very lucrative bank boxes that traveled by stage between the mines and Wells Fargo offices. The public was enthralled with this mysterious character because of his unique brand of criminality. He targeted only Wells Fargo valuables, as demonstrated by the story of a frightened passenger tossing her purse out the stage window to Bart, who remarked, "Madam, I do not wish your money. I honor only the good office of Wells Fargo." Occasionally he left behind at the robbery site poems he had written, including this one:

> I've labored long and hard for bread,
> For honor and for riches,
> But on my corns too long you've tred,
> You fine-haired sons of bitches.
> —Black Bart, the Po8

People who came into contact with this mysterious bandit mentioned his deep, mesmerizing voice, piercing eyes, and refined manner. Witnesses seldom saw his full face, which he covered with a flour sack with slits cut for his eyes. And he always wore a long light-colored duster to cover his six-foot frame. Some found his habit of never harming passengers or drivers endearing. But between 1875 and 1883, Black Bart had robbed twenty-eight stages, making away with thousands of Wells Fargo dollars. Wells Fargo detectives were not amused.

On a morning in November 1883, Olivia Rolleri and her family became part of the legend surrounding the poet bandit. Reason McConnell was driving a stage carrying more than four thousand dollars in gold between Tuttletown and Copperopolis. He knew quite well the breakfast he could get at Olivia Rolleri's inn on his way. As he pulled up for a hasty meal, Olivia's son, Jimmy, offered to watch the stage and asked if he could hitch a ride up to Funk's Hill, where he wanted to do a little deer hunting. After breakfast the two set out, with Jimmy and his rifle perched on top next to Reason. There were no passengers, so the Wells Fargo box bolted to the floor of the carriage was his most precious cargo.

At the approach to Funk's Hill, Reason slowed to let Jimmy off for his deer hunt. The two planned to reconnect on the far side of the hill. Within a short distance, Reason was startled by noise in the brush along the road and found himself "looking down the twin barrels of a sawed-off shotgun." The robber with the bright blue eyes peering through the slits in the flour sack demanded in a deep voice that the driver unhitch the team and disappear over the hill, which Reason did. He heard the bandit blasting open the Wells Fargo box but wasted no time looking back. When he crested the hill, Reason met up with Jimmy and the two quietly circled back to the stage. They took turns using Jimmy's rifle, directing their shots at the robber, who fled the scene carrying his flour sack filled with loot. Reason and Jimmy hitched the team and headed into Copperopolis to report the crime.

Together local lawmen and Wells Fargo detectives from their headquarters in San Francisco pieced together clues that were left behind at the scene of the robbery to finally bring in the infamous Black Bart. A handkerchief stamped with the letters "F.X.O.7" tipped off the San Francisco detectives, who recognized them as a laundry mark used by local launderers to identify customers. It took a little legwork, but before long a laundry owner informed the detectives that the handkerchief belonged to customer C. E. Bolton, who lived in a boardinghouse nearby. This was the beginning of the end for Black Bart, whose real name turned out to be Charles E. Boles. In the end, he was convicted only of the Funk's Hill holdup and served about four years in San Quentin State Prison. For his role in the capture of one of the most notorious robbers of the time, Olivia's son was awarded a new rifle by Wells Fargo.

We don't know if Olivia was impressed with Jimmy's role in the Black Bart story, but the Rolleris' brush with fame didn't change much for Olivia. While all this headline-grabbing drama captivated the nation,

Olivia Rolleri continued her day-to-day work raising her brood of kids and running her businesses. When Gerolamo died in 1889, she continued investing in properties and expanding her business. Her Hotel Calaveras in Angels Camp became legendary with its saloon served by bartenders sporting pearl-buttoned vests and dining rooms outfitted with cloth table coverings and flowers. Buying up several buildings to enlarge the business, she offered fifty rooms with a water bowl and pitcher in each room and always clean beds. Her meals consisted of her own homegrown produce and meat, not to mention fresh-churned ice cream and warm baked bread slathered with rich, creamy butter. And then there was her most sought-after dish: ravioli.

Olivia's descendants called her the "consummate entrepreneur" when they talked about her business enterprises; however, it was her kind-hearted, generous spirit they recalled most. Others called her an angel and a humanitarian. A news story at the time of "Grandma Rolleri's" death described the "loved figure" who for thirty-nine years had operated the Calaveras Hotel, where "no one ever was turned away from her door hungry."

"I'm a product of the 'Old West,' and in those days we didn't have much chance to practice the refinements and niceties of high society," Sarah Jane (Sadie) Creech Orchard told a New Deal interviewer for the Federal Writers' Project in 1936. Out-of-work writers, historians, librarians, and teachers contributed to the project by capturing the stories of Americans whose lives represented a snapshot of American life. As Sadie reminisced about her fascinating experiences in the stagecoach trades in New Mexico in earlier days, Clay Vaden meticulously recorded her words. Sadie recalled maneuvering a six-horse stagecoach over the rugged terrain: "My trips were surely trying—especially through picturesque Box Canyon between Kingston and Hillsboro." Sadie lived in both settlements in the mid-1800s and could have provided Clay with a treasure trove of stories to fill his pages. She did offer this: "At that time Kingston was a mining town of about five thousand population with a big silver boom going full sway. Dance halls and saloons did a rushing business almost day and night."

The Federal Writers' Project revealed only a small morsel of Sadie's fifty years of living and working in the pioneer days of New Mexico. Precious nuggets were buried in this colorful woman's past. It was a tale of survival in a dangerous, relentless environment that called for fortitude and resolute determination. Sadie proved she was a survivor as she navigated the business world of New Mexico's raucous past.

Born in Mills County, Iowa, somewhere around 1860, Sadie was living in the rip-roaring mining camp of Kingston, New Mexico, in the mid-1880s. Her initial business ventures almost certainly involved a period as a lady of the evening at Kingston and later at nearby Hillsboro in the late 1880s and early 1890s. She married a fellow named James Orchard in July 1895.

Together the couple operated stages between Kingston and Lake Valley by way of Hillsboro, carrying passengers and freight between railroad stations in their express wagon and two Concord coaches. The Orchards dealt with all the typical challenges associated with stagecoach ownership:

Sadie Orchard (on right) in front of the Ocean Grove Hotel, Hillsboro, New Mexico
GEORGE T. MILLER, COURTESY PALACE OF THE GOVERNORS PHOTO ARCHIVES (NMHM/DCA), 076560

competing for mail contracts, tending a healthy stable of horses, hiring reliable drivers, and maintaining the coaches and equipment. And as Sadie told Clay Vaden in 1936, she frequently took the reins herself. "I drove four and six horses every day from Kingston to Lake Valley." In 1899 a New Mexican newspaper called the Orchards' enterprise "one of the finest stage lines in the territory" and claimed it had the "best looking driver in the Southwest."

Sadie's venture into Hillsboro's business community included her two hotels, the Ocean Grove Hotel and the Orchard Hotel. The businesses were well known for offering clean rooms and outstanding food prepared by Sadie's cook, Tom Ying. Stage passengers and locals frequented the places, and as Hillsboro was the county seat, courthouse activities brought in business too.

In 1900 court documents and news articles hinted that the Orchards' marriage was on the rocks. There was a dispute over property and an incident involving Sadie's use of a "deadly weapon" on her husband. By 1901 they were divorced, and Sadie was operating her two hotels by herself. Over the next several years, Sadie appeared to once again be involved in the brothel business. However, an article in a 1915 newspaper featured "the Orchard House," a business owned by Sadie where guests could expect "good beds" and "grub" that was the "best served in southern New Mexico."

In 1936, when the Federal Writers' Project included Sadie in the collection of typical Americans, it's unclear what type of business she was operating. Clay Vaden wrote that Sadie "today is owner of the Orchard Hotel in Hillsboro, New Mexico." Another writer at the time claimed that "she is still the big-hearted, resourceful woman of frontier days who saw her job, tackled it stoically, and did it manfully with a twinkle in her eyes." When Sadie died in April 1943, the only hint that she was anything other than a typical citizen of Hillsboro was the headline announcing that the "salty innkeeper" had died.

Mother Nature consistently presented barriers to thwart owners of stage businesses—snowstorms that disrupted schedules and stranded guests at stage stations where food and good-naturedness became scarce, rain gushers that washed out roads and created quagmires resulting in damaged vehicles and costly repairs, dangerous mountain passages inviting upsets that led to lawsuits. Dealing with these quirks of nature was part of daily life for stagecoach and stage stop proprietors in any part of the country. Arizona's brutal heat and soaring mountain ranges could defeat even the most determined entrepreneur. But not Annie Box Neal, who embraced Arizona's natural elements and used them to her advantage.

Born on a Cherokee reservation in 1870 to a Native American mother and a dad who claimed British and African-American ancestry, Annie and her parents had traveled by covered wagon from Oklahoma to Arizona in the late 1870s. Wiley Box welcomed diverse opportunities for earning a living, including a stint as a stagecoach driver, but he was partial to prospecting and gambling. Hannah was flexible, so when they arrived in Tucson they dropped Annie at St. Joseph's Academy in the heart of town and set out to make a living through a variety of pursuits.

Annie blossomed at the boarding school, devouring every morsel the Catholic nuns offered relating to music, art, and cooking. It was here she developed the skills to compose a couple of musical pieces—"Oklahoma March," inspired by her journey from Oklahoma, and "Arizona Schottische"—and to refine her manners to become a charismatic adult. Her time at St. Joseph's shaped her into a young woman who was well prepared to become a gracious wife and housekeeper, or a highly successful businesswoman. After two failed marriages and two divorces, Annie finally met the true love of her life: William "Curly" Neal, a man twenty years her senior. She did become a housekeeper of sorts—and, most definitely, a businesswoman.

By the time Annie married him in 1890, Curly was an established businessman with several endeavors under his belt, including a cellar-building business and livery stables. He'd had success in operating the first stage lines between Tucson and Mammoth and provided a much-needed service hauling freight to and from Tucson and the many mines operating in the area. Over the years his government contracts to carry mail and his hauling of precious ores from the mines to banks in Tucson helped cement his reputation as a serious businessman. And all that came after he'd served as an army scout with the legendary Buffalo Bill Cody.

Annie's "gleaming chocolate skin and lovely thick hair" coupled with her "regal bearing" and flirtatious, high-spirited demeanor undoubtedly attracted Curly to this younger woman. But it was more than that. Her skills with a gun and capacity to survive a tough environment must have carried some weight with this very pragmatic man. When Curly took on the extremely dangerous duties of transporting gold from surrounding mines to the Consolidated Bank of Tucson, he rejected the services of an army escort. He believed he could outsmart any would-be robbers by using circuitous routes, alternating vehicles between buckboards and stagecoaches, varying schedules, and, possibly most useful of all, inviting Annie to accompany him on the route. Her reputation as one of the most beautiful women in the freighting business might have been thought a deterrent, but more likely it was her well-known ability to handle the rifle she carried as she perched next to Curly on the driver's seat.

It was Annie's prowess as a shrewd business owner and her knack for marketing that ultimately made the Neals famous. In 1894 they built their Mountain View Hotel on land they owned in the Catalina Mountain settlement of Oracle, about forty miles north of Tucson. Their grand opening in February 1895 was a well-attended affair. The guest list of Tucson elites was published in the *Arizona Weekly Citizen*, which covered the grand ball held on President George Washington's birthday. It was an opportunity to showcase the meticulously designed resort "built in one of the most enchanting spots in the southwest," according to the newspaper. On display were the lovely guest rooms with steel ceilings and gilded walls, each painted a different color at the direction of the artistic owner. With music provided by Tucson's Manuel Montijo Orchestra, guests danced until dawn in the billiards room decorated with fresh flowers from Annie's gardens, pausing only for a midnight supper.

The Mountain View Hotel was destined to become a celebrated resort prized by vacationers from around the country. It was especially appreciated by Tucsonans seeking a cool, clean refuge from the searing heat and pervasive dust storms of August. The beautiful vacation spot became a popular destination for people suffering from respiratory illnesses that

Picnic at Oracle, Annie Neal in white (seated)
ARIZONA HISTORICAL SOCIETY, WILLIAM NEAL COLLECTION

were alleviated by cool mountain air. Just as appealing to guests was the six-foot-tall owner, whose quiet voice and refined manners captivated anyone who dropped a foot over the threshold.

Annie's newspaper advertisements made sure readers knew about the amenities offered at the Mountain View: forty horses trained for saddle or harness, single and double carriages, bicycles, croquet grounds, tennis lawns, and a golf course. She reminded potential guests of the pure mountain air with "humidity almost nil." The trek up to an altitude of forty-five hundred feet need not trouble travelers who suffered from acrophobia, as Curly provided safe and reliable stage service every day (except Sunday) from Tucson. The Neals offered special rates to stage riders traveling to the hotel—a private coach for four dollars round-trip, compared to ten dollars for passengers going to other stops in the Catalinas. Annie promoted her resort as a "famous natural sanitarium for pulmonary invalids," and she provided a resident physician who catered to those needs.

Annie kept the Mountain View in the local news by offering titillating events that brought people up from Tucson as well as providing entertainment for her hotel guests, who had traveled from across the country and the world. In January 1896 she crafted this unique piece of poetry as an invitation for an upcoming event:

> *You are asked to present be*
> *At a "penny" jubilee*
> *Borrow if you haven't any.*
> *Come for a good time*
> *When seven o'clock doth chime*
> *Bring your answer in rhyme.*

Invitees eagerly responded with their similarly poetic acceptance letters. All agreed the best came from Lavinia Steward, a guest at Mountain View:

> *Many thanks for invitation to jubilee*
> *My earnest desire is a guest to be,*
> *And if a penny I can borrow,*
> *And have my bloomers mended by tomorrow,*
> *I shall be along on my bike*
> *By the time the clock doth seven strike.*

Christmas 1899 at Mountain View drew an interesting range of guests and offered something for everyone from "baby up to the grumpy old chap with whiskers." The beautifully decorated and lighted tree stood in a corner of the billiard room, where guests from Ohio, Iowa, and New York City enjoyed a dinner of oysters, turkey, cranberries, plum pudding, and a selection of wines. Annie provided gifts for everyone as well—a cowboy saddle for a little boy in knickers and a bottle of tarantula juice for the old chap with whiskers.

Annie's ingenuity in using her natural surroundings to attract paying guests from around the world, combined with Curly's resilience in finding ways to make money, kept the charming resort lucrative well into the 1930s. They adjusted to meet the needs of modern guests; for example, offering long-distance phone service and transportation from Tucson by automobile. However, they never stopped reminding potential guests of their most alluring enticements: the delightful natural beauty and cool mountain air.

Authorities in Sonoma County, California, had issued an arrest warrant for George Brereton in August 1876. He was wanted for assault with intent to do great bodily injury as a result of an accident in which a couple of women had been thrown from a buggy. He was accused of intentionally running into the rig from behind, causing it to overturn. Although the passenger had not sustained any injuries, the driver, Ina Case Miller, was suffering from some complications. Within a week of the incident, George had been apprehended, found guilty, and fined five hundred dollars by the judge. It turned out that Ina had recently fired George from his job as a stage driver, and he was out for revenge.

Ina was known as "The Little Boss" by her employees, and for good reason. Her husband, Lew Miller, had died a few months before, leaving her with much of his property and stage enterprises. Having taken an active role in Lew's stage businesses beginning with their marriage in 1869, after his death she began buying and selling properties and stage lines with gusto, as well as bidding on and winning mail contracts for routes in California, Washington, Nevada, and Idaho. It was the beginning of a lifelong career in staging.

"I think I have always been connected with the express and mail business," Ina told a *Boston Globe* reporter in 1893. "In the fifties I came to California, consigned as an express package. I was a wee bit of a girl, and father and mother had gone out before from Illinois, where I was born. I was shipped by way of the Isthmus (of Panama)."

Ina joined her parents in Yankee Jim's, a mining camp in northern California, and spent most of her childhood among the miners. At one point she was sent down to San Francisco for school, ultimately marrying Lew.

"At 19 I was left a widow with three stage lines on my hands and mail contracts with the government to be carried out. Why should I have hired a man when I knew how to run the business myself? There was no reason, so I turned stage owner and driver," Ina explained.

It's not known what George Brereton had done to bring about his firing, but everyone knew that Ina had no tolerance for drivers who "made too close fellowship with the flask." She was known to fire a drunk driver on the spot and take over the reins herself if necessary. People talked about the female driver with "dark auburn" hair and "flashing black eyes" deftly guiding her four-horse stages through some of the most rugged mountain passages of the Sierras. And when she sat on the driver's seat, mail and passengers were delivered on time. She took an active role in all aspects of her stage businesses, including inspecting the coaches to ensure the mechanicals were greased regularly and harnesses were oiled in a timely manner. She bought all the hay and grain for her horses, and when it came to acquiring fresh teams, people said she was as good a judge of stock as any man in the stage business.

Ina liked to regale friends with tales of her adventures as a driver, including the time she was hauling a load of mill machines to a mining camp high in the mountains. It was a perilous forty-mile climb that "most men would have willingly shirked." Partway through the trek she had to fix a broken wagon yoke as well as mend a harness—all in the dark. A short time after tackling those problems, she came upon a wild stretch of road where her horses began to act extremely jittery, suddenly leaping to the side of the trail and dragging the wagon up an embankment. The wagon teetered perilously as Ina gingerly stepped down from the driver's seat to investigate the situation and came face to face with a bear. "Now, I am not particularly afraid of bears, but horses always are; and it would have been unpleasant for anyone to be left alone in the mountains with an overturned wagon, so I kept very quiet," Ina said. "The four-footed road agent inspected the outfit in a leisurely fashion and then waddled away. I had to feel for the road and drag brush and stones out of the way, but somehow I avoided an upset, and at midnight the journey was ended."

If she wasn't driving, she was riding as a passenger, supervising her hired drivers. "The largest route I ever controlled was 1,800 miles long and ran from Reno, Nevada, to Fort Bidwell in northern California," Ina said. "Once every month for three years and a half I went over that line. I used to get on the stage beside my driver at 7 o'clock in the morning, and for thirty-six hours I never left that seat except to eat, inspect my stations and horses, and interrogate my men."

Ina soon was known as "one of the largest contractors in America." That meant she frequently sublet the mail contracts but kept decidedly close watch over all the operations. She boasted about the time she personally traveled to Washington, DC, with five hundred thousand dollars in bonds tucked into her luggage, prepared to submit bids for more than a thousand routes. She ended with far less—only 150—still an impressive accomplishment. After winning the contracts, the real work began; it was crucial that everything run efficiently in order to make the routes profitable based on the bids she had made. Ina traveled throughout Arizona, California, Oregon, Montana, Nevada, and Utah, lining up personnel to sublet the routes and ensuring the contracts were fulfilled to her satisfaction.

In addition to government mail contracts, Ina operated express lines delivering packages, freight, and other precious cargo. In 1891 she partnered with a legendary company. "I am the only woman who carries Wells Fargo express, and from July 1 to the time the snow set in we carried $100,000 in gold dust." With her reputation at stake, Ina said the nineteen agents delivering the highly valuable shipments were "under my personal supervision."

One of Ina's mail routes in 1882 ran between Reno and Cedarville, Nevada, and in July the US Post Office suddenly ordered daily delivery to scale back to weekly service. Locals were fiercely opposed to this change but were hopeful when Ina traveled to the nation's capital to convince postal authorities to reconsider. Success! On July 10 the US Post Office rescinded its previous order and six-day service resumed. It wasn't the first time Ina visited Washington to lobby for better mail delivery in the West, and it wouldn't be the last.

Ina was to have a long and contentious relationship with postal officials in Washington, prompting one newspaper to describe her as the "most successful lobbyist in America." She developed a particular dislike for Postmaster General John Wanamaker, who had been appointed in 1889 by President Benjamin Harrison—primarily because he had contributed one hundred thousand dollars to Harrison's campaign, according to Ina.

Making a trip east in 1891, she intended to demand a congressional investigation of Wanamaker. When asked by a reporter from the *San Francisco Examiner* what the charges would be, she replied, "I know that Brother Wanamaker will have to explain how he paid $100,000 for the office. Then he will have to explain how he came to make so many blundering changes in the postal service."

Ina compiled a list of grievances, including selection of a post office site far from the central business section of San Francisco on property belonging to a Presbyterian church that gave Wanamaker twenty-five thousand dollars, daily mail delivery to towns with only a handful of residents while cutting delivery to larger towns, ordering unnecessary overnight layovers that delayed delivery, fining stage companies that disregarded senseless schedules issued from Washington, and on and on. She complained about postal department directives that resulted in a letter taking nearly as long to travel between Chico and Quincy, California, as to travel between San Francisco and New York. And she questioned an order from Washington regarding the line that served Bartlett Springs, sending the mail stage eight miles over mountains to pick up and deliver *one* man's mail. She wanted to know what influence that man had over Wanamaker in order to give him such extraordinarily preferential treatment. Overall, Ina said the postal service throughout the Pacific Coast was "utterly demoralized" and mail was "blunderingly handled." In her eighteen years handling mail contracts, she added, she had "never seen mail service in the battered, knocked-out condition that now prevails."

Traveling with a bundle of photos as evidence of the deplorable situation of mail delivery in the West, Ina was prepared to make her case. One photograph showed her stagecoaches in front of "one of the four grog-shops on our routes where we have to leave mail." She explained, "Two are in mining camps, but the other two are in sections where women and children have to go and receive their mail over the bar." Another showed the place known as "Robbers' Roost" on a mountain route where stages were held up so often that shotgun messengers with a "trusty weapon and a belt full of cartridges" accompanied them.

Ina was furious with the reception she received from Postmaster General Wanamaker when she visited his office. She reported his reply to her complaints: "If the people on the Pacific Coast don't like the way I do business, let them take the business and run it to suit themselves."

After a trip to Washington in 1893, Ina accused Wanamaker of "willful disregard of the people of the Pacific Coast." When asked about postal services in the West, Ina replied that little had improved. "Oh, affairs are quite as bad as ever on our mountain routes," she said. But she perceived one bright spot: "Wanamaker's term is happily almost ended."

In response to a newspaper reporter's comment about her unusual life experiences, Ina said, "Women are quite as well qualified mentally for such a life as men. What I have done any woman can do."

While some men may have been put off by Ina's fierce independence, others must have found it alluring. Ina had never been one to shy away from marriage, tying the knot at least five times. After Lew Miller there was John Wade, Johannes Camphausen, George McLane, and finally Harry Langdon. Some of those fellows died; others merely disappeared from the public record. John Wade died only three months after the wedding, so Ina went to court to change her name back to Miller. She and Harry Langdon were married for almost thirty years.

Ina never publicly expressed any negative sentiments about her husbands, aside from complaining once that after she married Harry, she had to get her mail contracts in *his* name. It was an unfortunate sign of the times that successful businesswomen were robbed of the recognition they deserved as they invested their time and money in stagecoach enterprises. Take for example the omission of Sarah Erb's name from the newspaper advertisements boasting about the outstanding meals offered at the Erbs' stage station, while John's name always appeared in a prominent spot. And the common practice of recognizing women only by their connection with their husband: "Mrs. Harry Langdon" or "Harry Langdon and wife." More serious were instances when businesswomen who had established stage enterprises or were equal partners in such endeavors were robbed of their property. Sadie Orchard and Sarah Erb both had problems related to property rights when they divorced their husbands. Neither left the marriage without getting a share of the businesses they had operated with their husbands, but it didn't come easily. Too frequently women entrepreneurs were robbed of their property just because of their gender.

Occasionally justice prevailed, as in the case of a wealthy Nevada couple who had made their early fortunes running a stage road tavern. In 1897 the man was considering divorcing his longtime wife. The two had lived apart for a long time but had never legally divorced. A friend brought the fellow back down to earth after the businessman suggested he could pay his wife a paltry settlement of a thousand dollars per month. "It's your own affair about living together or apart, but if she goes, she takes her share of the fortune she helped to make. It's millions, and when you talk about giving her anything, you must talk about millions too," the friend said. It's unclear how his wife pulled it off, but she reportedly got millions from her ex-husband, living in luxury the rest of her life and leaving millions to her daughters.

CHAPTER 5

It Hardly Pays a Man, So Girls Do It

THERE WAS A HARD-AND-FAST RULE ON STAGE ROUTES IN THE LATE 1800s and early 1900s. One woman was allowed on the top seat with the driver; two were not. Did it have anything to do with female fashions at the time? Voluminous skirts, hand satchels, and parasols ate up a great deal of precious space on those narrow seats. Not to mention the difficulty a woman encased in yards of fabric faced in attempting to climb onto the seat seven feet above ground level. No, female fashion had nothing to do with it.

Perceived innate female constitution had everything to do with this unwritten law of stagecoach travel. Everyone knew that in the event of an accident, a woman would surely panic—screaming, trying to jump from her perch, or clutching at the reins and causing the horses to careen out of control. The rule existed because it was considered safer to have a man as the third person on the front seat so he could hold the hysterical woman while the driver held the horses.

How did those sentiments resonate with women like Hattie Agard, Mary Howell, and Sarah Garriman? At the age of nineteen, Hattie drove a stage thirty-six miles over rough and dangerous roads in all kinds of weather every day to deliver mail between Cooleyville and Orange, Massachusetts, in the early 1900s. Mary Howell, owner and driver of a stage between Warwick, New York, and Belleville, New Jersey, in the 1880s, encountered a large rattlesnake coiled in the middle of the road one day. It badly spooked her horse, but rather than screaming, Mary jumped from her seat and beat the snake to death with her driving whip. Then she tore off the rattles and took them to town as a trophy.

Sarah Garriman had driven a stage for years in Pennsylvania and was known as a "plucky horse-woman." One day in 1895 she and her horses were attacked by a swarm of angry bees. They went after her face and settled on the horses' backs, driving them nearly frantic. With one hand she held the lines and kept the galloping, maddened horses under control while, at the same time, using her other hand to swat the bees buzzing around her face. The wild escapade continued for several miles; by the time she reached her destination, her face was so badly swollen she could barely see. It was reported that the horses were unable to work for several days.

These women were just a sampling of the many female drivers over the decades when stagecoaches—also known as shake-guts—lurched and rattled from coast to coast over the rutted roads of America. Whether on short runs to deliver mail, freight, and passengers or longer relays from station to station, men and women sat atop the coaches, adroitly guiding teams of four or six horses with a snap of a whip.

Their pseudonyms were as varied and romantic as their reputations: brother whip, knight of the whip, knight of the ribbons, and Jehu, for a biblical king of Israel who drove his chariot fast and furiously. They were collectively labeled men "of importance," the "envy of many a small boy," and "a dignified and interesting class of men." But they also were characterized as big drinkers, reckless, and notorious for their profane language—except in the company of female passengers. When referencing stagecoach drivers, in most instances the existence of female drivers was ignored. But more than a few were women.

In reality, stage drivers came from all sorts of backgrounds and represented a mixed bag of favorable and unfavorable personalities. Mirthful, whimsical, legendary, surly, profane, a little rough—firsthand accounts describing stage drivers ran a gamut. What mattered most to stage owners was that the stage arrived on time with passengers, packages, and horses in good condition. And the driver was key to accomplishing this.

Ideally, what attributes were valued in stagecoach drivers? One popular description called for men who "could chew tobacco and tell of his adventures all at the same time." Because stage owners couldn't afford to employ risky drivers who would jeopardize the safety of cargo, most were careful to hire drivers who were "experienced, sober, and careful." One Massachusetts stage owner required his drivers to sign a contract promising to abstain from "the use of Ardent Spirits as a Drink" during the time of their service. No owner wanted to share the unfortunate experiences of a Kentucky stage proprietor who paid damages of nine hundred dollars to a passenger who was injured when his driver carelessly attempted to pass another stage. Human cargo had to be treated carefully not only for the obvious reasons but also because humans talked, and a stage line's reputation depended on word of mouth. Owners of the Griffin & McAchran stage line in Kentucky issued this rule for its drivers in 1838: "It shall be the duty of the stage driver to pay strict attention to the accommodation of passengers, and treat them with the utmost politeness."

A prized stage driver exercised physical prowess, mental acumen, and impeccable social skills. The job required lifting heavy passenger satchels, mail pouches, and trunks of gold bullion. Drivers were responsible for keeping the coach in good condition, as clean as possible, and in good working order. When breakdowns occurred, the driver better possess some mechanical and construction acumen. In the early days of stage travel, coaches didn't have mechanical brakes. That meant the driver had to scramble down from her or his seat to place a chain or drag under the rear wheels before descending a steep incline.

Quick thinking in dangerous and perilous situations went a long way with stage drivers. Should she take a chance and urge her team over that swollen stream after a thunderstorm or go miles out of the way, ensuring a late arrival at the next stop? Hand over the trunk with the bullion or unload her revolver into the robber who demanded the loot? And a valued driver became a diplomat when it came to dealing with passengers. Cigar smoking men in the confined carriage competed for space with squabbling kids and the smelly, unwashed bodies of fellow passengers who had been on the road for days. On a beautiful day, the outside seat next to the driver was a priceless commodity, and the driver made the decision about who got the coveted spot. A driver who could keep all his passengers happy was a prized employee.

The development of roads in America significantly impacted stagecoach travel. It was a slow process, one that evolved over decades. The poor condition of roads created a challenge for stagecoaches. Mud, tree stumps and roots, ruts, and boulders were all sources of danger. A driver speeding across the countryside had to be vigilant and demonstrate dexterity in steering his racing team around such obstacles. A New York passenger was impressed with his stage driver in 1788, writing glowingly of his "intrepidity" and "dexterity" as he "avoided twenty times dashing the carriage in pieces." Roads weren't considerably better in 1848; a passenger in Ohio complained, "Our course could not be called a road in any sense. . . . We made our way across gullies, rivulets, rising hillocks, and then again sunk up to our axles in bogs." And as travelers made their way beyond the Mississippi River in the mid- and late 1800s, towering mountains and thick prairie grasses offered their own unique barriers.

Stage drivers were admired for their special relationships with their horses. An expert driver directed her teams with a calm, reassuring voice. A subtle *cluck*, *tsk*, or *git up* guided a team in the desired direction or prodded a "snail-galloping" nag into a swinging trot. Always a whip in hand, a truly gifted stage driver never let the rawhide touch an animal. Rather, she sharply flicked the thongs at the end of the lash, setting off a popping sound like firecrackers—enough to urge the team into a spirited run. The ultimate compliment for a driver was to describe her as one who could "snap a fly off the flank of a lead horse" with a long-lashed whip.

Showoffs and daredevils were attracted to stage driving careers. A favorite ritual gave drivers an opportunity to demonstrate their driving proficiencies. Upon approaching a hill, the driver kept the team at a slow, steady pace. But as they neared the summit, the driver cut loose, racing the team full-speed down the slope. When the driver spotted a town up ahead, he urged the team into a vigorous gallop, making an entrance that was impossible to ignore. Sometimes he made an impressive turn in the middle of Main Street as he maneuvered the team and stage directly in front of the stage station. For thrill-seeking passengers, it was a great source of entertainment, and the local townspeople cheered as the spectacle played out.

In the early days of stage travel, especially in the East, drivers never left home without their horn. It was as essential to them as their whip. Rounding a curve out on the trail, the driver signaled oncoming traffic with three sharp blasts, meaning "clear the road." An exuberant blast was sounded within half a mile of the approach to a town. As the stage neared the tavern, one long blast put the tavern keeper on notice: "Set the table for guests" and "Stable boys, prepare the fresh team." After lunch, when the stage was about to depart, passengers better get back in their seats when they heard two short toots of the horn. Drivers with advanced musical talent added a little flourish to their calls to action. Rather than two short toots to indicate the stage was about to leave, the flamboyant driver blew a little ditty of eight notes—setting the horses dancing.

A job as a stagecoach driver afforded some definite perks and challenges: steady work, public adulation, a chance to see new places, long hours away from home, dirty and dusty work environment, high risk for accidents and injury, and cranky passengers. But how was the pay?

The US Post Office paid drivers fourteen dollars per month on the Baltimore and Philadelphia stage line in 1799. Drivers over the Allegheny Mountains in Pennsylvania in 1817 earned between sixteen and twenty dollars per month. By 1831, Philadelphia to Pittsburgh stage line drivers made twelve to fourteen dollars per month, and in 1837 the Eastern Stage Company in New England paid twenty-eight dollars per month. Drivers for the bigger companies on the major roads earned more than drivers for small mom-and-pop enterprises. Driver/owners realized much better earning potential.

Early on, stage and carriage drivers in larger cities organized in order to earn better wages and to protect their rights. The Stage Drivers' Association existed in Brooklyn, New York, as early as 1844. Philadelphia drivers had the Drivers' Beneficial Association to look out for their members in 1853. In the fall of 1872, the Coach Drivers' Association in New York held a special meeting to discuss demanding an increase in wages from twelve to fourteen dollars per week. They planned to strike if their demands were not met. The group also protested a proposed new city ordinance that prevented drivers from leaving their rigs temporarily at ferry landings and railroad depots to solicit passengers.

Was stagecoach driver a wise career path for a young person? Would a parent encourage a child to enter the profession? Conventional wisdom implies that the job typically went to males, and headlines called

Woman driving stage in Washington, 1909
ID NUMBER 2018.2.7, WASHINGTON STATE HISTORICAL SOCIETY, TACOMA

attention to the oddity of females who tried to enter the field: "A Real Female Jehu," "She Drives a Mountain Stage," "Pretty Girl Stage Driver."

Scratching below the surface reveals stories of many women who pursued a career as a female Jehu. Although a Minnesota newspaper reported that stage drivers' wages were so low "it hardly pays an able-bodied man to do the driving, so girls" do it, many enterprising and ambitious women saw stage driving as a fulfilling job. And they proved wrong those detractors who subscribed to the idea that women couldn't be trusted to remain calm in the face of adversity on the driver's seat of a stagecoach.

"Pay's small, work heavy, I'm no better off now than when I commenced," Charlie Parkhurst (aka Old Charley, One-eyed Charley, Cock-eyed Charley, and Six-Horse Charley) complained after driving stages for "nigh on to 30 years" in northern California. Charley was a bit of a legend by the time of his death in December 1879.

Although Charley's origins are a bit murky, it is believed he began his stage driving career in the East when he ran away from an orphanage in New Hampshire. He learned the trade from a man named Ebenezer

Balch, working for a time in Rhode Island. By the gold rush era of the 1840s, Charley was eager to venture west, where enterprising stage owners were luring skilled drivers with promises of steady work and highly attractive wages.

Charley made his way to California, where he continued driving stagecoach for several lines. At some point in his career, a horse had kicked Charley in the face, causing him to lose one eye—necessitating a debonair black leather patch over the injured socket and earning him the nickname "One-eyed Charley." Charley's rugged persona was enhanced by his reputation as a fellow who liked a little "chawin'," drank "moderately," and practiced a little "dice throwing for cigars."

In the 1870s a writer named John Ross Browne met up with Charley, sharing the driver's seat on a stage ride between Folsom, California, and Virginia City, Nevada. It was a fearsome 150-mile trail a "foot deep with dust and abounding in holes and pitfalls big enough to swallow a thousand stages and six thousand horses." The writer described the path as a place where the horses seemed to be "eternally plunging over precipices," the stage following with a crashing noise "horribly suggestive of cracked skulls and broken bones."

But Charley's reputation remained untarnished. It was said that no passenger of his had ever been injured. Browne wrote that the fearless driver, a "miracle of stage-driving," seemed to peer "through the clouds of dust and volumes of darkness."

"Do many people get killed on this route?" Browne asked Charley.

"Nary a kill that I know of. Some of the drivers mashes 'em once in a while, but that's whisky or bad drivin'," Charley replied.

"How in the world can you see your way through this dust?" Browne asked.

"Smell it. Fact is, I've traveled over these mountains so often I can tell where the road is by the sound of the wheels," Charley boasted.

Although that particular trip with Browne was relatively uneventful, Charley had encountered more than one stage robber during his driving years. The most famous was a notorious fellow called Sugarfoot (aka the Baling Wire Bandit), who had acquired the name Sugarfoot because he wore sugar sacks on his feet to avoid leaving footprints. This character had a nasty reputation and was renowned for carrying his Winchester slung over his right shoulder with a piece of baling wire attached at one end to the stock and the other end to the barrel. This unique holster of sorts allowed Sugarfoot to deftly swing his rifle around with his right hand while at the same time passing the hat among his "clients."

Sugarfoot made the mistake of robbing Charley's stage one day in 1858, making off with a bank box full of money. This was an occasion when quick thinking and patience probably saved the lives of the passengers as Charley weighed the potential consequences of standing up to Sugarfoot. When the notorious outlaw ordered Charley to "Throw down the box!" he complied, but he warned Sugarfoot and his gang that he would "break even with them" when next they met.

On the return trip from Mariposa to Stockton, California, Sugarfoot again approached Charley's stage. This time Charley "turned his wild mustangs and his wicked revolver loose" on Sugarfoot, who managed to escape to a miner's cabin, revealing on his deathbed that it was Charley Parkhurst who had plugged his stomach with lead.

Sometime in the 1860s Charley retired from stage driving and operated a saloon and stage station. He bought a farm and also brought in a little money lumberjacking. Rheumatism began to take a toll on the body that had bounced and jostled over thousands of miles during thirty years of exposure to all kinds of weather. Mouth cancer brought an end to Charley's life; the tough old Jehu drew his final breath during the last days of 1879. It was as his body was being prepared for burial that Charley's lifelong secret was revealed and announced to the world: Charley Parkhurst was a woman!

Charlotte Parkhurst, daughter of Ebenezer and Mary Morehouse Parkhurst, was born in New Hampshire, but after the death of her mother, she was placed in an orphanage. At a very young age she may have understood the advantages of making her way in the world as a male, donning boy's clothes to slip undetected out of the orphanage. It's possible that Charlotte never revealed her gender to anyone again; however, news reports after her death claim the doctor who pronounced her a woman declared she had given birth. A Yreka, California, newspaper offered this explanation for Charlotte's decision: "She may have been disgusted with the trammels surrounding sex and concluded to work out her fortune in her own way."

About the same time Charlotte Parkhurst was leading her covert life as a male stage driver in the West, another woman on the other side of the continent made no secret about her identity when she desperately appealed to the local stage company in Abingdon, Virginia, for a job as a driver in the mid-1850s. Everybody in the area knew Mary (Molly) Gragg Tate as the financially-strapped, grieving widow of Wilburn Tate. She had married Wilburn, who had already been married and widowed twice, when she was a mere fourteen. The Tates had several children by the time an epidemic of some sort swept through Abingdon, killing Wilburn and all the kids except a son, Talbert.

Looking for a way to support herself and her only surviving child, Molly turned to the Abingdon stagecoach company for work as a driver. Hired on a temporary basis, she soon proved to be skillful and was offered a full-time position as the night driver between Abingdon and Blountville, Tennessee.

A typical schedule for Molly meant leaving home about 1:00 a.m., a stop at Bristol to pick up passengers and cargo, and arrival in Blountville about six hours after leaving Abingdon. If she had time before the return trip, she squeezed in a little snooze on the floor of the repair shop at the stage station. Guiding four spirited horses over winding, rutted roads with little room for error was a demanding chore. Before long, people began to associate Molly with the nightly stage, and at some point she acquired the name "Old Moll," although it's unclear just how old she actually was.

Contemporaries of Old Moll described the legendary figure as "tall, raw boned, lanky and as quick motioned as a cat." They said she wore a long black dress and black stovepipe bonnet with the ubiquitous long leather whip wrapped around her body, the handle tucked into her dress pocket.

People all along the Abingdon to Blountville line were eager to share stories illustrating Old Moll's kindness and magnanimous spirit. There was the young bride who was spending her Christmas away from her mother for the first time. Hearing about the woman's desire to send her family fresh gingerbread for the holidays, Old Moll arranged to stop at the young woman's house at 3:00 a.m. to pick up the treat and deliver it to the delighted mother in Blountville.

And there was the child near Blountville who had lost his appetite after an illness. When Old Moll heard the boy had expressed interest in watermelon, she stopped at a farm along her route, pilfered a ripe melon from the vine, and delivered it to the overjoyed child. As the tale was repeated throughout the community, no one was willing to pass harsh judgment on Moll for her thievery.

Old Moll was a great source of news along her route. Sometimes she delivered messages from families and friends to loved ones. "Your Aunt Nan is improving fast," she might call out as she passed a house, adding, "They gave her solid food last night." If the news was about a death, she stayed for a bit to comfort the grieving recipients of the unwelcome news. People talked about the times she helped deliver babies along her route.

But it would be a mistake for anyone to get the impression that Old Moll was a pushover. "That woman were a hellcat when she got riled," an old-timer in Abingdon said about Moll.

It wasn't unusual for a stage driver to come across a fallen tree limb or even a tree trunk sprawled over the road. That's exactly why they carried tools such as axes and saws. As Old Moll raced her stage over the road one foggy evening, she came upon a large toppled tree blocking her path. It was an area with deep brush and misty forest on each side of the road, but, hoping to avoid a lengthy delay, the passengers were quick to leave the security of the carriage to help clear the obstacle.

Suddenly two bandits sprang from the roadside cover, pistols drawn. They made off with the passengers' money and the government mailbags. Old Moll was more than a little riled. When the news reached Blountville, the sheriff and his deputies set out to bring in the varmints. It wasn't long before the two scoundrels were safely locked in the Blountville jail.

When Old Moll got word that the two robbers had taken up residence in the local jail, she made her way to the jailhouse and informed the sheriff she was about to "whip the breeches off them devils." The locals who retold the story reported that the sheriff stood by with "gun in hand" as Old Moll took her whip to the jailbirds.

"Why, I believe that old woman could take a stage through the middle of hell, a-spittin' in the devil's eyes and come through without a scratch," one of the area's old-timers said about Old Moll.

In the fall of 1856 the railroad had become an integral part of life in the Abingdon and Blountville areas. It was the end of the line for the old stage line and Old Moll's job as a stage driver. For a time Moll took in washing and eked out a living for herself and her son. During the Civil War they moved to Texas, where she worked on a farm. Never one to loaf, locals claimed that Old Moll worked almost till the day she died in 1913.

Old Moll's stagecoach driving career ended with the arrival of the railroad in Abingdon, and, like Moll, many men and women who had made a living in stagecoaching were forced to find alternative work as the rails crept ever westward. Many former stage drivers transferred their skills to jobs with the railroads. Although the Civil War (1861–1865) gave the stage industry a temporary boost and extended its life for a time as all modes of transportation were stretched to transport soldiers and wartime supplies, the decline of staging was inevitable.

Stages were seen less frequently as a principal form of transportation; trains were more comfortable and faster. But stagecoaches continued to supplement the railroads—serving remote areas and small towns, as well as transporting people and products to and from the train stations. Well into the 1870s, 1880s, and 1890s, the stagecoach was a vital part of life in both the East and the West. And although Charlotte Parkhurst kept her stage driving activities as a woman hidden from the public, other Western women welcomed the celebrity associated with their involvement in stagecoach businesses. Adelia Haskett Phillips Rawson was one of those women who invited attention for her stage driving—and for other pursuits.

A gentleman named Henry Harrington had come to Los Angeles from his home in Cheyenne, Wyoming, in January 1893 to take advantage of the favorable climate. He had been ailing back home in wintry Wyoming and was convinced the California sunshine would improve his constitution. However, Henry soon suffered from another health condition, a result of his attempt at being a Good Samaritan.

"I came here last Saturday for my health," Henry said. "My experience so far has been a little unfortunate." He added that although he was mightily impressed with the climate, he was not so enthralled with the style of parasols in vogue in the city.

His remarks, part of his testimony in a standing-room-only court proceeding, stemmed from an incident that occurred in front of the post office, where Henry happened to be walking early one afternoon as two of Los Angeles's society ladies came to blows. When one of the ladies brought charges against the other, the pair and several witnesses ended up in a courtroom. There were at least two different versions of the story, but the judge believed only one.

Lucy Rawson, divorced wife of Abel M. Rawson, a well-known businessman, spotted Mr. Rawson's new wife, Delia Haskett Phillips Rawson, "a very pretty brunette, with flashing black eyes," in front of the post office and the ex-wife asked her carriage driver to stop. What happened next was the subject of the court proceedings the following day.

"I might have broken my parasol. She had me by the hand; I was afraid she would kill me," Lucy Rawson testified. "If any witness were to swear that I struck the first blow, I should think they were mistaken," she added.

But Henry Harrington, who had witnessed the encounter, related his observations, which portrayed Delia in a different light. According to Henry, Lucy had indeed struck the first blow with her parasol. "The defendant (Delia) raised her parasol to ward off the blow, and as her parasol dropped to the ground, she caught the prosecuting witness (Lucy) by the hand."

As Henry stepped in to protect Delia, he was greeted with a "whack to the cranium," according to other witnesses.

"My attention was attracted by the striking of parasols; in my part of the country, it is rather an unusual occurrence," Henry said. He stressed he was from the state of Wyoming, where women voted; yet he had never witnessed two females fighting with their parasols.

In the end, the judge ruled "the testimony is insufficient and the defendant is discharged." Delia was free to go.

Delia's marriage to Abel Rawson had taken place in 1890. She had been married to James G. Phillips in 1880 but later divorced him. After Delia's marriage to Mr. Rawson, he spent time in an "asylum" but was released after a year and deemed a "reformed lunatic." He wrote a book, *The Junior Partners*, published by the Women's Temperance Publishing Association, in which he detailed his battle with alcoholism and the effects of "alcohol upon the brain and nerve centers." He and Delia traveled to promote the book, and she told a newspaper that they had "realized quite handsomely" from sales. But in 1898 Delia and Abel were divorced.

Delia's name showed up in the early 1900s, when she was referred to as "one of the leading business women of Los Angeles" in a newspaper article, but rarely appeared after that until the 1930s and 1940s, when her membership in the California Pioneer Stage Drivers Association was announced and her time as a teenage stagecoach driver was lauded. "Woman Stagecoach Driver Qualifies for Reunion" the headline proclaimed in the June 22, 1934, *Covina (CA) Argus*. By this time Delia was growing oranges and raising thoroughbred police dogs on her ten-acre ranch in San Dimas, California. A daughter, Dale Fuller, a successful film star, lived with her.

When Delia became a member of the stage drivers' association, she shared her story. Her father, Samuel Haskett, owned a stage line for a time and also drove for the W. H. Forse stage company of Ukiah, California. Her mother, Miranda, was a schoolteacher. At a young age, Delia joined her dad on his stage runs. Occasionally she held the ribbons over a four-horse team pulling the stage over the desert and mountain roads between Ukiah and Willits. When a regular driver became ill, she took up the reins as a full-time driver, carrying passengers and the mail.

In her later years she liked to reminisce about her first official trip as a driver. She had stopped to let her horses get a drink on a lonely stretch of road at about 11:00 p.m. when she heard the sounds of approaching horses and men's voices. There were no passengers on her stage, so she knew she would face her fate alone. As the riders appeared and surrounded Delia, she learned that the men were returning from a religious camp meeting and posed no threat to the fourteen-year-old.

Recalling her days in the driver's seat, Delia said her day began at 6:00 a.m., ending at three o'clock the next morning. She said she often sang to her passengers, earning the nickname "Singing Delia." By the time she was eighteen, it was said she was a "crack shot, able to plug a nickel as far as she could see with a long barreled pistol, and able to shoot off the heads of snakes as she drove along the dusty highway."

Delia said although her stage-driving father had been held up many times by the infamous Black Bart, she had avoided his criminal pursuits. She claimed he had been a passenger on her stage, however. Surprisingly, she said, "Bart was quiet and business like."

"My father had told me, in case of a holdup, never to question but to tell them where the express box of money was and they would never harm us. The outlaws would say, 'Don't make any noise and this gun won't make any noise,'" she added.

Delia drove for about six years. "My last trip was made in 1887," she said in a 1946 interview. "I took the stage from Walker Valley and drove until three in the morning, with my baby strapped on the seat beside me."

Delia's notoriety as a result of the unfortunate parasol episode in 1893 was short-lived. But her days as a young stagecoach driver prevailed over time. Her name consistently appears when the topic of female stage drivers comes up. Recent newspaper articles feature Delia as one of the first female drivers, and a children's book was published based on her experiences. Delia died in 1949 at the age of eighty-seven. She is buried in Forest Lawn Memorial Park in Glendale, California.

If Charlotte Parkhurst, Moll Tate, and Delia Rawson were asked by an aspiring stagecoach driver what to expect in terms of challenges associated with the job, all three would have replied, "weather" and "robbers." Those two elements posed problems for stage drivers over the decades and across the continent, and the gender of the driver defying those adversities mattered little.

Stagecoaches were easy targets for robbers, and firsthand accounts of stage robberies abound. In 1818 three highwaymen armed with double-barreled pistols surprised the driver of the mail and passenger coach between Baltimore and Philadelphia. They barricaded the road with a hastily constructed rail fence, forcing the driver to halt. A passenger later recounted that the robbers threatened to "blow our brains out" at any sign of resistance. The armed bandits carried the driver and the passenger into the woods, tying them to trees while they proceeded to open every piece of mail in the pouch looking for bank notes—an endeavor that took nearly four hours. It was a lucrative few hours, as they secured "a large bundle of bills," ninety thousand dollars—the biggest stage robbery ever accomplished. But authorities were tipped off when the robbers made the mistake of spending lavish amounts of cash at a Baltimore clothing store a few days later.

It wasn't a good ending for the three stage robbers. One was sentenced to ten years' imprisonment; the other two were sentenced to death. One attempted escape as he and the constable walked from the courthouse to the prison—a jaunt that involved fording a stream by way of an improvised bridge in the form of a large tree trunk positioned over the water. The robber tried knocking the constable off-balance into the stream but failed. Again at the prison and facing execution, the convicted criminal attacked a jailer, nearly biting off his finger. In the end, the execution took place, with the gallows elevated above the walls of the prison to "afford a distinct view" for those who had come for miles to witness the spectacle.

In regard to that other troubling aspect of stagecoaching—weather— drivers and travelers would be hard pressed to say which conditions were more unsettling. Leaky stagecoaches offered little protection from the elements. Drenching downpours in summer and blinding blizzards in winter provided passengers an experience few could view as pleasurable. A passenger described his experience during a rainstorm in 1831: "Your feet get wet; your clothes become plastered with mud; the trunks drink in half a gallon of water apiece." And travel in winter was by some accounts "a slow form of lingering death." Firsthand accounts offer vivid descriptions of winter stage travelers who "looked like moving pillars of salt . . . hats and coats covered to the thickness of an eighth of an inch with ice."

Personal diaries and letters that have survived illustrate the "tough fibre" and "vast powers of endurance, both mental and physical" possessed by stage travelers who dared winter travel. Firsthand accounts from disenchanted passengers show they found "scant romance in travel by stagecoach." And if these were true of passengers *inside* the coach, the situation for drivers who sat outside was even more intolerable. A sixteen-year-old stage driver in Connecticut in the late 1800s had tales to tell about surviving both winter storms and threatening highwaymen.

The Yarrow Valley in the eastern part of New London County was a region of prosperous farmers and sheep growers in the 1890s. Bumpy, uneven country roads covered this backwoods region of the state. Farmers paid an annual road tax that ensured delivery of mail and packages as well as transportation to the railroad station by Silas Stewart, a local stagecoach driver. But in the great blizzard of 1888, Silas was exposed to the elements a good many hours, something that permanently affected his health; in 1890 he was forced to abandon his stage driving. Locals were sympathetic but couldn't overlook the tax they were paying for services.

Sixteen-year-old Ellen Stewart announced to her parents that she would take over her dad's route, which she did. Three years later, she was the sole means of support for the family. The business grew under her management. According to a newspaper that ran a feature article on her, Ellen's complexion had taken a beating due to her long exposure to the elements, but that didn't detract from her commitment to her job and her customers. Every day Ellen was up at 4:00 a.m., driving twenty miles over treacherous roads to deliver mail and cargo.

About a year into Ellen's takeover of the stage, she experienced the inevitable on a lonely stretch of road with heavy forests blanketing each side. The woods had served as cover for the lone figure who stepped into the path of Ellen's stage. As he snatched hold of the horses by their bits, he ordered, "Throw out that mailbag!" Ellen responded by slipping her revolver from her pocket and aiming the muzzle "squarely on the robber's head."

"Get up on that rear horse!" she barked. When the bandit ignored her initial request, Ellen reacted with a more forceful invitation, "Get up there or I'll shoot you."

This time the would-be thief obeyed. "Now sit still, sir, till we get to the post office or you'll be sorry," Ellen ordered, keeping her revolver aimed at the fellow. Upon their arrival in town, a group of local farmers secured him "beyond the possibility of escape."

The ill-fated individual was awarded a stay in the penitentiary for his actions, and Ellen received a one-hundred-dollar reward from her customers along the stage route.

In February 1893 Ellen's survival skills were tested again. It had been snowing for several days when Ellen set out for her regular run to meet the train, which had been delayed by the snow. By the time she set out for her return trip, night had fallen. As the roadway became blocked by the swift-falling snow, she decided her best course was to stop at the next house, about two miles ahead. Luckily, she had packed a shovel and began the slow process of digging through the drifts. Her lantern helped light her progress. By midnight Ellen decided the task was fruitless; climbing into the carriage of her stage, she covered herself with several blankets and a buffalo robe. She positioned the lantern to warm her feet, but soon the lantern oil was exhausted and Ellen's feet were numb. She lapsed into unconsciousness and "suffered severely" during the five hours she spent in the stage before daylight. About 9:00 a.m. a party of farmers with several yoke of cattle broke through the drifts and rescued Ellen. For a time her recovery was uncertain, but she did survive and was back at work driving her stage by spring.

Many women who successfully obtained work as stage drivers share a common story. If they weren't willing to live a secret life as a man, as Charlotte Parkhurst had, it helped to have a male family member who was desperate enough to allow a female to take over the reins. As in Ellen Stewart's situation, a father's inability to continue as a driver created the opportunity for a woman to snap up a coveted job. Annie Morrison was another one of those lucky beneficiaries.

Annie was the daughter of Henry "Hen" Morrison, "one of the most famous characters on the coast," a trustworthy old driver who brought miners and their precious cargo down from the mountain recesses to Oroville, California. He was said to be as honest as they came, a characteristic absolutely imperative in a driver who was transporting gold and other riches. He was described as fitting the model for a typical stagecoach driver: "hale, bluff, hearty, and good-natured"—and male.

It's not surprising that Hen's customers were distressed when his stage overturned on a rocky mountain trail one day in 1893 on a return trip from a mine, tossing him from the seat and hopelessly shattering his leg. Surely they were sorry to hear the affable driver was suffering physically from the mishap, but they probably were more concerned about securing a reliable replacement for the guy who held their fortunes in his hands with the "aid of his ready gun."

But the miners need not have fretted. The very day after Hen's accident, the horses were hitched and the stage set out from the Morrison stables at Cherokee Flat as usual. The only difference was the driver. It was Hen's twenty-year-old daughter who jumped up into the driver's box, took up the reins, cracked her whip, and drove up the mountain.

Annie developed a reputation as a "refined, well-educated" girl, who charmed her customers. "I am not surprised to hear that she relieved her father," a local fellow said. "She is a noble and splendid girl."

Not many years after Annie Morrison substituted for her dad on his stage in Oroville, another young woman also convinced her father she could handle the ribbons on a stage. Her trial run turned into a career.

"Give me a chance to try," Alice Westover begged her father.

"Those leaders would whisk you off the box before you could say 'Jack Robinson.' You would never reach Santa Isabel Creek, much less Ramona," W. N. Westover chided Alice.

Mr. Westover had a contract to carry mail between Mesa Grande and Ramona, California, in the late 1890s. A busy rancher, he usually hired drivers for the route, but he had a heck of a time finding reliable men to do the job. Still, when his daughter begged for a chance at the run, he was hesitant.

The route entailed eighteen miles of lonely steep mountain grades littered with sharp turns, boulders, and winding curves. W. N. didn't stop Alice when she hitched up the four horses, grabbed a whip, and set out the following morning over the "roughest road in the West." With her six-shooter securely nestled beside her on the seat, she picked up mail and passengers in Mesa Grande and made her way to Ramona. She deftly maneuvered her team over a particularly frightening stretch near Lace Falls, where the water tumbled "a sheer one hundred feet" down a canyon into a rushing creek. Passengers held their breaths when she urged her team up the dangerous Graves Canyon road.

Along the way, one of the frisky horses kicked a harness strap loose, threatening a runaway. Alice, "instead of being terrorized and calling a male passenger to assist," wrapped the reins around the brake bar, dismounted, and reattached the harness strap. By the time she had started up again, the passengers were hardly aware she had stopped the coach.

When Alice pulled the stage into Ramona, a crowd had gathered as word spread about the girl driver who had brought the stage down from Mesa Grande. The postmaster confirmed what they had heard. "Yes, it's so, and if the stage always got in on as good time as it did to-day, I'd never kick," he said.

One bystander could hardly believe a girl had managed a team and stage on the Graves Canyon grade. "Dunno as I'd care to try it myself, only as you give me time and a good brake," he admitted.

After her initial run, Alice continued to drive for her dad, making trips every day. In addition to driving, she supervised the care of the horses. The local blacksmith in Ramona came to know her well, as she "had her own ideas" about how her team should be shod and believed it required her supervision. She became known as a courageous, plucky driver, and people afforded Alice the ultimate compliment when they claimed she could "fleck a fly from the back of the leader with the skill of an experienced Jehu."

It's possible that Delia Haskett Rawson set the stage for others to follow when she drove stagecoaches in Mendocino County, California, in the 1880s. Maybe fourteen-year-old Alice J. Johnson, growing up there in the early 1900s, had heard stories about that earlier daring girl who had realized her dream of driving a stage. Alice spent as much time as possible riding and grooming her beloved horses. "It's sort of lonesome here—that is, it would be if it wasn't for the horses," Alice said. "They're my best friends."

Alice's dad, Alec, was a veteran stage driver and had a contract to deliver mail between Mendocino City and Ukiah, a fifty-mile drive over precipitous mountain roads where holdups were common. When she was just a young girl, Alice rode with her dad, and before long she was begging to hold the reins—even if just for a bit. Alec gave in one day, and that opened the floodgates. Alice started guiding the team for very

Alice Johnson
SAN FRANCISCO CALL, SEPTEMBER 8, 1901. CALIFORNIA DIGITAL NEWSPAPER COLLECTION,
CENTER FOR BIBLIOGRAPHIC STUDIES AND RESEARCH, UNIVERSITY OF CALIFORNIA, RIVERSIDE,
CDNC.UCR.EDU.

short distances every time she went with her dad. One time the spunky little girl wouldn't let go of the reins as they rounded a sharp curve. Alec couldn't think of anything to say except, "Well!"

Alice replied, "You see!"

By the time she was ten, Alec allowed Alice to drive most of the way—with him sitting next to her. Then one day when Alice was fourteen, Alec was too sick to drive. With his daughter insisting she could handle the job, he gave in—but he, sick as he was, would ride along stretched out on the floor of the carriage. At first he "fussed like a grandmother," but within a few miles he had fallen fast asleep.

The roads angled through mountains and canyons and dizzying precipices. Meeting farm wagons and other stages on the narrow passages called for a driver who could control a nervous team with a reassuring voice and a steady hand. Alice drove throughout the nine-hour trip, making three stops for fresh horses.

It was the first of many trips for Alice as she took over her dad's route. She earned the nickname "Mascot" and became known as one of the "wonders of the whole county," as she was said to complete her routes with "perfect nonchalance and sureness." Passengers said she was the "safest driver we know."

She was said to be a good student at the high school, but she had little time for womanly tasks such as dishes, sewing, cooking, and bed making. In fact, she said she despised those traditional female responsibilities, eschewing them for her love of horses and stagecoaching.

On the opposite side of the country about the same time that Alice J. Johnson adeptly galloped her team across the mountains and canyons of Mendocino County, another intrepid teen—"one of the most remarkable girls New England had ever produced"—also spurned housework for more nontraditional activities.

At seventeen, Maggie Hardy operated a daily stagecoach service delivering mail, passengers, and express packages from West Springfield to West Andover, New Hampshire, a twenty-eight-mile trip over desolate country roads. Her dad, John A. Hardy, had owned the business for as long as anyone could remember. But when John's health took a turn for the worse, no one was surprised to see the "plucky, winsome" Hardy girl step up to the driver's seat. It was nothing new for Maggie; she and John had shared the duties before he became ill.

Summer tourists to the beautiful area had been met at the train station in West Andover for years by the "winsome blonde" girl. They'd watched as she tossed their one-hundred-pound trunks and bags onto her stage before settling in for a rocky ride over the county's old corduroy roads. At stops along the way, she hopped down from her perch on the driver's seat to heave the bulky seventy-five-pound mailbags into the boot. She had become a favorite of the tourist crowd. In 1906 a Boston newspaper reported that Maggie was the "most talked about native of the Granite State."

Local housewives, farmers, and their kids looked forward to the "jovial greeting" they'd come to expect when Maggie arrived bringing mail and express packages. "Brawny woodsmen" at the area lumber camps eagerly awaited the arrival of Maggie as she delivered mail and brought news from town. And all along the train stops, the railroad employees delighted in Maggie's lively conversation. While she waited for the arrival of the train, she took the horses to a nearby barn for food and water and shared a meal with a local family.

During the winter months, passenger travel was lighter; but Maggie never missed a day fulfilling her family's commitment to deliver the mail. She traded her stagecoach for a stage sled and bundled up in a fur greatcoat.

California stage driver Nellie Egan
COURTESY OF THE CALIFORNIA HISTORY ROOM, CALIFORNIA STATE LIBRARY, SACRAMENTO, CALIFORNIA

Back at the family home in West Springfield, Maggie left the house-work to her older sister, Bertha, after their mother died. Every morning Maggie was up at sunrise, cleaning the barn and grooming the horses in preparation for the next stage trip. Any injuries or illnesses suffered by the horses were tended by Maggie herself—no need for a costly veterinarian at the Hardy stables.

Somehow Maggie found time to devote to her education, attending West Springfield High School. The locals said she was a prime example of the "indomitable will of the true Yankee girl."

Charlotte Parkhurst, Molly Tate, Delia Haskett Rawson, Ellen Stewart, Annie Morrison, Alice Westover, Alice J. Johnson, and Maggie Hardy. No panic, hysteria, screaming, feverishly clutching at reins, or jumping from seats in this collection of women. Is it possible the old unwritten law of stagecoach travel that limited the number of women on the driver's seat to one was a good one after all? Maybe that one woman should have been the driver.

CHAPTER 6

Hands Up! Hand Over the Gold!

IT WAS A LATE SUMMER EVENING JUST BEFORE DUSK WHEN A MONIDA-Yellowstone stage rounded a corner at the west edge of the park about three miles from the Grayling Inn and Bill Ripley pulled his tourist-filled stage to an abrupt halt. A horse stood in the middle of the road, blocking passage; atop the horse was a slight fellow wearing leather leggings, boots, and a sombrero and pointing two pistols at Bill. "Halt!" the robber demanded. Bill, a grizzly old frontiersman who was an old hand at driving and had met his share of robbers, ignored the request and pulled out his own revolver, leveling it at the horseman. As he was about to pull the trigger, the bandit shrieked, dropped the guns, and begged for mercy. The tourists burst into laughter as the would-be robber revealed herself—a teenage girl who obviously posed no threat to anyone. Alice Pulsipher, a wealthy New Yorker visiting Yellowstone with her dad, had pulled the prank on a dare by another young friend. Bill Ripley failed to see the humor in the situation and warned Alice that her foolishness was a dangerous undertaking in the West, where stage robbers were dealt with very harshly.

Stagecoaches loaded with cash-carrying travelers and valuable cargo proved to be lucrative sources of revenue for robbers, and unscrupulous men as well as women took advantage of these rich resources. As one historian wrote in 1962, women who pressed for equality "insisted on the privilege of waylaying stages" too, adding "the hand that rocked the cradle also toted the gun that halted fearless" stagecoach drivers. The men and women who stopped the stages and drew their guns to extort loot from travelers and couriers were at the front lines of the trade, but others

A Monida-Yellowstone stage similar to the one Alice Pulsipher tried to rob
YELLOWSTONE HISTORIC CENTER COLLECTIONS

behind the scenes supplied vital information, offered a place for bandits to rest and relax between robberies, and provided a safe location to stash stolen booty. For their efforts, they received a cut of the spoils. Elizabeth Hood was one of those individuals who never robbed a stage herself but made a living, at least for a time, catering to a notorious gang of stage robbers and cattle rustlers in northern California in the 1850s.

"As a mother, I could not pass by in silence a slander so infamous, on an artless child," Elizabeth Hood wrote in a Stockton, California, newspaper in late October 1856. "Statements are made concerning myself and family that are without the slightest foundation in truth."

Elizabeth's motherly concern may have touched the hearts of some readers, but it's likely others felt little sympathy for the woman who was a known accomplice to the gang of bandits who had been terrorizing the area around Sacramento. Her comments were a response to a confession by Bill Gristy (alias Bill White), one of the gang members, when he was arrested a few days before. He was hopeful of a pardon or at least leniency when he spilled his guts about his participation in the criminal activities of a gang headed by Dr. Thomas J. Hodges (alias Tom Bell), a veteran of the Mexican War who had turned to a life of crime after abandoning a medical career for a stint as a gambler and drinker. Everyone knew this ruthless criminal as Tom Bell, who, along with his gang of renegades, had been terrorizing local teamsters, miners, and stagecoach passengers. Elizabeth, a "large fat woman with red hair and a red face," if Bill Gristy is to be believed, lived with her three daughters at her boardinghouse along the Sacramento to Nevada City stage road. Her establishment was called the Western Exchange Hotel by the reputable guests who stayed there, but the less-savory clientele knew Elizabeth's place as the Hog Ranch. As Tom Bell's gangsters roamed the countryside committing their dastardly deeds, they used the Hog Ranch as a safe place to rest between jobs. (The term "hog ranch" was often used to identify a brothel in the West.)

Local sheriffs and detectives kept busy trying to catch the outlaws, and at one point during the crime spree, someone pounced on a pattern that seemed to be emerging. It couldn't be a mere coincidence that stages carrying passengers who had stayed at the Western Exchange Hotel were being targeted by Bell's men.

Elizabeth had indeed been an accomplice of Bell's gang, identifying stage passengers who carried hefty sums of cash. Gang members made themselves known at the Hog Ranch by stating a secret password and flashing a telltale sign—a bullet with a hole bored through it attached to a string. When Elizabeth saw the trinket, she discreetly pointed out passengers who would be profitable targets to the gang members. In return, Tom shared a cut of his profits with her.

After a while, Tom came up with an idea to set up a stock raising business using cattle he had stolen. He needed someone reliable to live at the ranch and decided Elizabeth would be a likely partner for this venture. When Elizabeth's role in the scheme was uncovered, she claimed Tom had used "threats and persuasion" to force her to assist him. She told a local newspaper that the gang consisted of almost fifty men who hid out in secluded caves in the mountains, venturing out in groups of four to five to carry out their robberies. And she said they took oaths to ensure loyalty to one another.

When Tom Bell was finally captured on October 4, 1856, no one mentioned a trial. The posse that caught up with the bandit, believed to have murdered multiple innocent victims, strung him up on a branch of a sycamore tree, but not before granting his final wish to write two letters—one to his mother and the other to Elizabeth Hood, his "dear and only friend." In it Tom lamented that although he had committed only three robberies in his entire life, he was being unjustly accused of every highway robbery that had occurred in the past year. "There is but one thing that grieves me," he wrote, "and that is the condition of you and your family. Probably I have been the instrumentality of your misfortunes." He then directed Elizabeth to send her daughters to San Francisco to be educated by the Sisters of Charity. He asked her to tell the girls to be good and to be "very careful to whom they pledge themselves for life." He left ten dollars to Sarah, one of Elizabeth's daughters.

It's unclear why he favored Sarah, but Bill Gristy had stated in his September confession that Sarah was fourteen years old and the "mistress" of Tom Bell. This was one of the falsehoods Elizabeth accused Gristy of making. She said Sarah, her middle child, was only nine years old. She claimed the statements made by Gristy were "totally untrue" and that his confession had caused her daughters to be dismissed from their school as "unfit associates of children of a like age." Elizabeth was not heard from again, but she and two daughters, including fourteen-year-old Sarah, were living in Douglas City, California, according to the 1860 US Census. A long list of individuals was registered in her household, which indicated she may have continued to run a boardinghouse. Also listed in the household was A. H. Farnsworth, a members of Tom Bell's gang who had been living with her at Hog Ranch during the gang's most productive days.

Back in the early 1850s when Tom Bell was making a living gambling and practicing medicine under the name Dr. Thomas Hodges, a story circulated around the mining camps and communities about an incident involving some diehard gamblers taking bets on the outcome of one of his patients. A fellow named Ezra Williams had been shot in a saloon brawl, and Hodges spent the night tending him as he lay on a barroom table straddling life and death. Never willing to pass up a game of chance,

Hodges and a crowd of gamblers gathered around the patient, drinking and placing bets on his chances of survival. As Hodges tended Ezra, the patient showed signs of recovery, only to drift back into unconsciousness. As he groaned or coughed up blood, the gamblers cheered or moaned, depending on how they had wagered. Ezra almost died a couple of times, only to revive for a time, but in the end Hodges lost his patient—along with the fifty dollars he had bet. Among the crowd was a woman everybody called Dutch Kate, who bet ten thousand dollars—some of which spectators had kicked in because Kate was such a popular gal—that Ezra would be dead by morning.

If the fellows at the saloon knew Dutch Kate's real name, they never used it, nor did the local newspapers when they carried articles about her. And history has not preserved it, so she may forever be known simply as Dutch Kate. To add insult to injury, the one act that she is remembered for was an embarrassing failure.

Kate was a frequent visitor at saloons in the Maryville, California, mining region in the 1850s. Usually wearing men's clothes, she drank whiskey, smoked cigars, played cards, and swore like a pirate, having no trouble holding her own "among the most accomplished ruffians of the mining country." It was her gambling habit that propelled her into more serious troubles.

In July 1858 a Sacramento newspaper carried a short blurb reporting that Dutch Kate had survived ingesting poison in a suicide attempt. "Gambling was the cause of the affair" was how the newspaper explained it.

By September, Dutch Kate was once again in the news—this time for robbing a stage. She'd lost more than two thousand dollars at a game of monte in Marysville, and her creditors were pressuring her to pay up. In desperation, she convinced some of her old friends to help rob the Forest City Stage, known to regularly carry a hefty express box loaded with riches from the mines. As the stage, packed with ten passengers, crested the top of a hill on a Monday morning in mid-September, the robbers, including Dutch Kate dressed in her usual men's clothing and toting a rifle in one hand and a pistol in the other, stopped the stage and demanded that driver William Wilson pass down the express box, which he immediately did. One of the robbers questioned Wilson about a sack under the backseat, but in the confusion it was left in the coach. At the direction of Kate, the robbers brushed off the idea of appropriating any valuables from the passengers, choosing to stick with the contents of the express package, from which they expected a high return. After directing the driver to get on his way and not look back, the robbers eagerly broke open the express box—and found it empty. The express company had gotten wind of a possible robbery (thanks to Kate, whose loose talk had been overheard by someone) and decided to send the valuable cargo on another stage. And when the robbers looked to open the sack they had spotted under the seat in the coach, they realized no one had snatched it. But that wasn't the worst of it for Dutch Kate. The next day she learned that the sack, which belonged to one of the passengers, had held fifteen thousand dollars in gold dust! Dutch Kate not only failed to gain the money to pay her gambling debts, but she was portrayed in news reports as an inept stage robber! A humiliating experience for a brash female bandit.

People in San Benito County, California, especially those living around the town of Hollister, had plenty to gossip about in the summer and fall of 1874. Teams pulling wagons overflowing with grain blocked the town's thoroughfares as ranchers brought their crops to the storage warehouses, most already running out of space. Thomas Butterfield & Sons advertised high-quality rams—clear of scabs—for sale at nearby Tres Pinos. Bred with merinos, these rams promised to produce offspring larger in size than most sheep and with longer wool. People were talking about the mountain lion Samuel Mattison claimed to have encountered when he was horseback riding in the hills. He said he'd used his trusty lariat to lasso the critter, buckled a strap around its jaws, and dragged it to his home. Skeptics were mollified by people who swore to have seen the skin, which Samuel displayed as a trophy. The county was still reeling from visits by a notorious desperado named Tiburcio Vásquez, who had been stealing horses, robbing stages, and killing innocent people along the way. When news reached the area in May 1874 that he had been captured and hanged, there was a collective sigh of relief. And everyone was still talking about Cy Wilcox's brazen confrontation with a stage robber on the road between Tres Pinos and Hollister in February. He had been riding along minding his own business when a man on horseback stopped him in his tracks and demanded, "Halt, and throw up your hands."

"Halt yourself, damn you," Cy responded as he went for his "messenger of death." The robber managed to fire one shot before fleeing, but not before Cy unloaded six bullets in his direction. As Cy told it, no one was hurt except his horse.

Just about the time people were getting tired of talking about Cy's heroic adventures, their attention turned to the exploits of a teenage petticoat bandit who was being held under tight security at a Hollister hotel, one of her lovers behind bars at the city jail. On a Saturday morning in mid-July sixteen-year-old Elizabeth (better known as Lizzie) Keith Fowler, dressed as a male, and an accomplice, nineteen-year-old Frederick J. Wilson, stopped the New Idria stage on its way from Hollister to the nearby mines. Their faces covered by hoods with slits for their eyes, the two brandished firearms and shouted for the driver to throw down the express bag. The driver, identified simply as Burnett, said there was no money on the stage other than the change in his pocket. As he climbed down from his seat, the pair aimed their weapons, but he proceeded to open the empty bag, showing the bandits that there was no money. One of the robbers climbed onto Burnett's seat, searching for any hidden bags; surprisingly, when the unarmed driver ordered the fellow down, he obeyed. Fortunately, none of the passengers were harmed, and the pair of robbers mounted their horses and left with nothing to show for their work.

The next day on his return trip, Burnett met a young couple on horseback in the vicinity of the incident. He immediately recognized the pair—despite their disguises during the holdup—as the bandits who had stopped the stage the previous day. This time, Burnett carried a six-shooter and ordered the two to raise their hands. He asked one of his passengers to search the man's pockets, from which he pulled a derringer—exactly like the one the robbers had aimed at him the day before. As Burnett directed the two to get into the stage, Lizzie innocently asked what he wanted with her. Probably tinged with a bit of sarcasm, Burnett replied that he simply wanted their company on the trip into Hollister, although he asked one of the passengers to keep his gun on them.

When the stage arrived in Hollister, Fred was taken to the city jail and Lizzie to a hotel, where she remained under guard. She explained to the sheriff that her parents had died years before. At the age of fourteen she had married a man named Samuel Fowler, a miner who was extremely jealous and demonstrated his fury by whipping her. When he took off to the mines, she teamed up with Fred.

Fred and Lizzie appeared in court and were each held on bonds of two thousand dollars while awaiting trial. Sometime before going to trial, Lizzie turned state's evidence against Fred and the charges against her were dismissed. Fred ended up in San Quentin State Prison, but not before a couple buddies tried unsuccessfully to break him out of the Hollister jail.

The citizens of San Benito County weren't the only people talking about Lizzie and Fred. Even the *New York Times* covered the story of the California kids who tried to rob a stage. The article was largely sympathetic to Lizzie, describing her as a "pretty, good-looking" girl, while calling Fred a "lunatic" and "undoubtedly crazy."

A Sacramento newspaper carried a follow-up story about Lizzie in September. Under the headline "Eliza the Brave," the paper claimed that two other men had fought for Lizzie upon her release from custody. According to the story, one "beau" trounced a "rival knight" in the competition for Lizzie's affections. "Our sympathies are with the winner," the article concluded.

———

"A Beautiful But Bad, Bad Black Hills Woman"—the headline in the October 22, 1881, *Black Hills Daily Times* couldn't be more clear about Belle Siddons, alias Madam Vestal, alias Lurline Monte Verdi. Her story began with her days as a Confederate spy in St. Louis, Missouri, where she was arrested by Union officers and served a short jail sentence during the Civil War. After the war she married Dr. Newt Hallett and moved to Texas, where her husband died in 1869, but not before sharing some nuggets of his medical training with his wife, something that would serve her well later in life. It was after Dr. Hallett's death that Belle became Madam Vestal and could be found in Denver running her gambling establishment. It was a profitable endeavor for Belle, and newspaper accounts described her dealing cards and spinning the roulette wheel dressed in velvets and laces adorned with diamonds, her dark hair held in place with gold clips, and a pistol in plain sight next to her stack of cards. "It excites curiosity and draws in the suckers," she is reported to have said about her flashy attire.

When miners started to leave Denver for the possibility of more riches in the Black Hills, Belle had the foresight to follow. It was said she secured a second-hand yellow omnibus to lead a caravan of wagons carrying her dealers, bartenders, bouncers, maids, baggage, and gambling paraphernalia to her new home in Deadwood. According to reports, her vehicle was decked out with curtains, a bed, a cookstove, and shelves for her books. The party was detained in Cheyenne for a few months in early 1876, but when they reached Deadwood, Belle—now known as Lurline Monte Verdi (sometimes spelled Verde)—made a flamboyant entrance if the legends can be believed. Perched atop a sturdy platform carried by four hefty men, she introduced herself to residents of the rough-and-tumble town that would be her home for the next few years.

Belle was a versatile businesswoman—again dealing cards, singing, dancing, and performing her original play titled *Outcast*, based on her own life and so moving it was said to draw tears from her admirers. When Belle made the acquaintance of Archie Cummings (alias McLaughlin), a known road agent who had terrorized travelers throughout the Black Hills, she fell in love and soon joined his enterprise by supplying him with valuable information she gleaned from travelers at her restaurant. She was discreet, and for a time no one caught on that she was a spy for Archie and his cohorts. By some accounts, she even began to direct the activities of the bandits and used the medical techniques she had learned from her late husband when the road agents met up with bullets. Of course Belle also shared in the profits.

By the time the stage lines hired detective Boone May to rein in the outlaws of the Black Hills, he was well aware of Belle's connection with the desperadoes around Deadwood and used it to his advantage.

Boone smoothly extracted information from Belle without her realizing her mistake. But when he arranged to have Archie and some of his gang detained by authorities as they boarded a westbound train for Laramie City on their way to San Francisco, where Belle planned to join Archie, it became obvious that Boone had played Belle for a fool. When word reached Deadwood that Archie and his cohorts had been lynched by a gang of vigilantes who intercepted the coach bringing them back to Deadwood to stand trial, Belle was devastated. She probably felt worse when she learned the details—that Archie had been promised a reprieve if he revealed where his stash was hidden and had been hanged despite complying. The scene couldn't have been pleasant, as the lynchers used the same rope for each outlaw, forcing those waiting for execution to watch their comrades swing one by one.

Belle's life went downhill after this; she moved from Deadwood, showing up in New Mexico, Arizona, and again in Colorado over the next few years. She may have married a fellow named Eugene Holman along the way and possibly had a child. There were rumors that she was performing at James McDaniel's theater in Leadville in November 1880—standing on her head while playing "Home Sweet Home" on a banjo with her toenails. But someone quashed that story, stating, "In the first place, her toenails ain't long enough, and she can't stand on her head anyhow."

There were reports that her beauty was fading as she turned to alcohol and opium to salve her emotional wounds. In October 1881, when a night beat reporter for the *San Francisco Examiner* dropped in at the city jail to visit with the guard, he was directed to one of the cells. "There is a woman sitting there in that cell whose history is a very remarkable one," the guard said. The woman once known as Madam Vestal and Lurline Monte Verdi sat hunched on a wooden bench with her head hanging; she had been arrested for intoxication on a city street. It's unclear when and where Belle died, but some sources indicate she met her end in an opium den.

"Notorious," "remarkable," and "frightful" were the tamest words used to describe Mother Osborne. "Hideous old creature," "old virago," "wicked, shrewd, and ugly old harridan," and "as gross in person as in passions" were more provocative descriptors and ignited more attention. This intriguing woman, who reportedly maintained a roadhouse on a Black Hills stage road, may have been a figment of a lonely cowboy's vivid imagination or a character in a popular crime magazine. Or maybe she did actually run a stage stop where an army of thieves and cutthroats preyed on unsuspecting miners and stage travelers between 1873 and 1879.

A bunch of cowhands driving a herd to fresh grazing grounds in northern Wyoming in August 1878 claimed to have spent an unforgettable night with Mother Osborne, her gang of desperadoes, and a bevy of "brazen, shameless women."

The cowboys had just settled in for the night after consuming a supper of antelope ribs around a campfire when they heard the pounding throb of horses approaching their site. Suddenly they were surrounded by a score of rough-looking individuals who said Mother Osborne was a bit lonely and wished for them to join her for a late tea and dancing. As the ruffians were well armed, the cowboys didn't feel they could politely refuse the invitation. After a thirty-minute horseback ride under guard of the armed posse, the men reached a cabin from which the haunting sound of a violin beckoned and where upon entering they were met by a "wonder of obesity" comfortably entrenched in the cushions of an immense armchair. They couldn't ignore the belt fastened around their hostess's girth, from which dangled a couple of pistols, nor could they avoid looking down the barrel of the Winchester rifle she aimed their way. Despite the arsenal, the cowboys swore they were greeted warmly and offered a generous supper topped off with whiskey and cigars, followed by a riotous night of dancing with the cheeky hussies. As the night wore on, pandemonium broke out as "vile language and dire threats" spewed through the dense haze of tobacco smoke and pistols and knives threatened to find a home in someone's belly. Only through the efforts of the officious Mother Osborne using the muzzle of her Winchester to drive some of the most boisterous of her boys from the cabin were fatalities avoided. As daylight began to seep across the horizon, Mother Osborne ushered all her guests from her home, sending them on their way replete with fantastic tales to fill a lifetime of lonesome nights around cowpoke campfires.

The cowboys' memorable tryst with Mother Osborne occurred toward the end of her reign as a road agent. Her colorful escapades began around 1873 when, by one account, she arrived in the Black Hills from the western mining towns, where her husband and kids had been killed—her husband shot before her eyes. She quickly established her roadhouse near the Cheyenne River, becoming the principal dealer in whiskey and tobacco and eventually a beneficiary of at least a percentage of the proceeds from most of the robberies that occurred in the area.

Her transition to the wrong side of the law was said to have taken place when a band of thieves fell behind on room and board payments at her roadhouse—partaking freely of her "expensive provender" and "mule-toted whiskey." When she told them to pay up or get out, they approached her with a plan that involved holdups and profit sharing. "Red-faced and hard-fisted," Mother Osborne went along with the suggestion, and her cabin ultimately became the base of operations for several gangs.

The first shared endeavor proved so successful for the bandits and Mother Osborne that the arrangement became permanent. However, that first ordeal was deadly for at least one participant. As a stage filled with passengers pulled up to Mother Osborne's establishment, she welcomed them with her customary graciousness and offered food and refreshments. A casual observer might not have noticed the absence of the seedy-looking band of ruffians who recently had been hanging about the place. But less than an hour after stopping at Mother Osborne's, the stage was robbed; and when it arrived at Deadwood, it carried several wounded passengers and one corpse. Back at Mother Osborne's, the gang and their new accomplice divided up the spoils: a wad of cash and several nice watches.

It was the first of many robberies committed on the stretch of road within a few miles of Mother Osborne's stage stop, an area that became known as "Mother Osborne's Trail," where the roads were alive with miners, investors, and freighters carrying goodly amounts of cash. The desperadoes who reaped rich harvests there became the terror of the road; they looked to Mother Osborne for motherly advice, earning her the name that stuck. They secretly hung out in her attic, lying low until it was safe to venture out to Deadwood for a night of drink and revelry. After a while, the connections were too obvious for anyone to ignore, and stages found a way to bypass Mother Osborne's. Vigilantes and the law made surprise visits to the cabin, but the bandits were never found at the old woman's abode. In time, however, the gangs took to operating farther out, and visits from her boys happened less and less frequently. There was the occasional late-night call, resulting in a flurry of wild carousing with the woman who by this time had a face that had "lost almost the last trace of womanhood" and "sported quite a beard."

By the time a Cheyenne and Black Hills Stage carrying a safe holding thousands of dollars of gold bullion was robbed at Canyon Springs in October 1878 and the gang of vigilantes who managed to capture one of the varmints sent word that "He's swinging," Mother Osborne decided it was time to pull up stakes and head north to Montana. There were rumors she had found work as a cook at some cattle camps and had once again entered the whiskey selling business.

It wasn't until her purported death in the fall of 1885 that evidence of the existence of a woman called Mother Osborne appeared in newspapers in New York, Texas, Montana Territory, Wyoming Territory, and San Francisco. With the announcement of her death in an old derelict cabin near Landers, Wyoming, came tales of the adventurous life she had lived. The *Police Gazette*, a tabloid-like men's magazine censored by the likes of the Woman's Christian Temperance Union, featured her in an early-1800s issue: "Old Mother Osborne, the Female Road Agent, dies destitute in a lonely cabin in the Yellowstone country, after a stirring life of outlawry in the Black Hills." Fact or fiction? Mother Osborne's story could be one of the mysteries of history where the lines between reality and legend have been irrevocably blurred.

⁓

While the true identity, even existence, of Mother Osborne remains uncertain, federal criminal case records preserved for more than a century through the National Archives authenticate the exploits of a young Arkansas woman, wed just over a year and barely out of her teens, who was charged with helping orchestrate a stage robbery in 1890. Tattered and yellowed for sure, but legible court papers undeniably document the misdeeds of twenty-year-old Louisa Belle Rose, who might have eluded the law had it not been for some determined law enforcement officials.

It was around midnight on September 29, 1890, when the Harrison and Eureka Springs, Arkansas, stage loaded with a couple of passengers and US mail was halted about a mile and a half west of Batavia by a couple of masked bandits on horseback. While one of the robbers leveled his pistol at driver Ed Linzy and demanded the mailbags, the other interviewed the passengers to see what they had to offer. Gathering up the mail pouches and any valuables harvested from the passengers, the bandits mounted their horses and rode off into the shadows of the surrounding forest. The stage resumed its journey a few pounds lighter—the passengers a bit frazzled but unscathed.

Although several law enforcement officials, including officers from the US Postal Inspection Service (the security arm of the US Postal Service), worked on the case for months, no arrests were made until May 1891, when Inspector Frank A. Beebe took two individuals into custody at Batavia. After traveling with the two to Fort Smith, Arkansas, Frank turned them over to US Marshal Jacob Yoes on May 17. Walter Markley and his sister Louisa Belle Rose confessed to the crime. The actual robbery was committed by Walter and his brother-in-law Edgar Rose, Louisa's husband, who had committed suicide near Kingston, Arkansas, a couple weeks before the arrest. Louisa confessed to making the disguises, including masks for the two men. Although the *Daily Arkansas Gazette* described Louisa as "young, dashing, pretty" and an individual who didn't "look like a criminal," she was charged with obstructing the US mail. On May 20 Louisa, with her dad by her side, appeared before a judge of the Western District of Arkansas and posted one thousand dollars bail. She was ordered to appear at the courtroom at Fort Smith at 10:00 a.m., October 5, 1891. On October 6, a grand jury dismissed the charges against Louisa, and she was free to leave. Walter wasn't as fortunate; he was sentenced to eighteen months in prison at Detroit, Michigan, having pleaded guilty to a charge of cutting open mailbags.

Inspector Beebe provided a detailed account of his investigation in a letter to his division chief, in which he recognized other law enforcement officials and detective agencies that had tried unsuccessfully to solve the baffling case. The local terrain, consisting of dense forests, caves, deep ravines, and mountain ranges, coupled with sparse human habitation gave the robbers secure cover so that, according to Beebe, the search was like looking for a needle in a haystack. It wasn't until he took charge of the case, pursuing numerous clues over eight months, that the crime was solved. It turned out that Edgar and Walter had earned $89.15 from the stolen mail, and Edgar hadn't shared any of it with Walter.

While the official court documents offer some facts about Louisa's role in the robbery, they don't provide anything about the personal side of her situation. Frank Beebe indicated that Edgar Rose had deceived the Markley family from the start and had been relentless in his pursuit of the very young Walter for his part in the scheme. And, said Beebe, the Markley family intended to pay back the stolen money when they were in a position to do so. Louisa apparently considered the adventure a silly

Warrant for the arrest of Louisa Rose and Walter Markley
NATIONAL ARCHIVES AT FORT WORTH, ANCESTRY, "FORT SMITH, ARKANSAS, CRIMINAL CASE FILES, 1866–1900"

Case files of the Louisa Rose stage robbery

prank, which she put behind her as a youthful misstep. She later completed a shorthand course and remarried, her name never again associated with any crimes.

━ ◆ ━

"I got a letter saying my mother was dying and asking me to come home if I wanted to see her alive again. I had no money." Pearl Hart offered that explanation for robbing a stagecoach near Globe, Arizona, in May 1899.

Her interview with *The Cosmopolitan* magazine in the fall of that year presented Pearl's version of how the robbery unfolded. Newspapers at the time sensationally reported details of the event—usually somewhat different than Pearl's.

When Pearl was sixteen and attending boarding school in her native Canada, she eloped with a man from the local community. Within a very short time he started abusing her, and over the next few years Pearl was in and out of the relationship. Together the couple drifted from location to location, eventually moving to the United States. They spent time at the World's Columbian Exposition in Chicago in 1893. That fall, Pearl boarded a train by herself for Trinidad, Colorado. "I was good-looking, desperate, discouraged, and ready for anything that might come," Pearl told *The Cosmopolitan*. She was only twenty-two years old when she made her way to Phoenix, where she ran into her husband, who convinced her to rejoin him.

"I was not then the innocent school-girl he had enticed from home, father, mother, family and friends—far from it. I had been inured to the hardships of the world and knew much of its wickedness," Pearl said.

Pearl had a son and a daughter with her husband, but he continued to be abusive throughout their tumultuous marriage. When he joined the military during the Spanish-American War in 1898, she sent the kids off to live with her mother and went to work as a cook at a mining camp in Mammoth, Arizona. Here she met Joe Boot; the two moved to Globe, where she worked in a miners' boardinghouse for a time. Joe had a claim, which the two worked day and night with pick and shovel. "I have never worked so hard in my life, and I have had some pretty hard experiences too," Pearl told *The Cosmopolitan*.

When the letter about her dying mother reached Pearl, she was desperate. "That letter drove me crazy," she said. "I longed to see her again before she died." But Pearl had no money, partly because she had recently sent her savings to a brother, who had asked Pearl to "help him out of a scrape."

According to Pearl, it was Joe who came up with the intriguing idea of robbing the Globe stage on May 30, 1899. "A bold front is all that is necessary to rob any stage," he assured Pearl. But, Pearl said, "It seemed a desperate undertaking for a woman my size." (She was reportedly around five feet tall and weighed about a hundred pounds.) In the end, desperate to see her dying mother, Pearl donned men's clothes topped off by a broad sombrero, grabbed her .38, and saddled up for the trek over mountains and through canyons to meet the stage as it rounded a bend on the Globe road.

"Throw up your hands," Joe shouted to the driver. He ordered the passengers out of the coach as Pearl searched them for concealed weapons. Some people were surprised that the stagecoach driver didn't resist when the female robber ordered him about, but he later explained that Pearl's gun was a notable deterrent—"the most eloquent thing he ever looked into in his life."

The theft turned out to be a lucrative job for only a few minutes' work, yielding Joe and Pearl about four hundred dollars. Before leaving the scene, they handed a dollar to each of the passengers—a "charitable contribution," according to Pearl.

The pair spent the next few days on the run, riding over the rough Arizona terrain chasing a mountain lion for food and encountering their share of assorted desert wildlife, including rattlesnakes and wild hogs. One day they crawled about twenty feet into a dark cave hoping for a few hours of rest; they were greeted by a pair of shining eyes belonging to what turned out to be a wild hog, whose home they had invaded. "I confess I felt very creepy, but we were between the devil and the deep sea," Pearl told *The Cosmopolitan*. Joe pulled out his pistol and ended the creature's life. The air became so foul from the smoke of the gun that Pearl and Joe were forced to move back toward the cave entrance, where they spent the day free of the suffocating smoke and the distasteful hog carcass, although Pearl could not rid herself of Joe's thunderous snoring during an afternoon nap.

By that time, their days of freedom were drawing to a close. Their horses were suffering from lack of food and water, and so were they. Joe chanced a trip into Mammoth one day to get food and tobacco, but both horses and humans were exhausted. On June 3 they were within twenty miles of their destination—the train station in Benson—when they both lay down for a few hours of sleep after riding through the night. Awakened by the sound of yelling and shooting, the two desperadoes found themselves "looking straight into the mouths of two gapping Winchesters" wielded by a couple of fellows in the sheriff's posse. (No evidence exists that Joe's snoring called attention to their location.) "Resistance was worse than useless," Pearl recalled.

The prisoners were taken to Benson and ultimately to the prison at Florence. Pearl said they were treated well, with the exception of the curiosity seekers who came to witness the now-famous outlaws and to "make fun" of them. She was saddened to learn she was being transferred to jail in Tucson, with Joe remaining behind in Florence. Pearl claimed the two had pledged to commit suicide rather than endure incarceration. She told *The Cosmopolitan* that she had unsuccessfully attempted to end her life at that time and regretted her failure.

There's where Pearl's firsthand account ends. In October newspapers carried widely varying reports that Pearl had escaped her Tucson jail cell as she awaited trial, possibly aided by a love interest, who had helped her jump from a hole chiseled through the walls of her cell. Some claimed she made a statement about women's rights before making her escape, boasting she would never submit to laws "neither she nor her sex had a voice in making." In late October, Pearl was recaptured in Deming, New Mexico. Early in November she stood trial for robbery, and, to the disbelief of many, she was acquitted by a jury that deliberated only thirty minutes. The judge who presided was so outraged he quickly brought new charges against Pearl—either for US mail interference or for stealing the stage driver's six-shooter (reports vary). This time she was found guilty and sentenced to five years at the penitentiary in Yuma. Joe Boot was sentenced for his part in the stage robbery; his sentence was either ten years or thirty, depending on which account people wanted to believe. He also went to Yuma.

People had been enthralled with the saga of Pearl Hart as it unfolded in the newspapers, magazines, and gossip mills. Opinions were split between outrage at her audacity and disgraceful lifestyle and empathy for a woman who merely wanted to visit her dying mother. When the *Arizona Republic* published a letter in late November written by Pearl's brother in Ohio, some readers may have softened their stance about the female bandit. In the letter, James T. Taylor explained that the family had lost contact with Pearl, and all the news reports of her exploits had finally solved the mystery of her whereabouts. He added that their mother had been heartbroken at Pearl's disappearance. But because she suffered from heart disease, the family had not revealed Pearl's actual situation to their mother.

A fellow named Joe Mulhatton submitted to the *Florence Tribune* a poem he had written comparing Pearl to Mary Magdalene (misspelled "Magdelene"), the repentant fallen woman of Bible fame, and chastising Christians for scorning Pearl. In part, it read:

> *Poor Pearl Hart, a Magdelene,*
> *In prison sick, by no one seen,*
> *Spurned by her sex, no helping hand,*
> *And yet this is a Christian land,*
> *Should Christ come down to Florence to-day*
> *Would he admire such Christian way . . .*

As for Joe Boot, he had no intention of remaining a guest of the territory of Arizona for his full term of incarceration. He had been such an exemplary prisoner that he landed a plumb job as a cook at the superintendent's residence. One night in January 1901, after cleaning up the kitchen, Joe left the place, never to be heard from again. According to news reports, authorities believed he was headed to Los Angeles, and there was talk of the Yuma sheriffs using bloodhounds to track him down. Once again, the details varied; the truth may never be known. Some interested observers liked to believe that Pearl had arranged his escape,

Pearl Hart

as she felt responsible for his participation in the robbery. Pearl writing poetry about Joe while she pined away in jail was another popular tale. By most accounts, Joe Boot (whose name may have been an alias) was never recaptured.

In December 1902 news reports revealed Pearl had been pardoned by Arizona territorial governor Alexander O. Brodie on the condition that she leave the territory until the end of her sentence. (Some accounts claim she was pregnant.) Word was that she was headed to California to live with her son. Rumors also suggested she had become an expert lace maker while incarcerated and had earned quite a substantial sum selling her products to visitors at the penitentiary. There was talk that while in prison she had written a play about her life and planned to star in an upcoming theater production. Supposedly she had already lined up an agent to manage her new career. After her release there were reports she became an actress in Buffalo Bill's Wild West Show, or operated a cigar store in Kansas, or settled down with a rancher in Arizona.

One of the first rules of successful stagecoach robbing was "Wear a mask to conceal your identity." The second rule should have been "Don't call the driver by name when demanding the loot." More specifically, "Don't use a nickname preferred by a limited number of people." The masked bandits who robbed the Rainbow-Durkee Stage in Oregon on April 5, 1915, made the unfortunate mistake of addressing the driver, Ralph Moorehouse, by his nickname "Slim." That was a tipoff to Ralph, and he let Baker County sheriff Price Anderson know about it when he reported the crime shortly after it occurred.

The exceptionally observant Slim, who found himself "looking into the muzzle of a revolver" at the scene of the robbery, also noted the small stature of the robber who had stopped his stage carrying seven thousand dollars in gold from the Rainbow Mine. And he was sure he recognized the voice behind the mask as that of Joe Carlson, a fellow who lived nearby with Molly Burget, who operated an establishment that some called a resort and others a dance hall, while most called it what it was—a notorious, raucous dive of a saloon. Slim and his only passenger couldn't ignore a second masked bandit directing a gun their way as they sped away after tossing the gold brick down to the outlaw. They saw the two robbers make their way toward the San Pedro Mountains, another piece of information Slim shared with the sheriff. Entrusting his stage to another driver, Slim joined one of the posses that had been formed to comb the countryside in search of the desperadoes. Sheriff Anderson had borrowed an automobile to pursue the men, who were believed to be on horseback.

Twenty-four hours after the robbery, the *La Grande (OR) Observer* reported that despite all the posses scouring the hills, the searchers were "still baffled," and the sheriff had "nothing to report except failure." However, William "Sour Dough Bill" Halter, a well-known acquaintance of Joe, had been arrested by Huntington's city marshal, Ed Hannon, at the request of Sheriff Anderson, who possessed some information that made him suspicious of Sour Dough. For one thing, Sour Dough had been a suspect in a murder case a few years before, naturally causing the sheriff to distrust him; secondly, people around town had noticed Sour Dough and Joe Carlson engaged in what appeared to be furtive conversations the day of the robbery. Before long Sour Dough confessed to being one of the two stage robbers; at the same time, he implicated Joe as the mastermind behind the robbery and identified him as the other man at the scene. It was no secret that a stage carried the precious cargo from the mine to Durkee about the same time each week, so it was an easy target. The three bandits hatched their scheme to relieve the stage of its gold, with the men doing the actual deed. Molly acted as a scout, standing at a high spot of land near the Rainbow Mine waiting for the gold to be loaded on the stage and then signaling Joe and Sour Dough.

Meantime, a posse, unaware of Sour Dough's confession, had discovered some of the robbers' disguises, a gun, and, most importantly, the gold brick buried in a badger hole not far from the scene of the crime. On April 8 the Associated Press reported that Joe Carlson and Mollie Burget had been arrested the day before and charged with "being implicated in a plot to hold up a stage." According to the report, Sheriff Anderson had "conclusive evidence," including one of the robber's coats found in Molly's house and Sour Dough's gun found at the robbery site.

Joe went to trial first. The state introduced Joe's old leather boot as evidence against him. A print found near the robbery site matched the size seven boot with four rows of hobnails running down the sole. A newspaper reported that Joe was so nervous the judge allowed him to smoke throughout the trial. Joe's worries were justified—the jury convicted him for his role in the crime, and he was sentenced to three to fifteen years in prison.

Sour Dough and Molly were tried together. According to a news account, Molly, dressed in an old gray sweater buttoned up to her throat on a warm June day, appeared anxious, having lost her previously defiant demeanor. During testimony she tried to pin the crime on a man named W. G. McCoy, who had been held for a time in connection to the robbery and whose charges were dismissed for lack of evidence. The jury deliberated about four hours before returning guilty verdicts for Molly and Sour Dough. Although there was some dissention, with some jury members wanting a lesser sentence for Molly, the two were both given three to fifteen years.

According to the *La Grande Observer*, after hearing of his conviction, Halter claimed, "They convicted an innocent man." To which Molly responded, laced with several "choice epithets," "Shut up you old fool. If you'd had sand enough to keep your gun instead of hiding it, you'd be a free man today." She showed little regard for her accomplices, adding that neither Joe nor Sour Dough possessed "enough brains to hold up a stage." Molly also had this to say about her future: "I've lived a fast life. Now I'm forty-eight years old and unattractive, so I guess the pen is as good as any place."

Molly joined a half dozen women prisoners at the Oregon State Prison in Salem in July, where at first she must have been extremely bored; after all, she had owned and operated an exceptionally lively saloon serving the parched miners from the Rainbow Mine. But in December the state board of prisons gave Warden Harry Minto permission to implement a work program for the women. The program came about after he informed the board that the female prisoners had nothing to do "except to eat and grow fat." It was the warden's suggestion that they take up some of

Molly Burget mug shot
OREGON SECRETARY OF STATE

the domestic duties at the prison, including sewing buttons on coats and trousers of the male convicts.

While the three robbers went to the state pen, Sheriff Anderson was the happy recipient of the reward money provided by the Rainbow Mine's insurance policy. He said he planned to share the thousand-dollar prize with his fellow law enforcement personnel.

In July 1916 the governor announced that he was giving Molly a conditional pardon. The condition being that she move to California, which she did.

Regardless of the facts that punctuate the tales of the female robbers of the stagecoach era, news reporters, magazine writers, and book authors of the time couldn't resist the temptation to sensationalize these questionable characters and romanticize their situations. Usually the young women were portrayed as attractive and dashing, their adventures exhilarating, and older women beloved and pampered. But how enchanted could a person feel after riding horseback over the dusty Arizona desert without bathing for days, as did Pearl Hart? And it's difficult to believe that anyone raising three little girls in a place called Hog Ranch, as Elizabeth Hood did, would find any comfort in her surroundings. The reality of incarceration at the Oregon State Prison in 1915 had to have taken a toll on Molly Burget, and fourteen-year-old orphan Lizzie Keith Fowler couldn't possibly have perceived any romance in her marriage to an abusive older man. If the decidedly gross yet irresistible Mother Osborne actually did disperse motherly advice, where was the glamour in her woefully lonely death in a crumbling cabin in the middle of nowhere?

CHAPTER 7

Just for Fun

"THE BRUTE, UNMINDFUL, TEARS MADLY ON—JOLTING OVER ROCKS, goading his horses down the hollows, only to run up the opposite side at an insane gallop, sending battered inmates to the roof, where their heads are banged and beaten; around jutting and dangerous precipices, where one inch too near the edges will pitch the stage, crashing through pines, to destruction." Celebrated actress-turned-writer Olive Logan demonstrated her flair for the dramatic in her gripping description of a tour of Yosemite at the hands of a colorful stagecoach driver in 1870.

Plenty of well-wishers offered advice to Olive as she prepared for her journey. When someone suggested she outfit herself in the notorious bloomer costume that would allow more freedom of movement on the demanding trek, Olive replied, "I feel that my charms are not so numerous that I can afford to lessen them by the adoption of this most ungraceful and unbecoming of dresses." And although she relented, asking a dressmaker to stitch up a pair of the pantaloons, she characterized them as "simply hideous."

As it turned out, her unflattering clothing was the least of Olive's complaints. Starting out on the first day at four in the morning after a "dirty and disgusting" meal consisting of food left behind after a swarm of flies had their fill, Olive and her fellow tourists found themselves "ensconced in a hard, lumbering, springless, unpainted fiend" of a stagecoach. Admitting the scenery was wild and grand, the air pure and sweet, Olive grumbled at the perpetual dust—"your eyes are smarting, your tongue is clogged, your hair is caked, your limbs are sore, your flesh is inflamed." And this after only the first day!

The roads grew intolerable as the stage began its ascent into the foothills; stage stations offered meals of salt beef, cold beans, watery potatoes, and weak tea and log cabin accommodations more expensive than the finest hotels in San Francisco. In at least one, all the guests—men, women, children, total strangers—slept together in one large room with little regard for modesty. At the Hutchings Hotel, Elvira Sproat Hutchings offered wine for refreshment and whiskey rubs for aching muscles. The stage driver expected his passengers up at 4:00 a.m. every day, despite the adventure having been promoted as a pleasure trip.

Olive had to admit throughout the days in Yosemite that the scenery was grand, but she always couched her praise in unflattering terms, claiming that

Olive Logan

NEW YORK; WASHINGTON, DC: BRADY'S NATIONAL PHOTOGRAPHIC PORTRAIT GALLERIES, LOC.GOV/ ITEM/96524617

other places in America offered just as satisfying vistas and reminding readers that the tourists were in no condition to enjoy the beauty after days in a jolting stagecoach or astride a skittish horse. As a tourist who had endured the rigors of Yosemite by stage, she felt obliged to warn the plucky tourists entering the area, "You'll feel it for a month!" She questioned if her twenty-dollar investment had been worth the agony. Instead, she advised vacationers to travel over the Great Plains by rail, soaking up the scenery of prairie dogs, antelopes, and sage deserts that cost nothing in the way of bruises, sprains, and torn flesh. She encouraged travel to various California towns—San Jose, Oakland, Los Angeles, and San

Francisco, where cool summer breezes had compelled her to wear a fur-lined jacket in July. She called on Americans' patriotic spirit to spend their tourist dollars in America rather than Europe. However, Olive implored, "Don't go to Yo Semite—in short, never ride of your own free will in a California stage."

Fortunately or unfortunately, depending on one's perspective, tourists in larger and larger numbers disregarded Olive's advice and ventured into the interiors of Yosemite. In spring 1872 a *New York Times* reporter warned that the arrival of a railway connecting San Francisco with Yosemite would lead to the same ruinous fate afflicting the Adirondack woods in New York, where a fisher could no longer enjoy a quiet afternoon on Tupper Lake without sharing the experience with a swarm of fashionably dressed spectators from the city or a hunter couldn't shoot at a deer without "running the risk of wounding a New-York belle." In the reporter's opinion, the Adirondacks had become more crowded than Central Park on a summer's Saturday afternoon, and it was the fault of the stage lines that brought tourists into the area from various locations in the Northeast. The reporter's predictions for Yosemite included the arrival of greedy entrepreneurs who would erect "exasperating hovels" where they would engage in "the sale of bad whisky to reckless visitors." And not far behind would be monte dealers at the "summit of each available precipice," not to mention the enterprising druggist constructing signs on "every inch of rock surface" hawking remedies for every imaginable disease. And what would stop the inevitable circuses from pitching tents and the almost certain arrival of establishments offering "public dancing and unlimited consumption of beer."

"The once majestic wilderness will be converted into a gigantic beer-garden, and in place of flowers will grow only pint-pots and defective whisky-bottles," the *Times* reporter wrote of Yosemite.

Undoubtedly, the reporter would have expressed not a molecule of surprise had he or she noticed a blurb in the *San Francisco Examiner* only a few years later in June 1875 that stated travel to Yosemite in May had been double that reported the year before. Stage proprietors in the city of Merced were sending as many as eight four-horse stages daily to accommodate tourists wanting to see the natural wonders of Yosemite.

According to the report, which may or may not have been based on actual data, in previous years tourists had originated from Europe and the eastern United States; whereas, increasingly, local residents now were visiting Yosemite. Women visitors to Yosemite outnumbered men two to one. "They crowd the inside of the stages, and not a day passes but half a dozen can be seen perched up alongside of the driver, and upon the top of the vehicles, both going to and coming from the valley," the *Examiner* reported. The reporter couldn't resist comparing the female travelers from the opposite coasts of the United States, stating the "fresh, rosy-cheeked" California women shone alongside the "sleepy, vinegar-visaged, grasshopper maidens of the far off Atlantic."

Stagecoaches had long been part of the tourist industry—from the 1820s, when they provided one of the few ways to access the falls at Niagara, New York. In summer 1836, stages left Buffalo every day at 8:00 a.m., arriving at Niagara Falls by noon. In 1844 three shillings bought tourists a tour on the Canadian side of the falls by stage, including stops at battle sights of the War of 1812, where the stage wheels "pressed that earth which had drank deep and long of human gore." In 1885 a popular resort in Los Angeles offered stage connection for a fifty-cent fare to Dr. Arthur Sketchley's ostrich farm a few miles from town, where visitors watched the voracious birds consume fresh-cut alfalfa by the forkful and chow down on bushels of stones and seashells. In the 1890s the Suburban Road Coaching Club offered nostalgic trips from Philadelphia to New York City, garnering attention at every tavern stop for a change of horses, just like in the old days, as curious onlookers gaped at the outdated form of transportation. Those venturous souls who visited far-off Hawaii in 1893 could board a stagecoach to the top of Mauna Loa, where they were rewarded with a grand view of the countryside and the sea beyond. They might stay a night at the Volcano House resort before continuing their journey to witness Mauna Loa's bubbling lava, complete with hissing steam and rising smoke.

George and Sarah Romrell Marshall were among the first to cater to the tourist trade in Yellowstone Park when they offered stage tours in the park and constructed a hotel within its boundaries in 1880. They recognized that even the most ardent of nature lovers yearned for an occasional night with a roof over one's head and a mattress under one's body, as well as a meal around a table rather than a campfire. The Marshalls' stage carried tourists from Virginia City, Nevada, to Yellowstone for twenty-five dollars per person, with board set at $2.50 per day at the Marshalls' hotel, situated on the Lower Geyser Basin. Saddle horses were available for an additional $2.50.

Robert and Carrie Adell Strahorn were two of the very first customers at the Marshalls' enterprise in October 1880, when the log cabin hotel was only partially completed. Carrie described the experience in her book *Fifteen Thousand Miles by Stage*: "The part we occupied was partitioned off with a canvas wagon cover . . . a window or two was missing in the upper part while the unfilled chinks between the logs allowed the rigorous October breezes to fan us at will . . . a single stove did its best toward heating the whole house."

George and Sarah accompanied the Strahorns in some of their travels in the park, including a trip to Mammoth Hot Springs, a distance of forty miles in a wagon, which the travelers hoped to cover in two days. Carrie was at a loss for words in describing the abysmal condition of the only trail at the time. "There are no adjectives in our language that can properly define the public highway that was cut through heavy timber over rolling ground, with the stumps left from two to twenty inches above ground," she wrote. In the end, the four turned back to the Marshall cabin to get saddle horses, hoping to make the journey more tolerable. However, Sarah decided to stay home rather than make the trip on horseback. It wasn't that she was a timid soul; it likely had to do with the fact that she was six months pregnant with her fourth child.

Some visitors to the Marshalls' hotel couldn't say enough flattering things about Sarah's hospitality. H. Bernard Leckler wrote about his experience in 1884, "Mrs. Marshall prepared a nice supper for us upon our arrival . . . cooking the dishes we liked best, opening cans of our favorite fruit, and in every way trying to make our stay with her as pleasant as possible."

Guest Frances Roe wrote in her book *Army Letters from an Officer's Wife, 1871–1888* about meals at the Marshalls' hotel that included choices of black-tail deer, white-tail deer, bear, grouse, prairie chicken, squirrels, and fowl—"the latter still in possession of their heads." She also was greatly impressed with the pipe that brought warm water from the nearby springs into the hotel. "Just fancy having a stream of water that a furnace somewhere below has brought to boiling heat, running through your house at any and all times," she wrote.

However, it was a different story from Margaret Andrews Cruikshank, a Minneapolis teacher who visited in 1883 and described the Marshalls as overworked and cross. According to her, while some meals were "tolerably good," others were "abominable messes" that likely included horsemeat. She bitterly resented paying fifty cents for some hot water; and the "dark and stifling" sleeping loft, subdivided by burlap partitions, was far from satisfying for this discerning traveler. "The bed was stuffed with sagebrush and had a horrid medicinal, quininey smell." She was suspicious of the bedclothes too: "I fancied that they had covered every teamster in the valley." (It should be noted that Margaret was highly critical of many other aspects of her trip, including some of Mother Nature's creations— canyons that she found not very impressive, boiling springs that made travel difficult, mountains that were not at all grand, and the legendary paint pots of colorful mud that were inferior specimens in her opinion.) Another guest was critical of Sarah's laundry practices, which made use of the natural geothermal water surrounding the hotel. In her little log laundry room located across the Firehole River from the hotel, Sarah washed the hotel's dirty clothing and linens without the benefit of soap, which she claimed wasn't necessary considering the warmth of the natural water.

Sarah's perhaps unconventional housekeeping and cooking habits might be overlooked considering the responsibilities thrust upon her as a pioneer in Yellowstone. She served as postmaster and cooked, cleaned, and arranged stagecoach tours for guests in addition to delivering, raising, and schooling six children over an eleven-year span. And George liked to tell the story of his wife's encounter with a couple of bears in June 1881. Shortly after he had left Sarah and the four kids for a monthlong trip to Omaha and San Francisco, two bears arrived at the Marshall cabin, attracted by the scent of meat stored in a root cellar for the family and future guests. Frantic to save their food supply, Sarah landed a shot in one of the burly fellows and managed to slam the cabin door in his face

Sarah Romrell Marshall

as he lunged toward her. As the wounded creature lumbered up a mountainside, Sarah took after, bringing him down with another, fatal, shot. According to George, upon his return he was pleased to learn his family was safe, but he expressed some disappointment that Sarah had failed to clean and preserve the skin that could have become a cozy rug for the hotel floor. As Margaret Andrews Cruishank wrote, Yellowstone was "no place for the delicate."

For a time the Marshalls were in partnership with George Henderson and his family in providing hotel and stagecoach services to Yellowstone visitors. At their establishment tourists enjoyed delicious meals including fresh milk from the eleven-cow herd on the premises, hot baths, and laundry facilities. The two families became renowned for their delightfully educational guided tours by stage and horseback.

Typically, by November a trip in Yellowstone could be risky, but thanks to the forces of nature and the foibles of humans, the fall of 1884 was not like most. The weather had been unusually mild, and politics had been particularly stormy. One visitor to the Yellowstone area described the uncommon weather conditions as "a delightful winter summer." As for politics, voters grappled with choices for president: A veteran politician, James Blaine, accused of various forms of corruption and who some said, "wallowed in spoils like a rhinoceros in an African pool," and, Grover Cleveland, whose alleged illicit affair years before had resulted in the birth of a child and thus the campaign slogan "Ma! Ma! Where's My Pa? Gone to the White House, ha, ha, ha." The nomination of a woman, Belva Lockwood, by the National Equal Rights Party only added to the drama. Her slogan, "I cannot vote but I can be voted for," helped her capture a few thousand votes that year. Even poet Walt Whitman was compelled to enter the fray with his poem "Election Day, November, 1884," in which he described Yellowstone's majestic "spasmic geyser-loops" as insignificant compared to the consequences of Election Day 1884.

In a nod to the fair weather and the fractious political situation, George Henderson's daughter Helen—also known as Nellie—suggested a tour of Yellowstone for those hardy visitors who could appreciate the park in wintertime, with the added possibility of a bone-chilling blizzard, and who needed a quiet distraction from political strife. A tour might be just the thing.

The Marshalls agreed to do their part, and on the morning of November 13, George and Sarah started out on foot with a group to explore an area south of the hotel. One of the tourists expressed his enthusiasm for George's unique perspective on the sights: "He knows where everything of interest is to be found without loss of time." And as early as 1884, this environmentally conscious visitor appreciated George's sensitivity to the fragile nature of the park: "He has also the good sense to keep the most beautiful nooks and basins hidden from the vandal and the specimen fiend who is continually seeking that he might destroy." The group continued on their trek to "Effervescent spring," which "effervesces like champagne," the "Chemical Basin filled with paint of every hue," and "the Bulldog" volcano that opened "like the jaws of a bulldog." It was in the area of these craters that Sarah barely averted catastrophe according to the visitor who witnessed the incident. "Mrs. Marshall broke through the thin crust, but being as elastic as steel she sprang forward and upward like a bird on the wing, and thus escaped serious injury." Sarah's involvement in this dicey venture was especially notable, as she had given birth to her fifth child in October, only two months before.

Nellie and George took a small group of men for a daylong trek beginning at sunrise with a climb up "the rocky ribs" of Terrace. After forty miles of sometimes walking other times riding horseback through canyons and basins, the group arrived back at the hotel about 7:30 p.m., just in time to enjoy a hearty meal before retiring.

This was one of the many tours Nellie conducted while the Hendersons operated in Yellowstone. Eventually the Marshalls dropped out of the enterprise, and the Hendersons operated the business with another partner. In the summer of 1885 they began construction of the Cottage Hotel in Yellowstone, providing many of the same services. By then they had already earned a reputation as stage drivers who enthralled passengers with their lively guided tours of the park. With a fleet of carriages and a staff of knowledgeable tour guides, the 150 guests who filled the rooms of the Cottage Hotel were assured of a breathtaking view of the park through the expert guidance of one of the Hendersons or their employees.

A guest at the Cottage wrote a letter to George expressing his pleasure with the experience: "The past six days in Yellowstone Park were the most delightful ones. Your daughter, Mrs. H. H. Stuart, [Nellie had married Charles Stuart] took myself and wife up to the Orange geyser in one of your magnificent Quincy carriages, conducting us thence from subject to subject among ever increasing wonders. . . . Such an accumulation of indescribable wonders with such a guide to point out their beauties, made our first day something like a bewildering dream."

Those awe-inspiring vistas and interactions with nature drew tourists to Yellowstone from the start. The informative tour guides and accommodating stage drivers enhanced the experience, but it was the natural environment that captured the hearts of visitors. Majestic wildlife offered rapture-inducing entertainment against a backsplash of magnificent varieties of vegetation and land formations. Ella McIntyre Smith visited Yellowstone in 1892 with her husband; from their room at the Mammoth Hot Springs Hotel, she described their wonder in letters to their young daughters, who had remained behind with caretakers. Their two-hundred-mile stagecoach tour of the park had been made most pleasant by the well-behaved teams of horses pulling the stage and by the very careful driver, whose skills had prevented accidents even as the party traversed the roughest mountain passes. Ella marveled at the eagles that had built nests on the summits of the tallest peaks overlooking streams and at the profusion of wildflowers sprinkled across the landscapes. She described the bears they had encountered—some "brought in from the woods and tamed"—and a huge one that visited the back of the hotel until he spotted the tourists, causing him to run away into the woods. It may have been a mother's attempt to rationalize leaving the kids at home when Ella wrote that the trip would have been very hard on the little girls. Perhaps as a gesture of appeasement, she promised to purchase some new paper dolls for them when she reached Helena. If that didn't appease them, she promised that when they were older and could take care of themselves, their papa would probably "take you through this wonderland."

In summer 1894, Jennie Coltman made her first attempt to tour Yellowstone Park, her curiosity piqued by the reports of early explorers such as John Colter of the Lewis and Clark Expedition, who may or may not have visited Yellowstone in 1807, and Jim Bridger, who explored in the 1830s. Jennie, a college student at the time, embarked with some friends, her parents, and the family dog, Buster, from Laramie, Wyoming, heading across the state toward Yellowstone. It was a camping expedition that tested the stamina of the hardy travelers as they made their way at a snail's pace—only about twenty miles per day. Their transportation consisted of riding horses, a wagon, and a surrey. Jennie rode in the surrey with Buster. Each night the travelers pitched tents and ate what game they managed to hunt—prairie chicken and rabbits—around a campfire. Each morning's departure was delayed by the antics of Buster, who pretended to need help getting into the surrey. It was a game he enjoyed and one Jennie found extremely amusing, but which tried her dad's patience as he attempted to round up the group for another day of travel. As it was, it

Camping in Yellowstone, 1903
LIBRARY OF CONGRESS PRINTS AND PHOTOGRAPHS DIVISION, WASHINGTON, DC,
LC-USZ62-41334

took more than a week for them to reach Casper, and when they arrived, the tiny town with its two blocks of wooden sidewalks, log cabin hotel, and saloon was a disappointment to the weary travelers. The multipurpose brick town hall that served as church, school, dance hall, and morgue failed to impress them. By the time they reached Hyattville, the dispirited explorers realized that summer was quickly running out and decided they weren't going to make it to Yellowstone. Confusing maps had kept them lost most of the trip, and they turned back without satisfying their desire to explore the great park.

People who knew Jennie probably weren't surprised to hear that she wasn't about to let a few obstacles stand in the way of eventually seeing the park. Her second attempt, in 1910, was successful. By then she had traveled the globe after graduating from college to work as a missionary in China, avoiding seasickness during a typhoon simply by looking herself in the mirror and scolding, "If you grow a shade greener, I'll throw you overboard." Her travels across China by rail, houseboat, and donkey cart and mastering a meal of sea slugs with chopsticks certainly proved her endurance. Her escape from China with her new husband, Professor Oliver Clifford, during the Boxer Rebellion of 1900, when they dodged hostile troops to board a military train with moments to spare and witnessed the shelling of the American gunboat *Monocacy*, said something about this woman's stamina.

When Jennie, her husband, and three kids set out on their tour of Yellowstone, traveling to Gardiner, Montana, by train to the north entrance of the park in 1910, the five-mile horse-drawn coach ride to the Mammoth Hot Springs Hotel posed no inconvenience. And their five-day tour of the park in a beautiful red-and-yellow stagecoach pulled by four prancing horses guided by the driver in his bright red coat, sporty cap, and high black boots seemed a luxury. No camping for Jennie on this trip—only comfortable and spacious rooms at the Fountain Hotel, Old Faithful Inn, Lake Hotel, and elegant Canyon Hotel.

Jennie expected this to be an educational adventure for her children. "Listen to the guide. Listen and learn; but watch where you step," she warned. When a photographer wanted to capture an image of a bear eating out of a human's hand, he convinced the tourists that the photo would be most impressive if the person was as small as possible to emphasize the enormity of the furry creature. Jennie's youngest and smallest child, five-year-old Helen, was selected. As everyone moved to the trash dump outside the hotel where the Cliffords were staying, the bears moved in from the woods and the photographer fumbled to set up his camera. Helen was encouraged to approach one of the bears, her tiny outstretched hand offering a lump of sugar, something everyone knew bears couldn't resist. But as the huge animal grew closer, Helen hurled the sugar at the bear and ran for cover in Jennie's arms. While the onlookers and the photographer grumbled about the missed opportunity, Jennie defended her daughter's reaction: "It was a very big bear, and Helen is a very little girl."

Recalling the encounter as an adult, Helen admitted it was indeed a learning experience—she vowed never again to feed a wild animal. However, she did return to Yellowstone many years later, when she and her husband toured the park by car rather than stagecoach in 1971.

Stagecoaches were ubiquitous in Yellowstone well into the 1900s. Lillian Fellows toured Yellowstone in 1910 when she was only eleven years old, traveling in a covered wagon and camping with a friend's family. When stagecoaches pulled by four- or six-horse teams and loaded with well-dressed passengers approached on the narrow roads within the park, other vehicles, such as the family's covered wagon, pulled to the edge to give the stagecoaches right-of-way—earning them the name "sage brushers," as they frequently brushed up against sagebrush alongside the paths.

Traveling with the Wylie Camping Company in 1911, a ticket purchased at the entrance to the park entitled Dorothy Brown to six days camping in a tent in Yellowstone, including tours by knowledgeable guides. Each day began at 6:30 a.m. with a gong to awaken guests and rouse them from their tents, followed by breakfast and the loading of the stages. Each passenger was expected to remain with the stage assigned the first day and to bring only one piece of luggage. Dorothy felt lucky to have a driver named Shorty, who was squint-eyed and pigeon-toed but good natured and eager to point out areas of interest. Lunch was enjoyed along the way at the dining camps maintained by the Wylie Company. Shorty accommodated his passengers' wishes every day, wowing them with the majestic sights. "Here was at last a spot where man might come to enjoy what man had left undone," Dorothy wrote in her diary. "At times high up on the mountain side, with our horses sweeping around a bend in the road—canyons lying deep below us, wooded and dark—and glimpses in the distance of mountain peaks—of a lake—vistas and visions of a promised land." As the days passed and the end of the stagecoach tour approached, Dorothy wrote, "I regretfully turned my face away from the enchanted land, even then laying plans for my second visit to the Park."

In 1914 Mary Chapman and her husband, Clarence, experienced a hybrid tour of Yellowstone, combining the traditional with the modern as they arrived at the park in an open observation car attached to a train. A six-horse stagecoach transported the visitors from the entrance of the park to the Mammoth Hot Springs Hotel. The Chapmans used the Yellowstone Park Transportation Company, one of the in-park stage lines, for some of their tours, possibly because the company's drivers had stellar reputations. At one point they hired "one of the most popular and well-known stage men in the northwest," Tex Holm, and saw more wildlife than at any other time. Finally they hired a Stanley Steamer automobile to finish out the tour; it's unclear if this came about as a result of reported stage holdups in the park, in which a lone robber made off with twenty-five hundred dollars from passengers on nineteen stages near Shoshone Point.

A trip through Yellowstone by stagecoach offered unique scenery and surprising interactions with wildlife, but it was not for the faint of heart. Especially in the early years, such an adventure required a certain degree of endurance and more than a little fortitude of spirit. So it was understandable that Margaret Andrews Cruikshank, the Minneapolis teacher who visited the park in 1883, consumed a little brandy and whiskey during her stagecoach travels in Yellowstone, sometimes with breakfast. "There was no getting through such an experience without frequent 'little goes' of strong waters," she explained.

Dressed in her pink gingham ankle-length dress, a wide-brimmed straw hat perched atop her tawny hair, with her feet tucked snuggly into a pair of russet-colored high-button, pointy-toed boots, Nina Morey settled

Coney Island, 1897
LIBRARY OF CONGRESS PRINTS AND PHOTOGRAPHS DIVISION, WASHINGTON, DC,
LC-DIG-STEREO-1S07248

into the driver's seat of her bright white stagecoach. Although slightly
built, she experienced little resistance as she maneuvered her team and
coach through the streets of Brooklyn, New York. So far, the summer of
1896 had proved to be a banner year for her stage business. Every day at
two o'clock, she positioned herself on the Coney Island beach with her

rig—vying with other eager drivers to transport tourists and day-trippers to the nearby beaches and resorts. One of the more popular drivers, she was known to make as much as twenty dollars a day.

Nina was already known to many of the locals for her pluckiness. In 1890, when she was only fifteen, she had participated in the annual ladies' ocean swimming match with eight other contestants ages eight to twenty-eight. The roughly mile-long race started from a point opposite the Brighton Beach Music Amphitheatre, where a yacht named the *Loretta S* carried the contestants. The seas were so turbulent that August day that the start of the race was delayed for an hour. At least two of the contestants became severely seasick, causing one to drop out of the contest. At exactly 4:30:50 the swimmers dove as one from the deck of the yacht; one by one they began to drop out as they tired, picked up by the waiting lifeboats. Nina was one of those who did not complete the race, but that didn't mean she was a weakling. During her stagecoach driving days, she demonstrated her strong swimming skills more than once by rescuing individuals from drowning—one a woman she saved as a crowd cheered her on to safety.

Nina lived with her mother and other siblings near Coney Island's Brighton Beach race track in an old blacksmith shop that had been converted into their house. The livery housing Nina's stagecoach horses and other livestock including pigs and poultry was attached to the house. At twenty-one years of age, Nina was already an accomplished business owner, having started an oil and kerosene delivery service in addition to her furniture delivery enterprise. Keeping her horses and equipment in working order consumed a great deal of her time. Cleaning and oiling harnesses, replacing buckles, adjusting straps—all part of the job. Shoeing her stage horses and repairing a wheel were tasks that Nina took on herself. She was the main support of the family. "Nina has always been our mainstay," her mother said.

When her stagecoaching enterprise slowed, Nina took a job as a snow shoveler for the city. Dressed in a "short bicycle skirt," a military overcoat, and boots, she scooped snow by hand, tossing it into her horse-drawn wagon and hauling it to the city dump. For her efforts she was paid sixty-four cents per load. During a four-day storm in 1899 she earned $23.68.

Anyone foolish enough to threaten Nina's livelihood quickly came face to face with her weaponry. She carried a pistol on her stage for protection and was known to flash it at intruders on the family property on Coney Island. A former employee learned his lesson when he returned to retrieve some personal belongings and Nina met him at the gate, indicating he should expect to be riddled with shot if he didn't leave the premises. If he dared look over the fence as he left, he would meet the same fate, she assured him.

Over the years Nina's notoriety extended to the local law enforcement agencies. She made frequent appearances at the local courts as a result of various entanglements with individuals she accused of stealing her property or trespassing on the family land. And Nina was occasionally in trouble for allowing her cows and stage horses to roam unfettered on Coney Island. The *New York Times* reported in May 1901 that Nina's appearance in the Coney Island Police Court was a result of her half dozen cows grazing on the grass in Seaside Park, a common occurrence that she refused to remedy. When the magistrate offered Nina the option of a ten-dollar fine or ten days in the county jail, she considered for a moment and replied that since the stage business was a little slow, she would spend the time in jail. In August she again was sentenced to ten days in the Raymond Street jail on a charge of violating a city ordinance related to permitting horses to roam on Coney Island. Nina replied that she would never pay a fine that would only add to the city's treasury and would gladly serve the time instead.

By 1901 the *New York Times* reference to Nina's Coney Island stage as "an old and much battered stage coach" that offered transportation "between Brighton Beach and the West End" didn't inspire confidence in the once-sought-after attraction, and future news articles about her centered on the family's long legal battle over ownership of their property on Coney Island.

About the time Nina Morey ran her stagecoach business in New York, Nora Greenfield was making a name for herself as an operator of a tourist stagecoach in and around Colorado Springs, Colorado. Nora was married so many times, it's nearly impossible to pin a name on her. She was born Nora Miller and married George Greenfield, O. C. Fenalson, Dan

Gaines, and perhaps Louis Whittaker. She buried two of those fellows next to each other. They share a tombstone along with Nora. But Nora's notoriety didn't come from her multiple relationships—well, except for the time she married Dan Gaines, thinking George Greenfield was dead when he wasn't, causing some to accuse her of bigamy. Her fame was due to the remarkable service she provided to tourists, exceptional partly because she was a woman in a male-dominated business.

As summer vacationers flocked to the Colorado Springs area in 1898, Nora quickly became known as one of the area's most popular and busiest stage drivers. As Nora and the male drivers met the incoming train each day, visitors seemed to gravitate to the sole woman in the crowd. Dressed in a skirt and blouse with a sombrero on her head and high boots on her feet, she easily guided her team up the steep mountain roads. At the end of the tour, her passengers told others about the energetic woman who revealed the most beautiful spots around the area and deftly maneuvered her coach through the countryside. Nora told people her husband was an invalid and she was the breadwinner of the family, so she cherished the fifty dollars she could make in a day. Her success led the other drivers to look for ways to discredit this female interloper, going so far as to bring charges against her for stealing business from them. Still, they couldn't deter the tourists who were drawn to the woman driver.

Maybe it was because Nora could be quite entertaining. It was said she could "swear like a pirate and drive like the devil." Weaving through the streets of downtown Colorado Springs, she swore at pedestrians to get out of her way. Once when she was taking a coach full of passengers to the popular tourist spot Seven Falls, Nora overheard a fellow in the crowd direct a disparaging comment toward her. She let loose with a stream of such vitriolic language that the locals insisted she stop bringing her rig into the area. Still, Nora went out of her way to accommodate her passengers, seeing to their comfort by covering them with lap robes and raincoats when the stage encountered sudden rainstorms. When a would-be robber sprang into the path of her stage, aiming a revolver and demanding she halt, Nora knocked the bandit to the ground and galloped away, leaving the fellow to wonder what had happened to his grand scheme.

Nora was a favorite of wealthy tourists and famous theatrical talent in 1905. She admitted her clientele were "people who possess a penchant for fine scenery at high prices." By this time she had been driving tourists to points of interest around the Pikes Peak area for years during the summer season and had net earnings averaging about 250 dollars per month. This had allowed Nora to invest in several carriages and "some of the sleekest horseflesh in the city." She had several employees who helped drive, including her husband, Dan Gaines. However, Nora's prosperity didn't keep her from performing some of the less glamorous aspects of the business. When she wasn't driving her fashionable clients around, she donned a pair of overalls and rubber boots and headed to the stable, where she curried her horses and laid down straw for them.

"I am a businesswoman. Men may come and women may go, but I go on forever—earning money," Nora said.

It's unclear if Nora knew Florinda (alternately spelled Florenda) Chapin, another stage driver who catered to tourists in Colorado Springs in the 1890s and early 1900s, but Florinda may have been making a point in 1905 when she told a news reporter, "Yes, I am the leading female hack driver of Colorado Springs and Manitou, this being my seventh season and they have all been very successful."

Like Nora, Florinda was licensed to operate a stage service that carried sightseers to popular points of interest around the area. She claimed she owned "four of the finest mountain conveyances" in town and her "seven head of good reliable horses" offered her an advantage over other coach operators. Unlike her competitors, who she alleged categorized easterners as easy targets for outrageous prices, Florinda provided her passengers engaging, safe tours at reasonable and consistent rates for all.

A frugal business owner, Florinda tended her horses herself—brushing, combing, and harnessing, having learned the useful skills on the family ranch when she was a young girl. When business was brisk, Florinda hired additional drivers to keep her vehicles and horses on the move. Being a shrewd businesswoman, she paid her employees according to the number of trips they completed rather than a salary. Her thrifty business practices meant that during the summer months, Florinda's average income hovered around 350 dollars per month, dropping to never less than 125 dollars per month in the fall.

An eastern newspaper reporter painted a verbal portrait of this intriguing woman he had encountered on a visit to Colorado, writing that Florinda's courageous character was reflected in her penetrating blue eyes and strong convincing voice. "I'm not the kind of a woman that is always throwing bouquets at herself," she told him. But there was plenty about Florinda that deserved accolades. She had climbed to the summit of Pikes Peak—although she admitted she spent a month recuperating—and she was operating her business enterprise single-handedly, as her husband had died less than two years before. All this while raising six kids. And like Nora Miller Greenfield Fenalson Gaines Whittaker, Florinda continued to work into her sixties, operating her Mountain Side Camp in the 1920s, offering "cabins for campers, automobile sheds, all conveniences."

When the monstrous lumbering elephants and proud prancing horses emerged from the train cars, the hundreds of exotic performers and harried workers began to pour into town, and the billowing yards of canvas transformed into massive tents, townspeople knew the circus had arrived. John Robinson's was considered one of the best. People flocked to the awe-inspiring performances, knowing the jaw-dropping acrobats, fiery spectacles, and dazzling costumes would soon be on to their next town, leaving kids with dreams of someday running away to join the circus and adults secretly wishing the same.

Frank Knapp happened to be in town when the Robinson Circus arrived in Dunkirk, New York, on a summer's day in 1905 and found himself drawn to a fellow unloading some of the high-spirited circus horses. Something about the way the worker handled the horses brought to mind his long-lost sister Florence, who had disappeared six years before after being jilted by her wealthy western stockman fiancé. Frank and his sister had grown up on a farm near Rochester, New York, and Florence had become an expert horse handler at a young age.

When Frank approached the circus worker known as James McIntosh, it became obvious that this individual posing as a man was actually

SHE PASSED AS A MAN FOR SIX YEARS AND DROVE CIRCUS WAGON

MISS KNAPP AS A TEAMSTER

FLORENCE KNAPP, A FARMER GIRL, FOUND HANDLING HORSES WITH THE JOHN ROBINSON CIRCUS—DESPITE FALSE MOUSTACHE BROTHER RECOGNIZED HER—SHE TIPPED THE MUSICIANS OVER, BUT THE CIRCUS PROPRIETOR THINKS SHE'S THE STUFF AND WON'T FIRE HER.

Miss Florence Knapp

MISS KNAPP AS QUEEN OF THE BALLET

It has just been discovered that Miss Florence Knapp, a Monroe county, New York, girl, who has been mysteriously missing for six years, has been working all that time as a man.

The last two years she has been driving horses for the John Robinson circus.

Her brother, Frank Knapp, No. 173 East Ferry street, Buffalo, N. Y., recently visited Robinson's circus at Dunkirk, N. Y. While the equipment was being unloaded Mr. Knapp, being a good horseman, was struck by the manner in which a man handled some high spirited steeds. There was something familiar in the man's appearance and on inquiry he was told that his name was James McIntosh. As he watched the horseman, the image of his sister, Florence, an expert horsewoman, who disappeared from home six years ago, came to him, and he divined that she was before him in the person of the driver.

With Manager John G. Robinson, he met "McIntosh" and claimed him as his lost sister. The "man" at first said Knapp was mistaken and declared "himself" to be truly "James McIntosh" but finally confessed to being

Miss Knapp. She wore a false moustache to make the deception more complete.

She left home after Charles Worthington, a wealthy western ranchman, broke off his engagement to marry her. There was much mystery about the disappearance at the time; she disappeared as if the earth had opened and swallowed her. And so did Worthington. His whereabouts are unknown. She says she came direct to Ohio and has supported herself as a workman for four years, but where she will not say. Two years ago she entered the employ of Robinson's circus at Cincinnati, and her sex was not discovered until at Dunkirk.

As a girl on her father's farm in Monroe county, New York, she became an expert horsewoman. She says she likes the circus life and refused to return home with her brother. Miss Knapp is not over 24 years old and will hereafter be seen in woman's attire. Manager Robinson promptly promoted her and made her queen of the ballet in the big spectacular first part. She also appears in the daily street

parade of the circus, driving a six horse team hitched to one of the band wagons, and attracts unusual attention. The musicians object to her driving the wagon because she had a little bad luck in making a quick turn on a road leading to a county fair ground. The horses became unmanageable and the wagon was dashed into a bridge and upset. The musicians and their instruments were spilled into the ditch. One musician, Joe Madru, of Terre Haute, Indiana, sustained a broken arm and all were more or less bruised.

The musicians complained to Manager Robinson about the woman driving, but he refuses to take her from the seat, Governor Robinson, owner of the show, says he can get all the musicians he wants, but there is only one woman driver in the world, and that is Miss Florence Knapp. The musicians went on a strike and the matter is to be arbitrated in Cincinnati.

W. T. M'CREIGHT'S TALK ON NEW MEXICO

Mr. and Mrs. W. T. McCreight, of Albuquerque, N. M., are house guests of Mrs. Bertle McCreight, mother of Mr. McCreight, says the Shelbyville, (Ky.) Record.

The gentleman is a Shelbyville reared boy, and learned the "art preservative, of which it is known he is proficient, in the same room now occupied by the Record some thirty odd years ago.

He has been a resident of New Mex-

Colic and Diarrhoea—A Remedy That is Prompt and Pleasant.

The prompt results produced by Chamberlain's Colic, Cholera and Diarrhoea Remedy, together with its pleasant taste, have won for it a place in many households. Mr. W. T. Taylor, a merchant of Winslow, Ala., writes: "I have used Chamberlain's Colic, Cholera and Diarrhoea Remedy myself and also with men on my place, for diarrhoea and colic and it always gives relief promptly and pleasantly." For sale by all dealers.

A blessing alike to young and old: Dr. Fowler's Extract of Wild Strawberry. Nature's specific for dysentery, diarrhoea and summer complaint.

Florence Knapp

ALBUQUERQUE EVENING CITIZEN, AUGUST 22, 1905. COURTESY *ALBUQUERQUE JOURNAL*

Florence. At first she denied Frank's suspicions but soon broke down, admitting that she was indeed the sister he had given up for lost. If Frank had hopes of Florence happily returning to the traditional life of a twenty-something woman at the beginning of the twentieth century, he would be sorely disappointed. Florence had no intention of leaving the life she had come to love—driving a six-horse team pulling a circus stage. To everyone's surprise, John Robinson did not fire this masquerading employee; rather he embraced her audacity and added to her driving duties by including her in the lineup of ballet performers, featuring her as "queen of the ballet."

In September, when the Robinson Circus rolled into DeKalb, Illinois, a crowd had gathered at the train station eagerly awaiting its arrival, and they weren't disappointed. Cheers greeted the sleepy elephants as they lined up to mosey over to the circus grounds where show people had gathered in the dining tent, filling their bellies before a long day and night of circus duties. The parade would kick off the events with enthusiastic drummers and trumpeters leading the way, announcing the approach of six bands, a herd of Shetland ponies, beautifully costumed women atop gold-bedecked steeds, colorful chariots, clowns, and rolling cages of wild animals eyeing the crowds while emitting terrifying growls. Florence Knapp, the "only woman six-horse driver in the world," evoked a vigorous round of applause. Some may have been surprised to see Florence, as word had gotten out about the unfortunate accident involving the circus musicians and the world's only female six-horse driver, who had lost control of the wagon carrying the music makers and caused it to upset. At least one person was injured, sustaining a broken arm. The group had lost confidence in Florence and weren't eager to ride with her. But when they complained to John Robinson, he said he could get all the musicians he wanted, but there was only one woman driver in the world. He was sticking by Florence, and the musicians could leave if they didn't like it. There were rumors that the musicians were considering a strike.

NOTES

CHAPTER 1: THE STAGECOACH: JOB CREATOR, MONEY MAKER

1. ". . . a huge uncouth, unmannerly": Anne Newport Royall, *The Black Book; or, A Continuation of Travels in the United States*, vol. 1 (Washington, DC: Anne Royall, 1828), 9.

1. "greasy, black coach": Royall, *The Black Book; or, A Continuation of Travels in the United States*, 43

1. "beastly drunk": Royall, *The Black Book; or, A Continuation of Travels in the United States*, 297.

2. ". . . there is a large variety": Harriet Martineau, *Retrospect of Western Travel in Three Volumes* (London: Saunders and Otley, 1838), 71, https://archive.org/details/retrospectofwest01mart.

2. "most trying ordeal": Earle, *Stage Coach and Tavern Days*, 228.

2. "not to exceed"; "two-inch ring.": US Department of Transportation, Federal Highway Administration, "The Paintings of Carl Rakeman," https://www.fhwa.dot.gov/rakeman/1823.htm.

2. "dreadful"; "roads will then": Adrienne Koch and William Peden, eds., *The Life and Selected Writings of Thomas Jefferson* (New York: Random House,1993), 502.

2–3. "Your papa"; "It is a very unsafe": Earle, *Stage Coach and Tavern Days*, 369.

3. "In the 1790s it cost": Earle, *Stage Coach and Tavern Days*, 238.

3. "By 1820, almost 40,000": Oliver W. Holmes and Peter T. Rohrbach, *Stagecoach East* (Washington, DC: Smithsonian Institution Press, 1983), 75.

3. "Many were given": Holmes and Rohrbach, *Stagecoach East*, 76.

4. "once a Fortnight"; "Ways are passable"; "Reasonable Rates": Holmes and Rohrbach, *Stagecoach East*, 6–7.

5. "And while the existing railroads": Leroy Pratt, "Ten Cents a Mile and a Fence Rail," *Annals of Iowa* 39 (1969): 603.

5. "stagecoaches sped over": Ralph Moody, *Stagecoach West* (Lincoln: University of Nebraska Press, 1967), 10.

5. "In 1850 the US Census Bureau": US Bureau of the Census, *Statistics of Occupations*, Washington, DC, 1850.

5. "in 1860, over nineteen thousand": US Bureau of the Census, *Statistics of Occupations*, Washington, DC, 1860.

6. "superior quality"; "first class"; "rare ability": *Grand Forks (ND) Herald*, August 10, 1883.

6. "highest reputation"; "pleasanter than ever": "New Stages," *Reno (NV) Gazette-Journal*, July 14, 1886.

8. "of any consequence"; "These charmingly": Moody, *Stagecoach West*, 294.

8. "straw color"; "English vermillion"; "highly ornamented.": Merri Ferrell and Christopher Augerson, "Concord Ornamental Painter John Burgum and the Artistry of Carriage Painting," *Historical New Hampshire* (Summer 2011): 39.

9. "Abbot-Downing offered top-of-the-line": Moody, *Stagecoach West*, 12.

9. "At least that was the intent": C. Robert Haywood, *Trails South* (Norman: University of Oklahoma Press, 1986), 197.

10. "Today the average twenty-one-year-old": Centers for Disease Control and Prevention, National Center for Health Statistics, Atlanta, GA, https://www.cdc.gov/nchs/fastats/body-measurements.htm.

12. "would not last until": Sam Moore, "James Reeside: Stage Coach Colonel," *Farm Collector* (March 2013), https://www.farmcollector.com/farm-life/reeside-stage-line-zmlz13marzbea.

12. "By opposition the people": Archer B. Hulbert, *Pilots of the Republic* (Chicago: A. C. McClurg, 1906), 200.

15. "Big Horse Market": "The Big Horse Market," *Kansas City Gazette*, March 1893.

15. "The Big Horse Sale": "The Big Horse Sale," *Indianapolis News*, March 21, 1888.

15. "Big Horse Sale!": Display ad, *Sentinel* (Carlisle, PA), June 12, 1888.

16. "common horses and plugs": "St. Louis Horse and Mule Market," *St. Louis Post-Dispatch*, November 3, 1875.

16. "By 1900 livestock officials estimated": Emily R. Kilby, "The Demographics of the US Equine Population," *State of the Animals IV* (2007): 176.

17. "mecca": "Chicago: The Mecca of Men Who Make the Horse an Idol," *Inter Ocean*, December 1, 1901.

17. "greatest horse market in the world": John Cooper, "The American Horse, Proceedings of the Annual Convention, National Live Stock Association National Stock Growers' Convention" (1900): 332.

17. "new life": "Chicago: The Mecca of Men Who Make the Horse an Idol," *Inter Ocean*, December 1, 1901.

18. "protect, promote and": "Local Trade Review," *Indianapolis Journal*, September 2, 1895.

18. "Horses were labeled according": "The Greatest Horse Market," *Country Gentleman*, vol. 70 (1905): 794.

18. "with the eye of an eagle"; "ever-watchful commission"; "all sorts and conditions of men"; "the acquisition": "Chicago: The Mecca of Men Who Make the Horse an Idol," *Inter Ocean*, December 1, 1901.

19. "tall and stately blonde"; "I have been engaged": "Miss Kittie Wilkins," *Democrat and Chronicle* (Rochester, NY), December 28, 1891.

20. "lady horse dealer,": "The Lady Horse Dealer," *Anaconda (MT) Standard*, March 4, 1892.

20. "She sold in large numbers": "Researcher Speaks Tuesday on Idaho's Famous Turn-of-the-Century Horse Dealer," *Times-News* (Twin Falls, ID), January 23, 2009.

20. "induced"; "When I was quite"; "When I got"; "I hold that"; "They are always": "Miss Kittie Wilkins," *Democrat and Chronicle* (Rochester, NY), December 28, 1891.

20. "Do you know": "She Sells Horses," *Wilkes-Barre (PA) Times Leader*, May 12, 1892.

21. "Horses know as well": "How to Treat Horses," *Forest Republican* (Tionesta, PA), November 11, 1891.

21. "noisy, a dirt": "The J Street Improvement," *Record-Union* (Sacramento, CA), November 28, 1892.

21. "inhumanly, unnecessarily": "A Word for Our Friend, the Horse," *Fort Wayne (IN) Gazette*, May 18, 1873.

21. "If you hit.": "Are You a True Friend of Animals?" *St. Louis Post-Dispatch*, September 28, 1902.

21. "When it fell": "Caused Arrest of Horse Beater," *St. Louis Post-Dispatch*, Dec. 1, 1902.

22. "well-fed,": Alyssa Bentz, "How Horses Have Been the 'Pride of Wells Fargo Service,'" November 17, 2017, https://stories.wf.com/horses-pride-wells-fargo-service.

22. "A well-tended stage . . .": "The Life of the Stagecoach Horses," International Museum of the Horse, http://www.imh.org/exhibits/online/legacy-of-the-horse/stage-travel-america.

22. "April 28, 1908, My dear Mrs. Lydic": Letter from Theodore Roosevelt to Mary D. Lydick, Theodore Roosevelt Papers, Library of Congress Manuscript Division, Theodore Roosevelt Digital Library, Dickinson State University, http://www.theodoreroosevelt center.org/Research/Digital-Library/Record?libID=o184818.

23. "place at the bench": "Woman Harness Maker," *Minneapolis Journal*, April 27, 1901.

23. "She can make": "Beats All Politics," *Minneapolis Journal*, June 27, 1903.

23. "I thank the": "Has Government Order," *Warren (MN) Sheaf*, June 7, 1906.

23. "At that time": "US Bureau of the Census, Part II, Comparative Occupation Statistics, 1870–1930": 115, 169.

23. "both sexes"; "remunerative": "Reports to the Legislature of the State of New Hampshire, vol. 2" (Manchester, NH: Arthur E. Clarke, 1901): 78, 126.

23. "It is an acknowledged fact": Display ad for J. R. Hill & Co., *Granite Monthly*, vol. 7 (1883): i.

24. "horse and mule jewelry": Arthur James Weise, *The City of Troy and Its Vicinity* (Troy, NY: Edward Green, 1886), 342.

24. "I make every part": "Only Woman Harness Maker on Coast Works in Salem," *Oregon Daily Journal*, October 1, 1911.

25. "The daughter of a": "A Woman Wheelwright," *New York Times*, August 6, 1895.

25. "by the clang"; "fashioning iron"; "I have found time": "Woman Wheelwright's Children Play in the Shop," *Evening World* (New York), July 19, 1911.

26. "I've seen dozens": "A Girl Blacksmith," *St. Louis Post-Dispatch*, September 30, 1888.

26. "din of ringing anvil."; "Yes, I know": "Santa Rosa Has a Woman Blacksmith," *San Francisco Chronicle*, October 7, 1901.

27. "I can handle horses": "Arizona's Woman Blacksmith," *Los Angeles Herald*, January 22, 1905.

28. "firm mouth"; "resolute way"; "five figures.": Arthur J. Burdick, "Western Highland Mary, Muscular Woman Teamster," *Atlanta Constitution*, February 8, 1903.

28. "swash-buckling": Haywood, *Trails South*, 82.

29. "the little black-eyed"; "cheerfulness and quiet demeanor": "Kittie Gibson," *Times* (Munster, IN), December 27, 1907.

CHAPTER 2: STAGECOACH AS PURVEYOR OF INFORMATION

32. "wou'd get tar'd and feather'd."; "hinder all acts"; "They are they say": Hugh Finlay, *Journal Kept by Hugh Finlay* (Brooklyn, NY, 1867), 23–24.

33. "convey all Packages and Letters.": Oliver W. Holmes and Peter T. Rohrbach, *Stagecoach East* (Washington, DC: Smithsonian Institution Press, 1983), 24.

33. "new arrangement in the post-office"; "the contract for transporting"; "unfavorable to the": Holmes, *Stagecoach East*, 30.

33–34. "evils"; "Stage drivers and private"; "the injury the general"; "perhaps no complete"; "poor people": "To Alexander Hamilton from Samuel Osgood, 20 January 1790," https://founders.archives.gov/documents/Hamilton/01-06-02-0095.

34. "That's the craziest thing": "Mural 'Crazy' Says Collier," *Arizona Republic*, October 9, 1937.

35–36. "I have carried"; "Well, I had some"; "dark as a pocket"; "pounded him in the face"; "until the blood ran down"; "He had tackled"; "I should like"; "Some have been"; "Look here"; "It seems like": "A Feminine Jehu," *Boston Globe*, May 5, 1884.

36–37. "It's the little incidentals"; "I suppose I have ridden"; "a man's work"; "do a few things": "Woman Carried Mail 28 Years, 80,000 Miles, Never Missed Train," *Pittsburgh Press*, April 1, 1917.

37. "along the lines": David Warren, "Women of the Old West," *Afro-American*, September 25, 1976.

38. "from the front, not the rear.": Gayle Shirley, *More Than Petticoats: Remarkable Montana Women* (Guilford, CT: Globe Pequot Press, 2011), 3.

38. "One of the nuns": Jean Conrad Rowe, *Mountains and Meadows* (Great Falls, MT: Blue Print & Letter Co., 1970), 157–58.

38. "her terrible temper": Rowe, *Mountains and Meadows*, 158.

39. "often spent the prairie nights": Marc Crawford, "Stagecoach Mary: A Gun-Toting Black Woman Delivered the US Mail in Montana," *Ebony* (October 1959): 98.

39. "managed the two teams of horses.": Jessie Carney Smith, ed., *Notable Black American Women* (Detroit, MI: Gale Research, 1992), 344.

39. "could break the"; "the gallows"; "licking": "Mary Fields Celebrates Her 83rd Birthday at Her Home in Cascade," *Great Falls (MT) Daily Tribune*, April 3, 1913.

40. "in the best sense,": Mark Harris, "The Legend of Black Mary," *Negro Digest* (August 1950): 86.

40. "syndicate bidders": "Star Route Mail Letting," *Natrona County Tribune*, October 3, 1901.

41. "Winner": Display ad, *Natrona County Tribune*, November 25, 1897.

41. "a four-span of wild-eyed broncs"; "We carried mail"; "There were few": "Lady Stage Driver," *Casper Star-Tribune*, January 8, 1928.

42–43. "truly half an acre of hell"; "burning sand of the desert"; "over hills"; "completely tired": "Over the Stage Line," *Natrona County Tribune*, August 1, 1901.

43. "soft-cushioned"; "heavily burdened": "Wants a Big Price," *Natrona County Tribune*, May 8, 1902.

44. "Yes, I meet some": "Woman Carries the Mail," *Boston Globe*, September 9, 1894.

44. "I'd as soon think": "She Carries Mail," *Buffalo (NY) Courier*, July 7, 1895.

44. "Afraid? Why, no!": "She Drives a Mail Coach," *St. Joseph (MO) Gazette-Herald*, November 29, 1898.

44. "I took up": "Girl Drives the Meeker Stage," *Ogden (UT) Standard*, January 2, 1913.

44. "great strength"; "resolute, determined": "Woman Carries the Mail," *Boston Globe*, September 1894.

45. "wild western type"; "I've never had"; "I've got to protect"; "I halted my"; "Poor fellow"; "My mother always": "She Carries Mail," *Buffalo (NY) Courier*, July 7, 1895.

46. "Modest as": "Oregon's Girl Stage Driver," *San Francisco Chronicle*, October 23, 1898.

46. "I considered it"; "Most of the time"; "I don't carry"; "It's pretty good"; "It wasn't any hotter": "She Drives a Mail Coach," *St. Joseph (MO) Gazette-Herald*, November 29, 1898.

47. "I think I've got": "She Drives a Mail Coach," *Freeland (PA) Tribune*, January 16, 1899.

47. "deadly weapon": "Lady Jury Refuses a Divorce," *Eastern Kansan*, July 4, 1912.

47. "First Girl": "First Girl Stage Driver," *Evening World* (New York), April 1, 1912.

47. "Girl Drives": "Girl Drives the Meeker Stage," *Ogden (UT) Standard*, January 2, 1913.

47. "Girl Runs": "Girl Runs Coach Line," *San Antonio Light*, August 31, 1913.

47–48. "four bronchos"; "no better driver"; "I always liked"; "I don't know as": "Girl Drives the Meeker Stage," *Ogden (UT) Standard*, January 2, 1913.

48. ". . . there is scarcely"; "boys and girls": Holmes, *Stagecoach East*, 126.

49. "shameful practice,": "A Hint to Newspaper Thieves," *North-Carolina Star*, May 20, 1825.

50. "strict impartiality,": Holmes, *Stagecoach East*, 128.

51. "You leave"; "You have our room.": Caroline Nichols Churchill, *Active Footsteps* (Colorado Springs, CO: Mrs. C. N. Churchill, 1909), 192.

51. "smother a woodchuck.": Nichols Churchill, *Active Footsteps*, 194.

51. "to keep a man's": Nichols Churchill, *Active Footsteps*, 193.

51. "people did not": Nichols Churchill, *Active Footsteps*, 19.

51. "an opportunity": Nichols Churchill, *Active Footsteps*, 22.

52. "belligerent"; "fists instead": Caroline Nichols Churchill, *Little Sheaves; Gathered while Gleaning after Reapers* (San Francisco: Mrs. C. M. Churchill, 1874), 18.

52. "Why is it": Nichols Churchill, *Little Sheaves*, 98.

52. ". . . this individual": Nichols Churchill, *Little Sheaves*, 54.

52. "It is surprising": Nichols Churchill, *Little Sheaves*, 84.

52. "so compact"; "I belong to": Caroline Nichols Churchill, *Over the Purple Hills* (Denver, CO: Mrs. C. M. Churchill, 1881), 46.

53. "baby or colty"; "outworked three"; "I just wish": Nichols Churchill, *Over the Purple Hills*, 207.

53. "regret that": Nichols Churchill, *Over the Purple Hills*, 210.

53. "Advantages Which"; "Its editor is"; ". . . it is the wittiest": "Advantages Which the Antelope Has over Other Papers," *Colorado Antelope*, January 1880.

54. "A Deadwood": "Is This Journalism?" *Daily Deadwood Pioneer-Times*, September 11, 1892.

54. "look to the interests": Nichols Churchill, *Active Footsteps*, 114.

54. "We are living": Nichols Churchill, *Active Footsteps*, 34.

54. "Not really great"; "more ideal civilization."; "best years"; "towards this attainment.": Nichols Churchill, *Active Footsteps*, 23–24.

54. "I guess some woman": Carrie Adell Strahorn, *Fifteen Thousand Miles by Stage, Volume 1: 1877–1880* (New York: Knickerbocker Press, 1911), 238.

54. "woman hater": Adell Strahorn, *Fifteen Thousand Miles by Stage, Volume 1: 1877–1880*, 234.

54–56. "full of ginger"; "with a tenacity"; "drove like fury,"; "within a hair's"; "turn out to"; "food for the bears."; "I knew he was"; "Well, I guess": Adell Strahorn, *Fifteen Thousand Miles by Stage, Volume 1: 1877–1880*, 235.

56. "a lot of our drivers"; "didn't yell": Adell Strahorn, *Fifteen Thousand Miles by Stage, Volume 1: 1877–1880*, 237.

56. "The real home": Adell Strahorn, *Fifteen Thousand Miles by Stage, Volume 1: 1877–1880*, 9.

57. "escape valve"; "squawk of": Adell Strahorn, *Fifteen Thousand Miles by Stage, Volume 1: 1877–1880*, 291.

57. "dirt roof,": Carrie Adell Strahorn, *Fifteen Thousand Miles by Stage, Volume 2: 1880–1898* (New York: Knickerbocker Press, 1911), 77.

57. "matted around": Adell Strahorn, *Fifteen Thousand Miles by Stage, Volume 2: 1880–1898*, 78.

58. "I always put": Adell Strahorn, *Fifteen Thousand Miles by Stage, Volume 2: 1880–1898*, 82.

58. "hordes of rats"; "scampered in"; "into our faces." Adell Strahorn, *Fifteen Thousand Miles by Stage, Volume 2: 1880–1898*, 204.

58–59. "mere scratch"; "washed away": Adell Strahorn, *Fifteen Thousand Miles by Stage, Volume 1: 1877–1880*, 206.

59. "to dispose of": Adell Strahorn, *Fifteen Thousand Miles by Stage, Volume 1: 1877–1880*, 215.

59. "hurled top down": Adell Strahorn, *Fifteen Thousand Miles by Stage, Volume 1: 1877–1880*, 217.

59. "wagged on worse": Adell Strahorn, *Fifteen Thousand Miles by Stage, Volume 1: 1877–1880*, 218.

60. "for the cheerless": Adell Strahorn, *Fifteen Thousand Miles by Stage, Volume 2: 1880–1898*, 19.

60. "worst looking,": Adell Strahorn, *Fifteen Thousand Miles by Stage, Volume 2: 1880–1898*, 20.

60. "veritable mudhole": Adell Strahorn, *Fifteen Thousand Miles by Stage, Volume 1: 1877–1880*, 363.

60. "one of the most picturesque": Adell Strahorn, *Fifteen Thousand Miles by Stage, Volume 1: 1877–1880*, 314.

60. "No one could feel": Adell Strahorn, *Fifteen Thousand Miles by Stage, Volume 1: 1877–1880*, 88.

60. "magic word": Adell Strahorn, *Fifteen Thousand Miles by Stage, Volume 1: 1877–1880*, 247.

60. "cyclonic wreckage": Adell Strahorn, *Fifteen Thousand Miles by Stage, Volume 1: 1877–1880*, 149.

60. "What in hell": Adell Strahorn, *Fifteen Thousand Miles by Stage, Volume 1: 1877–1880*, 11.

60. "the most picturesque inland": Adell Strahorn, *Fifteen Thousand Miles by Stage, Volume 1: 1877–1880*, 197.

60. "maddening salt plains,"; "kiss the sky,": Adell Strahorn, *Fifteen Thousand Miles by Stage, Volume 2: 1880–1898*, 301.

60. "marvelous bits": Adell Strahorn, *Fifteen Thousand Miles by Stage, Volume 1: 1877–1880*, 73.

61. "up and down"; "awful grandeur": Adell Strahorn, *Fifteen Thousand Miles by Stage, Volume 1: 1877–1880*, 282.

61. "carried on wings": Adell Strahorn, *Fifteen Thousand Miles by Stage, Volume 1: 1877–1880*, 310.

61. "to the magic work": Adell Strahorn, *Fifteen Thousand Miles by Stage, Volume 2: 1880–1898*, 89.

61. "The joys of motherhood": Adell Strahorn, *Fifteen Thousand Miles by Stage, Volume 1: 1877–1880*, 146.

61. "On days the stage came to town": Miss Leslie, "The Tenth Passenger: A Sketch," *Godey's Lady's Book* (June 1842): 321.

61. "unpublished news": Leroy Pratt, "Ten Cents a Mile and a Fence Rail," *Annals of Iowa* 39 (1969): 603.

61. "eager buzz of gossip": J. Winston Coleman Jr., *Stage-Coach Days in the Bluegrass* (Louisville: University Press of Kentucky, 1935), 83.

CHAPTER 3: TRAVEL BY STAGE:
TEETH-RATTLING, BONE-JARRING

62. "the purpose of": "Carelessness of Stage Drivers," *National Gazette*, January 11, 1822.

63. "spirited contest": No title, *Long-Island Star* (Brooklyn, NY), November 11, 1818.

63. "it is high time": No title, *Evening Post* (New York), March 28, 1833.

63. "full blood"; "with a crack"; "tremendous crash.": No title, *Selma (AL) Daily Reporter*, September 15, 1838.

64. "absolutely prohibited"; "every driver": "People's Line of Stages," *Mississippi Freed Trader* (Natchez), March 5, 1838.

65. "The United States"; "The people wanted"; "almost continuous wilderness"; "never will be settled.": "Railroads for Winter Wear," *Leavenworth (KS) Times*, March 12, 1869.

66. "teeth-rattling": Kenneth Colton, "Stagecoach Travel in Iowa," *Annals of Iowa* 22 (1940): 187.

66. "By the time the family": "The Overland Stage" (Wells Fargo Association, n.d.), 24–27.

67. "use every exertion": "The Epizootic Spreading," *Helena Weekly Herald*, February 6, 1873.

67. "a solid sick": "The Epizooty," *New North-West* (Deer Lodge, MT), February 8, 1873.

67. "the great horse": "The Epizootic Subsiding," *Helena Weekly Herald*, March 13, 1873.

67. "without doubt": "Epizoo in Helena," *Helena Weekly Herald*, March 27, 1873.

68. "ten cents a mile": Pratt, "Ten Cents a Mile and a Fence Rail," 601.

68. "a red head": Colton, "Stagecoach Travel in Iowa," 181.

68. "bridges built of"; "Pub. Docs."; "massive books"; "a solid foundation": Frank A. Root and William Elsey Connelley, *The Overland Stage to California* (Topeka, KS: Crane & Co., 1901), 73.

69. "two children,"; "though they are charged": Leslie, "The Tenth Passenger," 318.

70. "democratic"; "made for no particular": Holmes and Rohrbach, *Stagecoach East*, 46.

70. "absence of classes"; "dirty citizens": Winther, *Via Western Express and Stagecoach*, 21.

70. "who traveled"; "quarrelsome"; "squirted": Oscar Osburn Winther, *Via Western Express and Stagecoach* (Stanford, CA: Stanford University Press, 1945), 24.

70. "colored.": "Ejecting a Colored Passenger From a Stage," *Liberator*, March 25, 1853.

70. "the Great Salt Lake,": "Montana," *Montana Post* (Virginia City), November 10, 1866.

71. "truly grand"; "bordered with": "Diary of Mrs. Mary E. Cook, Written While Coming Up the Mo. River in 1868," SC 558, Montana Historical Society Archives.

71. "America went": Colton, "Stagecoach Travel in Iowa," 195.

71. "closeness of"; "fellow-sufferers": Morse Earle, *Stage Coach and Tavern Days*, 358.

71. "many pleasant intimacies": Morse Earle, *Stage Coach and Tavern Days*, 359.

71. "perfect vision": "The First Kiss," *Knickerbocker* 34 (September 1849): 221.

71. "warm rosy lips.": "The First Kiss," 222.

71. "at least a hundred": "The First Kiss," 223.

72. "Walter, dear": "The First Kiss," 224.

72. "attractive.": Haywood, *Trails South*, 244.

73. "Well, if me"; "You couldn't"; "five months"; "never saw"; "I've kep' up"; "Why, of course"; "You think"; "ain't suited to"; "ain't made no": J. L. Harbour, "Mrs. Bradley's Experience," *Leslie's Weekly* (August 24, 1893): 120.

73. "shrill-tongued"; "dared think": "Told of Anne Royall," *Washington Post*, March 13, 1906.

73–74. "the worst public"; "ignorant, proud"; "ruffian barkeeper.": Royall, *The Black Book; or, A Continuation of Travels in the United States*, 298.

74. "followed by": Royall, *The Black Book; or, A Continuation of Travels in the United States*, 35.

74. "influential centers": "About Our Hotels," *Republic* (Columbus, IN), December 6, 1886.

74. "one of the most"; "On a sixty-three mile": Holmes and Rohrbach, *Stagecoach East*, 143.

75. "temperance principles.": Coleman, *Stage-Coach Days in the Bluegrass*, 135.

75. "luxuries of life": Root and Connelley, *The Overland Stage to California,* 323.

75. "unhewn sampling": Winther, *Via Western Express and Stagecoach,* 24.

76. "a weak stomach,": Root & Connelley, *The Overland Stage to California,* 96.

76. "tough beefsteak": Winther, *Via Western Express and Stagecoach,* 24.

76. "dried fruit"; "half-cooked": Winther, *Via Western Express and Stagecoach,* 27.

76. "groans with": No title, *Avant Courier* (Bozeman, MT), December 31, 1875.

77. "well-stocked bar"; "good meals": Agnes Wright Spring, *The Cheyenne and Black Hills Stage and Express Routes* (Lincoln: University of Nebraska Press, 1948), 70.

77. "quite good": Laura Winthrop Johnson, "Eight Hundred Miles in an Ambulance," *Lippincott's Magazine of Popular Literature and Science* (June 1875): 695.

77. "Corn for the teams"; "some very stale"; "slightly warm"; "excellent substitute": "Journey from Cheyenne to Custer City and Its Incidents," *Atchison (KS) Daily Champion,* January 5, 1877.

77–79. "I am quite convinced"; "I didn't care"; "a belt": "Diary of Anna Gerard" [no page numbers].

79. "brave man"; "answering lead"; "turned coolly"; "I never saw": "Sidney Telegraph," *Nebraska State Journal,* August 9, 1878.

79. "iron clad": "Diary of Anna Gerard" [no page numbers].

79. "The unusual coach": Robert K. DeArment, *Assault on the Deadwood Stage: Road Agents and Shotgun Messengers* (Norman: University of Oklahoma Press, 2011), 151.

80. "armed with weapons": "Diary of Anna Gerard" [no page numbers].

80. "brave, fearless men"; "honorable scars": "To Puzzle Road Agents," *Southern Standard* (Arkadelphia, AR), June 8, 1878.

80. "Quick Shot": DeArment, *Assault on the Deadwood Stage: Road Agents and Shotgun Messengers,* 32.

80. "When we go back,": "Diary of Anna Gerard" [no page numbers].

82. "not look back.": "Mrs. W. R. Piper Reminiscences," Mss 1509, Oregon Historical Society Research Library (1955): 10.

83. "Young women, hungry": Root and Connelley, *The Overland Stage to California,* 67.

84. "the great white"; "a native-born"; "careening, bumping"; "labyrinthine maze"; "shaggy coat"; "cosy and pleasant"; "Can anybody tell"; "gentlemanly judges"; "determined to"; "her protector"; "snoozed cozily"; "thinks too much": "Eastern Oregon," *New Northwest,* November 11, 1880.

85–86. "A transplanted New Yorker"; "colored servant girls"; "twelve or fifteen"; "three ladies"; "electioneering": "Life in Wyoming," *West Schuylkill Press* (Tremont, PA), May 7, 1881.

88. "Ione City was a": Peter Bacon Hales, *Silver Cities: Photographing American Urbanization, 1839–1939* (Albuquerque: University of New Mexico Press, 2005), 107–8.

88. "snug and secure."; "and some awful"; "But I never"; "Newell bath-tub,"; "Last but"; ". . . it is at hand": Mrs. E. W. Withington, "How a Woman Makes Landscape Photographs," *Philadelphia Photographer* (December 1876): 357–60.

CHAPTER 4: SALTY, RESOURCEFUL, BIG-HEARTED BOSSES

90. "I cannot,": Morse Earle, *Stage Coach and Tavern Days,* 397.

90. "deserved a better"; "very fine": Morse Earle, *Stage Coach and Tavern Days*, 401.

92. "corpses never": "Cheerful," *Weekly Harrison Flag* (Marshall, TX), March 1, 1866.

93. "Although still": James Harvey, "The Twelve Mile House," *Colorado Magazine* (September 1935): 175.

94. "in spite of my": Harvey, "The Twelve Mile House," 176.

94. "No Better Supplied": Display ad for Bull Dog Ranch, *Black Hills Central* (Rochford, SD), January 5, 1879.

94. "champion cuisine": No title, *Black Hills Central*, January 5, 1879.

94. "Even the name": Jerry L. Bryant and Barbara Fifer, *Deadwood Saints and Sinners* (Helena, MT: Farcountry Press, 2017) [no page numbers on copy].

95. "cut out like": No title. *Black Hills Daily Times* (Deadwood, SD), August 5, 1879.

96. "warpath,": "Madame Erb on the Warpath," *Black Hills Daily Times*, August 6, 1879.

96. "Sarah was released": Bryant and Fifer, *Deadwood Saints and Sinners* [no page numbers on copy].

96. "one of the best": "Miscellaneous," *Black Hills Daily Times*, July 31, 1880.

96. "One newspaper claimed": No title, *Black Hills Weekly Pioneer*, August 21, 1880.

97. "Over the next several": Bryant and Fifer, *Deadwood Saints and Sinners* [no page numbers on copy].

98. "Madam, I do not": Moody, *Stagecoach West*, 310.

98. "I've labored long": Moody, *Stagecoach West*, 311.

99. "looking down": Moody, *Stagecoach West*, 316.

100. "consummate entrepreneur": "Olivia Elena Antonini Rolleri," Find a Grave, https://www.findagrave.com/memorial/66848530/olivia-elena-rolleri.

100. "Others called": Judy Georgiou, "Grandma Rolleri: the Angel of Angels Camp," *Calaveras Enterprise*, June 11, 2013.

100. "loved figure": "Grandma Rolleri," *Oakland (CA) Tribune*, June 19, 1927.

100. "I'm a product"; "My trips were"; "At that time Kingston": Clay W. Vaden, "Sadie Orchard, One of Few New Mexico Women Stage Drivers," *Folk Ways*, Federal Writers' Project, https://www.loc.gov/rr/program/bib/newdeal/fwp.html.

101. "Her initial business": Glenda Riley and Richard W. Etulain, eds., *Wild Women of the Old West* (Golden, CO: Fulcrum Publishing, 2003), 101.

102. "I drove four": Clay W. Vaden, "Sadie Orchard, One of Few New Mexico Women Stage Drivers," https://www.loc.gov/rr/program/bib/newdeal/fwp.html.

102. "one of the finest": Riley and Etulain, *Wild Women of the Old West*, 105.

102. "best looking": Riley and Etulain, *Wild Women of the Old West*, 106.

102. "deadly weapon": Riley and Etulain, *Wild Women of the Old West*, 109.

102. "Over the next several years": Riley and Etulain, *Wild Women of the Old West*, 112.

102. "the Orchard House"; "good beds"; "grub"; "best served": George H. Clements, "Wise Expenditure of Road Funds Has Gridironed Sierra with Fine Highways," *Sante Fe New Mexican*, March 30, 1915.

102. "today is owner of"; ". . . she is still": Clay W. Vaden, "Sadie Orchard, One of Few New Mexico Women Stage Drivers," https://www.loc.gov/rr/program/bib/newdeal/fwp.html.

102. "salty innkeeper": "Sadie Orchard, Salty Innkeeper, Dies at Hillsboro," *Albuquerque Journal*, April 4, 1943.

104. "gleaming chocolate"; "regal bearing": Barbara Marriott, *Annie's Guests* (Tucson, AZ: Catymatt Productions, 2002), 39.

104. "and possibly most useful": Marriott, *Annie's Guests*, 42; Donald N. Bentz, "William and Anna Neal of Oracle," *Oracle Historian* (Summer 1982): 11.

104. "built in one of": "Mountain View Hotel," *Arizona Weekly Citizen* (Tucson), March 2, 1895.

105. "humidity almost nil"; "famous natural sanitarium": Display ad for Mountain View Hotel, *Arizona Daily Star* (Tucson), February 6, 1901.

106. "You are asked"; "Many thanks": "Gay Times at the Oracle," *Arizona Weekly Citizen*, January 18, 1896.

106. "baby up to": "At Oracle," *Arizona Daily Star*, December 29, 1899.

107. "I think I have"; "In the fifties"; "At 19 I was": "She Is a Stage Driver," *Boston Sunday Globe*, March 12, 1893.

108. "made too close": "Plucky Mrs. Langdon," *Buffalo Commercial*, February 26, 1891.

108. "dark auburn"; "flashing black eyes": "A Female Stage-driver," *American Machinist* (August 18, 1892): 7.

108. "most men"; "Now, I am not"; "The four-footed": "She Is a Stage Driver," *Boston Sunday Globe*, March 12, 1893.

108. "The largest route"; "Once every month": "Plucky Mrs. Langdon," *Buffalo Commercial*, February 26, 1891.

109. "one of the largest": "The Boss Lady Mail Contractor," *Daily Appeal* (Carson City, NV), July 8, 1886.

109. "I am the only": "Plucky Mrs. Langdon," *Washington Post*, February 23, 1891.

109. "under my personal supervision.": "The Little Boss," *San Francisco Examiner*, May 10, 1891.

109. "most successful": "Good News," *Reno (NV) Gazette-Journal*, July 17, 1882.

110. "I know that Brother"; "utterly demoralized"; "blunderingly handled."; "never seen mail": "She's After Mr. Wanamaker," *San Francisco Examiner*, August 8, 1891.

110. "Two are in"; "trusty weapon": "Plucky Mrs. Langdon," *Washington Post*, February 23, 1891.

111. "If the people": "She's After Mr. Wanamaker," *San Francisco Examiner*, August 8, 1891.

111. "willful disregard"; "Oh, affairs are"; "Wanamaker's term"; "Women are quite": "She Is a Stage Driver," *Boston Sunday Globe*, March 12, 1893.

112. "Occasionally justice prevailed": "Last of the Bonanza Kings," *Times* (Philadelphia), December 26, 1897.

CHAPTER 5: IT HARDLY PAYS A MAN, SO GIRLS DO IT

114. "plucky horse-woman.": "Thrilling Experience," *Hamilton (OH) Daily Republican*, June 25, 1895.

114. "of importance"; "envy of": Pratt, "Ten Cents a Mile," 598.

114. "a dignified": Morse Earle, *Stagecoach and Tavern Days*, 323.

115. "experienced, sober,": Coleman, *Stage-Coach Days in the Bluegrass*, 81.

115. "the use of Ardent": Holmes and Rohrbach, *Stagecoach East*, 70.

115. "No owner wanted": Coleman, *Stage-Coach Days in the Bluegrass*, 95.

115. "Owners of the Griffin": Coleman, *Stage-Coach Days In The Bluegrass*, 94.

115. "in the early days": Holmes and Rohrbach, *Stagecoach East*, 66.

116. "intrepidity"; "dexterity": Holmes and Rohrbach, *Stagecoach East*, 63.

116. "Our course could": Holmes and Rohrbach, *Stagecoach East*, 64.

116. "snail-galloping"; "snap a fly": Dr. John E. Briggs, "Exploring the History of Iowa," *Ames Daily Tribune*, December 31, 1934.

117. "The US Post Office paid": Holmes and Rohrbach, *Stagecoach East*, 69.

118. "Although a Minnesota": "Woman Stage Drivers," *Minneapolis Journal*, October 9, 1901.

119. "chawin',": Ernest Otto, "Old Santa Cruz," *Santa Cruz (CA) Sentinel*, April 11, 1948.

119. "foot deep": John Ross Browne, *Adventures in the Apache Country: A Tour Through Arizona and Sonora* (New York: Harper and Brothers, 1871), 312.

119–20. "This character had a nasty reputation": Cliff Knight, "Outdoors," *Hartford Courant*, March 17, 1957.

120. "Throw down"; "break even"; "turned his wild": "Thirty Years in Disguise," *Buffalo Commercial*, January 10, 1880.

120. "Charlotte Parkhurst, the daughter": Mary Ellen Snodgrass, *Settlers of the American West: The Lives of 231 Notable Pioneers* (Jefferson, NC: McFarland, 2015), 127.

120–21. "she may have been disgusted": Ernest Otto, "Old Santa Cruz," *Santa Cruz (CA) Sentinel*, April 11, 1948.

121. "Old Moll,": V. N. Phillips, *Pioneers in Paradise* (Johnson City, TN: Overmountain Press, 2002), 1.

121. "tall, raw boned,": Phillips, *Pioneers in Paradise*, 35.

122. "Your Aunt Nan": Phillips, *Pioneers in Paradise*, 14.

122. "That woman were"; "whip the breeches"; "gun in hand": Phillips, *Pioneers in Paradise*, 19.

123. "Why, I believe": Phillips, *Pioneers in Paradise*, 35.

124. "I came here": "Their Parasols as Weapons," *Los Angeles Herald*, January 27, 1893.

124. "a very pretty": "The Two Mrs. Rawsons Meet," *Los Angeles Herald*, January 26, 1893.

124. "I might have broken"; "The defendant": "Their Parasols as Weapons," *Los Angeles Herald*, January 27, 1893.

124. "whack to": "The Two Mrs. Rawsons Meet," *Los Angeles Herald*, January 26, 1893.

124. "My attention was"; "the testimony is insufficient": "Their Parasols as Weapons," *Los Angeles Herald*, January 27, 1893.

125. "asylum"; "reformed lunatic.": "A Reformed Lunatic," *Los Angeles Herald*, June 1, 1891.

125. "realized quite handsomely": "The Two Mrs. Rawsons Meet," *Los Angeles Herald*, January 26, 1893.

125. "one of the leading business": "A Former Ukiah Girl," *Ukiah (CA) Republican Press*, September 21, 1906.

126. "crack shot,": "Not Always Speedway," *Oakland (CA) Tribune*, June 20, 1937.

126. "Bart was quiet": "Stage Day Thrills Told," *Los Angeles Times*, June 3, 1935.

126. "My father had told"; "The outlaws would"; "My last trip": "Old Stage Drivers Tell Some Colorful Stories at Meeting," *Havre (MT) Daily News*, March 26, 1946.

127. "blow our brains"; "a large bundle": Morse Earle, *Stagecoach and Tavern Days*, 385.

127. "afford a distinct view": Morse Earle, *Stagecoach and Tavern Days*, 388.

"your feet get wet": Morse Earle, *Stagecoach and Tavern Days*, 364.

127. "a slow form of"; "looked like moving": Morse Earle, *Stagecoach and Tavern Days*, 362.

127. "tough fibre": Morse Earle, *Stagecoach and Tavern Days*, 363.

127. "scant romance": Morse Earle, *Stagecoach and Tavern Days*, 372.

128. "According to a newspaper"; "suffered severely"; "Throw out"; "squarely on"; "Get up on"; "Get up there"; "beyond the possibility": "Captured a Footpad," *Boston Sunday Globe*, May 7, 1893.

129. "one of most famous"; "hale, bluff"; "aid of his ready gun."; "refined, well-educated"; "I am not surprised": "Queen of the Whip," *San Francisco Chronicle*, July 12, 1893.

130. "Give me a chance": "She Drives the Coach," *Philadelphia Times*, February 5, 1899.

130. "Those leaders would": "She Drives a Four-horse Coach Over the Mail Route," *San Francisco Call*, December 25, 1898.

130. "roughest road"; "instead of being terrorized": "She Drives the Coach," *Philadelphia Times*, February 5, 1899.

131. "Yes, it's so"; "Dunno as I'd care"; "had her own ideas"; "fleck a fly": "She Drives a Four-horse Coach over the Mail Route," *San Francisco Call*, December 25, 1898.

131–33. "It's sort of"; "Well!"; "You see!"; "fussed like a grandmother"; "wonders of the"; "perfect nonchalance"; safest driver": "Alice Johnson, California's Most Remarkable Stage Driver," *San Francisco Call*, September 8, 1901.

133–35. "one of most"; "plucky"; "winsome"; "most talked of native"; "jovial greeting"; "Brawny woodsmen"; "indomitable will": "Plucky Girl Guards Uncle Sam's Mail," *Boston Sunday Post*, January 28, 1906.

CHAPTER 6: HANDS UP! HAND OVER THE GOLD!

136. "insisted on"; "the hand that rocked": Eugene Block, *Great Stagecoach Robbers of the West* (Garden City, NY: Doubleday, 1962), 105.

137. "As a mother": "A Contradiction," *Sacramento Daily Union*, October 29, 1856.

138. "large fat woman": "Confession of Bill Cristy," *Sacramento Daily Union*, October 23, 1856.

138. "threats and persuasion": "Execution of Tom Bell," *Sonoma County Journal*, October 24, 1856.

139. "dear and only"; "friend now"; ". . . there is but one"; "very careful to whom": Block, *Great Stagecoach Robbers of the West*, 90–91.

139. "totally untrue"; "unfit associates": "A Contradiction," *Sacramento Daily Union*, October 29, 1856.

139. "A fellow named Ezra": Benjamin W. D'Ooge, "Diseases of the Gold Rush Examined," *Placerville Mountain Democrat*, April 1, 1998.

140. "among the most": W. Storrs Lee, *The Sierra* (New York: G. P. Putnam's Sons, 1962), 129.

142. "Halt, and"; "Halt yourself"; "messenger of": "Pacific Coast Items," *Sacramento Daily Union*, February 17, 1874.

143. "pretty"; "lunatic"; "undoubtedly crazy.": "Stage Robbers," *New York Times*, July 26, 1874.

143. "Eliza the Brave"; "beau"; "rival knight"; "Our sympathies": "Eliza the Brave," *Sacramento Daily Union*, September 8, 1874.

144. "It excites curiosity": "Madam Vestal," *Black Hills Daily*, October 22, 1881.

145. "She may have married": Donna Blake Birchell, *Wicked Women of New Mexico* (Charleston, SC: History Press, 2014) [e-book page number not available].

145. "In the first place": "A Bloody Mystery," *Leadville Daily Herald*, November 5, 1880.

145. "There is a woman": "Madam Vestal," *Black Hills Daily*, October 22, 1881.

145. "Hideous old creature": "Mother Osborne," *San Francisco Examiner*, January 17, 1886.

145. "old virago": "Mother Osborne," *Democrat and Chronicle* (Rochester, NY), June 6, 1886.

145. "wicked"; "as gross": "Mother Osborne," *Standard* (Clarksville, TX), December 11, 1885.

146. "brazen, shameless": "Montana Mention," *Weekly Yellowstone Journal*, January 2, 1886.

146. "wonder of obesity": "A Remarkable Character," *San Francisco Chronicle*, May 23, 1886.

146. "vile language": "Mother Osborne," *Standard* (Clarksville, TX), December 11, 1885.

147. "expensive provender"; "mule-toted"; "Red-faced": "Mother Osborne," *San Francisco Examiner*, January 17, 1886.

148. "lost almost": "Mother Osborne," *San Francisco Examiner*, January 17, 1886.

148. "sported quite": "A Remarkable Character," *San Francisco Chronicle*, May 23, 1886.

152–53. "I got a letter"; "I was good-looking"; "I was not"; "I have never"; "That letter"; "I longed"; "help him out"; "A bold front"; "It seemed": "An Arizona Episode," *Cosmopolitan* (October 1899): 674.

153. "Throw up"; "the most eloquent": "Woman Bandit Is Set Free," *Saint Paul Globe*, January 19, 1903.

153. "charitable contribution": *Cosmopolitan*: 675.

153. "I confess": *Cosmopolitan*: 676.

154. "Resistance"; "make fun": *Cosmopolitan*: 677.

154. "neither she nor": "Pearl Hart Is at Liberty," *Fort Wayne (IN) News*, October 13, 1899.

157. "looking into the muzzle": "Stage Robbed by Two Men: Get $7,000 in Gold," *Ontario Argus*, April 8, 1915.

158. "Before long": R. Michael Wilson, *Great Stagecoach Robberies of the Old West* (Helena, MT: TwoDot, 2007), 173.

158. "being implicated"; "conclusive evidence": "Two in Custody," *Statesman Journal* (Salem, OR), April 9, 1915.

159. "Molly also had this to say": Wilson, *Great Stagecoach Robberies of the Old West*, 177.

159. "except to eat": "Women Prisoners Will Sew Buttons on Pants of the Male Convicts," *Statesman Journal* (Salem, OR), December 4, 1915.

CHAPTER 7: JUST FOR FUN

162–64. "The brute"; "simply hideous."; "dirty and disgusting"; "ensconced in; —your eyes"; "Don't go to Yo Semite": "Does It Pay to Visit Yo Semite?" *Leavenworth (KS) Weekly Times*, October 6, 1870.

164. "running the risk"; "exasperating hovels"; "the sale of"; "summit of"; "every inch"; "public dancing"; "The once majestic": "The Impending Doom of Yosemite," *New York Times*, February 13, 1872.

165. "They crowd"; "fresh, rosy-cheeked"; "sleepy, vinegar-visaged": "Letter from Merced," *San Francisco Examiner*, June 3, 1875.

165. "pressed that earth": "Correspondence of the Star," *Brooklyn Evening Star*, August 5, 1844.

166. ". . . the part we occupied": Adell Strahorn, *Fifteen Thousand Miles by Stage*, vol. 1, 259.

166. "There are no adjectives": Adell Strahorn, *Fifteen Thousand Miles by Stage*, vol. 1, 268.

166. "Mrs. Marshall prepared": William J. Hunt Jr., Annalies Corbin, M. J. Harris, Christopher F. Valvano, *A Bath House and Plenty of Fresh Air: Archeology in a Thermal River Environment* (Columbus, OH: PAST Foundation, 2008), 39.

167. "the latter still"; "Just fancy": Frances M. A. Roe, *Army Letters from an Officer's Wife, 1871–1888* (New York: D. Appleton, 1909), 321–22.

167. "tolerably good"; "abominable messes"; "dark and stifling"; "The bed was stuffed"; "I fancied that": Margaret Andrews Cruikshank and Lee H. Whittlesey, "A Lady's Trip to Yellowstone, 1883: 'Earth Could Not Furnish Another Such Sight,'" *Montana: Magazine of Western History* 39 (Winter 1989): 12.

167. "Another guest was critical": Hunt, Corbin, Harris, Valvano, *A Bath House and Plenty of Fresh Air: Archeology in a Thermal River Environment*, 41.

167. "And George liked to tell": "Biographical Statement of G. W. Marshall, about 1885," Bancroft Library, Berkeley, CA, File P.M. 48:1.

169. "no place": Cruikshank and Whittlesey, "A Lady's Trip to Yellowstone, 1883": 4–5.

169. "a delightful winter": "The Geysers in Winter," *Livingston Enterprise*, December 6, 1884.

169. "wallowed in spoils;" "Ma! Ma!": "The Election of 1884," *Digital History*, http://www.digitalhistory.uh.edu/disp_textbook.cfm?smtid=2&psid=3117.

169. "I cannot vote": Jill Norgren, "Lockwood in '84," *Wilson Quarterly* 26 (Autumn 2002), http://archive.wilsonquarterly.com/essays/lockwood-in-84.

170. "He knows where"; "He has also"; "Effervescent spring"; "effervesces like"; "Chemical Basin"; "the Bulldog;" "like the jaws"; "Mrs. Marshall broke"; "the rocky ribs": "The Geysers in Winter," *Livingston Enterprise*, December 6, 1884.

171. "The past six days": Lee Whittlesey, "Yellowstone's First Female Rangers," *Buffalo Chip* (March–April 2002): 1.

171. "brought in from"; "take you through": Ella McIntyre Smith, "Letter from Ella McIntyre Smith to her daughters (Virginia Smith [O'Brien] and another unnamed daughter), August 19, 1892, about trip to Yellowstone," Yellowstone Research Library, VISITORS-1890(SMITH): 2, 4.

171. "In summer of 1894": Helen Clifford Gunter, "Yellowstone Park Three Times Around, 1894, 1910, 1971: A Chapter from an Unpublished Book of Memoirs" (Portola Valley, CA: Helen Clifford Gunter, 1987), Yellowstone Research Library, VISITORS-1890 (GUNTER): 2.

173. "If you grow": "From China," *College Life* (Emporia, KS), January 30, 1897.

173–74. "Listen to the guide"; "It was a very big"; Recalling the encounter": Clifford Gunter, "Yellowstone Park Three Times Around, 1894, 1910, 1971: A Chapter from an Unpublished book of Memoirs": 9.

174. "sage brushers": Lillian Fellows Kirkemo, "Letter giving account of a trip to Yellowstone in 1910," Missoula, Montana: Lillian Fellows Kirkemo, 1972. Yellowstone Research Library, VISITORS-1910 (KIRKEMO): 2.

174–75. "Here was at last"; "I regretfully turned": Dorothy Brown Pardo, "Dorothy in Wonderland," Yellowstone Research Library, VISITORS-1910 (PARDO): 16, 43.

175. "one of the most": "Great Work of Government," *Semiweekly Billings (MT) Gazette*, March 16, 1909.

175. "There was no getting through": Cruikshank and Whittlesey, "A Lady's Trip to Yellowstone, 1883," 7.

177. "Nina has always": "A Coney Island Girl of a Brand-new Type," *World* (New York), July 26, 1896.

177. "short bicycle skirt": "Woman Snow Shoveler," *Wilkes-Barre Times*, February 16, 1899.

179. "swear like a pirate": Inez Hunt and Wanetta W. Draper, *To Colorado's Restless Ghosts* (Denver, CO: Sage Books, 1960), 59.

179. "Once when she": Hunt and Draper, *To Colorado's Restless Ghosts*, 61.

180. "people who possess"; "some of the sleekest"; "I am a business woman": "Colorado Has a Woman Jehu," *St. Louis Post-Dispatch*, April 23, 1905.

180–81. "Yes, I am the leading"; "four of the finest"; "seven head of"; "I'm not the kind": "John C. King Meets Female Hack Driver," *Daily Home News* (New Brunswick, NJ), December 2, 1905.

181. "cabins for campers": Tim Blevins, Dennis Daily, Chris Nicholl, Calvin P. Otto, and Katherine Scott Sturdevant, ed., *Extraordinary Women of the Rocky Mountain West* (Pikes Peak Library District, 2010), 62.

183. "queen of the ballet.": "She Passed as a Man for Six Years and Drove Circus Wagon," *Albuquerque Evening Citizen*, August 22, 1905.

183. "only woman six-horse": "John Robinson's Big Shows," *Galena Tribune*, September 18, 1905.

SELECTED BIBLIOGRAPHY

Bake Birchell, Donna. *Wicked Women of New Mexico*. Charleston, SC: History Press, 2014.

Bentz, Alyssa. (2017). "How Horses Have Been the 'Pride of Wells Fargo Service.'" https://stories.wf.com/horses-pride-wells-fargo-service. Retrieved April 28, 2019.

Bentz, Donald. "William and Anna Neal of Oracle and the Mountain View Hotel." *Oracle Historian* 5 (Summer 1982): 1–18.

Block, Eugene. *Great Stagecoach Robbers of the West*. Garden City, NY: Doubleday, 1962.

Bryant, Jerry L., and Barbara Fifer. *Deadwood Saints and Sinners*. Helena, MT: Farcountry Press, 2017.

Coleman Jr., J. Winston. *Stage-Coach Days in the Bluegrass*. Louisville: University Press of Kentucky, 1935.

DeArment, Robert K. *Assault on the Deadwood Stage: Road Agents and Shotgun Messengers*. Norman: University of Oklahoma Press, 2012.

Ferrell, Merri, and Christopher Augerson. "Concord Ornamental Painter John Burgum and the Artistry of Carriage Painting. Abbot-Downing: Coach and Wagon Makers to the World." *Historical New Hampshire* (2011): 30–51.

Garceau-Hagen, Dee, ed. *Portraits of Women in the American West*. New York: Routledge, 2005.

Gerard, Anna. 1878. *Diary of Anna Gerard*. Deadwood History, Inc. Adams Museum Collection, Deadwood, SD.

Haywood, C. Robert. *Trails South: The Wagon-Road Economy in the Dodge City-Panhandle Region*. Norman: University of Oklahoma Press, 1986.

Holmes, Oliver W., and Peter T. Rohrbach. *Stagecoach East: Stagecoach Days in the East from the Colonial Period to the Civil War*. Washington, DC: Smithsonian Institution Press, 1983.

Horan, James D. *Desperate Women*. New York: Crown, 1952.

Jackson, Joseph Henry. *Bad Company: The Story of California's Legendary and Actual Stage-Robbers*. 1st edition, New York: Harcourt Brace, 1949.

Lee, W. Storrs. *The Sierra*. New York: G. P. Putnam's Sons, 1962.

Marriott, Barbara. *Annie's Guests*. Tucson, AZ: Catymatt Productions, 2002.

Martineau, Harriet. *Retrospect of Western Travel in Three Volumes*. London: Saunders and Otley, 1838.

Martineau Wagner, Tricia. *African American Women of the Old West*. Helena, MT: TwoDot, 2007.

Moody, Ralph. *Stagecoach West*. Lincoln: University of Nebraska Press, 1967.

Morse Earle, Alice. *Stage Coach and Tavern Days*. New York: Macmillan, 1901.

Nichols Churchill, Caroline. *Active Footsteps*. Colorado Springs, CO: Mrs. C. N. Churchill, 1909.

————. *Little Sheaves; Gathered while Gleaning after Reapers.* San Francisco: Mrs. C. M. Churchill, 1874.

————. *Over the Purple Hills.* Denver: Mrs. C. M. Churchill, 1881.

Palmquist, Peter E. "Stereo Artist, Mrs. E. W. Withington; or, 'How I Use My Skirt for a Darktent.'" *Stereo World* 10 (November/December 1983): 20–21.

Piper, Mrs. W. R. 1955. Mrs. W. R. Piper Reminiscences. Mss 1509, Oregon Historical Society Research Library.

Pratt, Leroy. "Ten Cents a Mile and a Fence Rail." *Annals of Iowa* 39 (1969): 597–603.

Reich, Alice, and Thomas J. Steele, S. J. *Fraser Haps and Mishaps: The Diary of Mary E. Cozens.* Denver: Regis College Press, 1990.

Riley, Glenda, and Richard W. Etulain, eds. *Wild Women of the Old West.* Golden, CO: Fulcrum Publishing, 2003.

Root, Frank A., and William Elsey Connelley. *The Overland Stage to California.* Topeka, KS: Crane & Co., 1901.

Royall, Anne. *The Black Book; or, A Continuation of Travels in the United States.* Washington, DC: Mrs. Anne Royall, 1828.

Schwantes, Carlos A. "The Steamboat and Stagecoach Era in Montana and the Northern West." *Montana: Magazine of Western History* 49 (Winter 1999): 2–15.

Shirley, Gayle C. *More Than Petticoats: Remarkable Montana Women.* Guilford, CT: Globe Pequot Press, 2011.

Spring, Agnes Wright. *The Cheyenne and Black Hills Stage and Express Routes.* Glendale, CA: A. H. Clark, 1949.

Stapp, Cheryl Anne. *The Stagecoach in Northern California.* Charleston, SC: History Press, 2014.

Strahorn, Carrie Adell. *Fifteen Thousand Miles by Stage, Volume 1: 1877–1880.* New York: Knickerbocker Press, 1911.

————. *Fifteen Thousand Miles by Stage, Volume 2: 1880–1898.* New York: Knickerbocker Press, 1911.

Turner, Erin H., ed. *Wild West Women: Fifty Lives That Shaped the Frontier.* Helena, MT: TwoDot, 2016.

Weise, Arthur James. *The City of Troy and Its Vicinity.* Troy, NY: Edward Green, 1886.

Wilson, R. Michael. *Great Stagecoach Robberies of the Old West.* Helena, MT: TwoDot, 2007.

Winther, Oscar O. *Via Western Express and Stagecoach.* Stanford, CA: Stanford University Press, 1945.

Withington, Mrs. E. W. "How a Woman Makes Landscape Photographs." *Philadelphia Photographer* 13 (December 1876): 357–79. Women in Photography Archive. https://www.cla.purdue.edu/waaw/palmquist/Photographers/WithingtonEssay.html.

INDEX

About the Author

Cheryl Mullenbach is a former history teacher, newspaper editor, and public television project manager. She is the author of five nonfiction books for young people. The American Library Association named *Double Victory* to its "Amelia Bloomer Top Ten List" in 2014. The FDR Presidential Library and Museum honored her as one of ten authors at their Roosevelt Reading Festival in 2013. All of her books (*Great Depression for Kids*, *Industrial Revolution for Kids*, *Women in Blue*, and *Torpedoed!*) have been included in the National Council for Social Studies "Notable Trade Books for Young People." The International Literacy Association recognized *Industrial Revolution for Kids* in 2015.